RACHMANINOFF'S RECOLLECTIONS

S. RACHMANINOFF

RACHMANINOFF'S
RECOLLECTIONS
TOLD TO

OSKAR von RIESEMANN

ILLUSTRATED

 BOOKS FOR LIBRARIES PRESS
FREEPORT, NEW YORK

First Published 1934
Reprinted 1970

TRANSLATED FROM THE GERMAN MANUSCRIPT

by

MRS. DOLLY RUTHERFORD

STANDARD BOOK NUMBER:
8369-5232-4

LIBRARY OF CONGRESS CATALOG CARD NUMBER:
74-111100

PRINTED IN THE UNITED STATES OF AMERICA

PREFACE

AN hour's motor drive from Paris, close to Rambouillet, the beautiful summer residence assigned to the President of the French Republic, in whose woods he and his friends enjoy pheasant shooting, lies the tiny village of Clairefontaine. It is famous for its lilies of the valley, the splendour and immeasurable multitude of which attract half Paris on a fine spring day. As one enters the village there rises a wall with a high gate, but this only opens to the pull of a bell, which must be a century old. Through the wrought-iron work of the gate one can see the corner of an unpretentious manor-house. It is "Le Pavillon," the country place in which Rachmaninoff has spent his recent summers. Not until one approaches the front of the house which, with its steeply ascending flight of steps, faces the park is one able to understand why the Composer should have chosen this particular spot as a refuge for his quiet summer holidays.

Before the house stretches the broad *pelouse*, surrounded by magnificent old chestnuts and lime-trees, through which one gets a glimpse of the tennis court, while immediately behind the lawn an arrow-straight avenue, flanked by the grey beech trunks and silver birches of the park, seems to dwindle into infinite distance. There are ponds close by bordered by lush meadows and soaring woods—loud with the croaking of frogs.

"I would not exchange this concert for the most beautiful chorus of nightingales," says the Composer.

For the rest there is silence. It seems as if the high surrounding walls arrested every sound from the outside world; for the stillness beneath these trees remains unbroken.

It was here, in this park—in a fresh clearing in the trees which crowd towards the garden gate—that Rachmaninoff told me the story of his life. I have tried to reproduce it in the following pages, my own contribution being merely the connecting text. Sitting on a tumbledown seat, or on a felled tree trunk, waging ceaseless war against an army of gnats, I took notes, while Rachmaninoff paced up and down in front of me and talked. In beautiful, simple sentences which nevertheless vibrated with force of expression, in words growing more vividly descriptive with the emotion stirred by his memories, he outlined for me the strange course of his fate.

Never before have I felt such regret at my inability to write Russian shorthand: I am afraid there are moments when the necessary translation into English prevented me from doing justice to the plastic clarity and calm strength of expression shown by the narrator.

It is not often that a biographer is able to draw from such a truly living source. In this case the opportunity was accepted all the more gratefully because this living source proved the only possible one. The material usually at the disposal of biographers, such as letters, manuscripts, newspaper cuttings, etc., was not opened up. It remained in Soviet Russia and its use was withheld. It seems to me, however, that when one considers the absolute authenticity of personal communication, this can hardly be counted as a loss; nor is the fact that the choice of material was largely left to the central figure in this biography of any real importance. From the biography of a living person consideration for the feelings of others demands, as a matter of principle, that certain matter should be omitted. Of the proper exercise of this principle the subject is in general the best judge. The missing chapters in the story are most fitly to be considered only in historic retrospect and should be added by later writers. I hope that the following pages will, one day, be richly supplemented; they need no verification and may,

6

therefore, constitute the foundation of every future Rachmaninoff biography.

*   *   *   *   *

Why did Rachmaninoff choose me to take down his life story? Was I better suited than others to write his biography? As it happens, I had some special qualifications for the task, and they may have persuaded Rachmaninoff to meet my first request so readily.

My life has, in part, run parallel with his own, and the first "blossoming" of his creative and executive powers took place under my eyes. During the years 1899–1917, in the concert-halls and the Grand Theatre of Moscow, I was present at each of the long series of triumphs that greeted the first performances of his works. In the year 1899 I entered Moscow University and, soon afterwards, met Rachmaninoff at the house of a mutual friend, Princess Alexandra Lieven. When I had finished my studies I settled down in Moscow, and the way to the plain, yellow-painted house behind the monastery "To the Sorrows of Christ," on the boulevard of the same name, became quite familiar to me. One of the outstanding memories of my career as a conductor in Moscow is a concert in which Rachmaninoff played his Third Piano Concerto for the second time.

And it was not only in Moscow that we met. During his stay in Dresden I lived in Leipzig, where I studied under Hugo Riemann and Arthur Nikisch. Whenever the "Gewandhaus" promised a concert of outstanding merit Rachmaninoff would come to Leipzig; if the Dresden Court Opera had some special treat to offer, he would ask me there. I had regular invitations—by post card—to attend the performances of *Die Meistersinger*, conducted by Ernst von Schuch. During my visits to the town on the Elbe I had the privilege of witnessing the actual birth at the piano of such works as were composed there: the

7

Second Symphony, the First Piano Sonata, the Symphonic Poem, *The Isle of Death*, and the songs of Op. 26.

When, together with a few friends, I travelled to Paris for the first Russian Season in May 1907, whom should I see, sitting in a carriage of the North Express to which our own of Magdebourg was coupled, but Rachmaninoff.

When, as a refugee from Soviet Russia, I landed in Germany in 1922, the Composer happened to be in Dresden, where I visited him, and I have since been a frequent guest at his country house in France. Now we are close neighbours on the borders of the Lake of Lucerne in Switzerland.

All the musicians of Moscow, and most of the musicians of St. Petersburg, mentioned in this book I have known personally and have frequently met; a fact which has helped to lighten the task of writing it. The danger that it might, on that account, develop into a collection of personal memoirs I have tried—and I hope successfully— to avoid.

*　　*　　*　　*　　*

In writing this biography I often made the annoying discovery that dates of events, especially of first performances and of the beginning and completion of compositions, were remembered neither by myself nor Rachmaninoff.

A mere coincidence came to our rescue. A small pamphlet entitled *S. W. Rachmaninoff*, by V. Belayev, published in Soviet Russia in 1923, fell, by some chance, into the Composer's hands. This little book has one interesting feature in that it contains an accurate index of Rachmaninoff's works, with all the dates of their beginning and completion, which had been marked on each manuscript. From this one may conclude that some Soviet Russian agency has made a thorough search in Rachmaninoff's house, found the collection of manuscripts which, on his departure from Russia, he left behind, and made their existence known to the public through the agency of the above-mentioned Belayev. The pamphlet also includes dates of the first performances of Rachmaninoff's compositions, but these are, unfortunately, incomplete. It is the only source apart from Rachmaninoff's own communications from which I have drawn material for this book.

The edition of my work has been substantially helped by the friendly and unselfish assistance of Mrs. Frieda Cramer of Kastanienbaum in Switzerland. It is my pleasant duty to express to her my sincere gratitude. My thanks are due also to the Composer's sister-in-law, Mlle Sophie Satin, from whom I have had many details of family history, some anecdotes, and pictures which she had the chance to take with her on her flight from Russia. I have, further, to thank Mrs. Lilly Diedrichs von Wogau and Messrs. Dührkoop of Hamburg for their kindness in lending me photographs of Rachmaninoff and his family, while my gratitude goes to the Russian Music Publishers in Paris and Messrs Breitkopf and Härtel for their readiness in placing his compositions at my disposal, and last but not least to Mr. Felix Aylmer of London, whose help has been very important for the English edition of this book.

If my work meets the desire of the Composer's innumerable admirers and friends to know more about his musical career and his development as an artist, its object will be amply fulfilled. May it also prove a useful reference to all that may wish to study the musical life of Moscow towards the end of the nineteenth century in relation to its central figure, Sergei Rachmaninoff.

OSKAR VON RIESEMANN

ST. NIKLAUSEN, NEAR LUCERNE
Autumn 1933

9

CONTENTS

11

CONTENTS

13

RACHMANINOFF'S RECOLLECTIONS

ILLUSTRATIONS

RACHMANINOFF'S RECOLLECTIONS

CHAPTER ONE

HAPPY CHILDHOOD IN THE COUNTRY

1873–1882

Life of the Russian aristocracy in the seventies and eighties of the nineteenth century—The parents and grandparents of the artist—First recollections of his childhood—The piano mistress, Anna Ornazkaya—The parents differ about the future of their sons—"Corps of Pages"—Fate decides—The Rachmaninoff children and their parents—Removal to St. Petersburg—Little Sergei enters the Conservatoire

THE Russia of the seventies of the last century is a vanished world, connected with the present only by feeble threads of a purely personal character. These threads reach across the borders of the country towards representatives of a generation who, although born as subjects of the all-powerful Tsar, were able to call themselves the first bourgois of the free state formed in 1917, and were then driven, or had to fly, from their native soil because they would not bow before the despotism of the mob and felt even less inclined to let themselves be morally and politically chastised, or "exterminated."

It is indeed a vanished world, this widely hated, widely admired empire of the Tsars, a target of scorn to one, an object of love to another; abused by the envious; but always sustained by the hopes of its children. Who remembers this Russia? Who is able to conjure up from a store of personal memories the magic spell of a world so rich in treasures of culture that one might well have wondered how best to enjoy them, how best to turn them to the fullest use? Even if their value is disputed to-day, it was very real at the time.

It was the period when Russian literature, science, sculpture, and, above all, music had come to its full growth.

The natural centres of this culture were the two great cities, St. Petersburg and Moscow, where it found its fullest appreciation. Glittering St. Petersburg, with its beautiful and monumental buildings, its palaces, its Court, the wealthiest and most splendid of all times, its theatres (which have made more than one theatrical manager in Europe pale with envy), its diplomats from all over the world, the nobles of the high bureaucracy, the General Staff and the Guards, resplendent in their purple and gold, and Moscow, the very heart of Russia, quieter, but of more intrinsic worth, with its snug retreats for ageing aristocrats and great gentlemen, its world-famous university, and, last but not least, its millionaire merchants— a Moscow that was almost a state within a state and certainly a world unto itself.

But the real roots of this peculiarly Russian culture, which was largely nourished from abroad by France and also Germany, but which owed its greatest charm and power to the native element added to these foreign influences, were to be found neither in the towns nor in the cities.

These roots, spreading like a network through the whole country, lay most deeply embedded in the soil wherever low walls enclosed the shady parks of old country estates, with their melancholy nightingales singing over slumbering ponds and adding instrumental brilliancy to the orchestra of frogs. It was a time when the country, for good or evil, was almost entirely ruled by the landed aristocracy. Although serfdom had been abolished for more than ten years the patriarchal spirit—a way of thinking and living which had existed for centuries—could not be changed as quickly as the external and legal forms for a state of human and social dependence. It continued for a long time and formed the inevitable and invariable background for the fascinating picture of Russian country life.

The manor-house generally was a low one- or two-storied wooden structure, built with logs from its own forest, whose sun-mottled gloom reached up to the garden gate; roomy verandas and balconies stretched across the whole front of the house, which was overgrown with Virginia creeper; behind lay the stables and dog-kennels that housed yelping Borzoi puppies; in front of the house was a lawn, round in shape—with a sundial in its centre—and encircled by the drive; a garden with gigantic oaks and lime-trees, which cast their shadows over a croquet lawn, led into a close thicket; a staff of devoted servants who, under good treatment, showed an unrivalled eagerness to serve, made house and yard lively. The girls wore light, rustling cotton frocks, and the men brightly coloured Russian shirts and boots, which were their greatest pride. In the distance flashed the blue ribbon of a river or the mirror of a lake, surrounded by birch-trees. One drove there in a special carriage, only known in Russia, which, on account of its shape, was called a *leeneyka* ("ruler"), in order to bathe, or picnic, or to row on the lake whose still beauty was crowned with water-lilies. In the autumn there was hunting behind a pack of eager greyhounds on a long leash, or shooting, when, accompanied by keen pointers, one tramped over marshy meadows, yellow stubble fields, and bright woodland carpets woven by falling leaves, or took up one's stand on brightly tinted slopes where the dogs, panting and making a great clamour, drove before them the terrified hares and foxes. Quiet evening hours, spent at the tea-table, set with all the delicacies of a Russian pantry and bakehouse, or in the library, which contained periodicals and newspapers of every country, together with the most popular Russian, French, and German books, concluded the day.

Such was the environment into which was born Sergei Vassilyevitch Rachmaninoff on April 2, 1873.

* * * * *

Vassili Rachmaninoff, son of the landowner Arkadi Rachmaninoff and Varvara Rachmaninoff, formerly Pavlova, was a captain of the Cavalry Guards, and belonged to a distinguished family of the Russian landed aristocracy. He resigned from the army at an early age and married Lyoubov Boutakova, the daughter of General Peter Boutakov, commandant of the Araktcheyev military college in Novgorod (where he taught history), and his wife, Sophie Litvinova.

The Rachmaninoffs traced their descent back to the "Hospodars" Dragosh, who had founded the realm of the Molday and ruled over it for two hundred years (from the fourteenth to the sixteenth century). One of them had married his sister, Helena, to the son and heir of the Grand Duke Ivan III of Moscow, and it was from a nephew of the former—who was named Rachmanin— that the family took their origin. A Rachmaninoff, an officer of the St. Petersburg Guards, had keenly supported the enthronement of the Empress Elizabeth, a daughter of Peter the Great, and was rewarded for this by his Sovereign, who endowed him with the estate "Znamenskoye" in the district of Tambov. This has remained in possession of the family ever since. The district of Tambov, boasting the rich "black-earth" soil, is a fertile stretch of land between Central and South Russia. The Boutakovs were domiciled in the district of Novgorod, which is situated in the north of the empire and is poorer in soil, though rich in myths and legends.

Vassili Rachmaninoff was a brilliant officer. He had great charm of appearance, being of medium size but very broad-shouldered, dark, with fine, quick, pronounced gestures, and endowed with unusual physical strength. While in his regiment he followed the prevailing fashion and led a rather dissipated life, spending a great deal of money. In character he was inclined to indulge in somewhat fantastic day-dreams. He was always conceiving grandiose projects, usually of a business nature, which cost him vast sums of money and were either never realized or suffered a sudden collapse. Although he was very musical, he used his talent only in order to fascinate a swarm of admiring society ladies with his beautiful touch on the piano when he played opera melodies and dance tunes to them. His musical talent, however, was undeniable and he inherited it from his father. The latter, the grandfather of the Composer, a calm, dignified, and gentle man, following the family tradition, had entered the army when he was young, and fought in the Russian-Turkish War. But the army afforded him little interest. He resigned his commission early and retired to his estate in the district of Tambov, which, afterwards, he seldom left. Music was his sole ambition, and, according to the undivided opinion of his contemporaries, he was an exceptional musician and an excellent pianist. In his youth he had been a pupil of John Field, who in his turn had studied under Clementi, and had spent half his life as a piano teacher in St. Petersburg and Moscow, there establishing a unique tradition in piano playing and winning especial praise for his *jeu perlé*, which he passed on to his pupils. Rachmaninoff's grandfather also distinguished himself by this manner of playing. He took it seriously and pursued his study with great devotion. Up to the very last he practised four or five hours daily, and no one was allowed, under any circumstances, to disturb him in this. The stables might be struck by lightning, his cornfields might be ruined by hail-storms, but he continued to mount his *Gradus ad Parnassum* without a halt. Sometimes he was persuaded to play at a public or private charity concert, and this always proved a feast for the district or the whole government. Grandfather Arkadi Rachmaninoff belonged without doubt to the highest rank of amateur musicians, a class of artists widely represented in Russia during the first half of the nineteenth century. To these belonged Oulibishev, Count Vyelhorsky, Prince Odoyevsky, Count Sheremetyev, and others. Also Glinka, Dargomyshky, and, later on, Rimsky-Korsakov, Borodin, and Moussorgsky, came forth from this caste.

Lyoubov Boutakova brought to her husband, the former captain of the Cavalry, Vassili Rachmaninoff, a rich dowry consisting of four or five beautiful estates. It is probable that Vassili Rachmaninoff resigned from the army as early as he did in order to devote himself to the management of these estates; a decision which, unfortunately, soon led to very sad consequences.

There were six children of this marriage: three daughters—Helena, Sophie, and Barbara—and three sons—Vladimir the eldest, Sergei, and Arkadi, who was eight years younger, and is the only one still alive besides the Composer.

Since their marriage Rachmaninoff's parents had resided on the estate "Oneg" in the government of Novgorod. With them, in a special wing of the house, lived the grandparents Boutakov. "Oneg" was situated on the River Volchov, that river which Rimsky-Korsakov has celebrated in his opera *Sadko*. The mermaid, Princess

HAPPY CHILDHOOD IN THE COUNTRY

Volchova, in parting from her lover, the legendary *gouslee* player Sadko, begins to cry and dissolves into a river, the very River Volchov whose silver ripples divide the plains of Pskow and flow into Lake Ilmen. The surrounding country is rich in picturesque beauty that could not fail to impress the sensitive mind of the growing boy who lived in its midst. The grave northern landscape, the poetry of its unchanging rhythm, left their mark on the soul of the child Rachmaninoff and found powerful expression, convincing and alluring, in all his later work.

* * * * *

Of his early childhood Rachmaninoff speaks as follows:

"My memory goes back to my fourth year, and it is strange how all the recollections of my childhood, the good and the bad, the sad as well as the happy ones, are somehow connected with music. My first punishments, the first rewards that gladdened my childish heart, were always linked with music.

As I must have shown very early signs of a gift for music, my mother started to give me piano lessons when I was four.

I remember that, soon afterwards, my grandfather on my father's side announced his intention of visiting us. My mother told me he was a great musician and a wonderful pianist, and would, most likely, wish to hear me play. It is probable that she herself intended to introduce to him the talents of his promising grandchild. But first of all she took me aside, attended to my hands, cut my finger nails, etc., and made me understand that this was necessary for piano playing. The proceeding impressed me deeply. My mother's own hands were lovely; white and beautifully kept; an example to us children.

My grandfather arrived, and I was placed at the piano, and while I played my little tunes, consisting of four and five notes, he added a beautiful and, as it seemed to me then, a most involved accompaniment. This was probably in the manner of such piano duets as the 'paraphrases' of the *Dog Waltz* or *Tati-tati*, composed about that time by the masters of the Neo-Russian school, amongst whom were Borodin, Cui, and Rimsky-Korsakov. My grandfather praised me and I was very happy. This was the only time that I ever saw him and played duets with him, for soon afterwards he died.

I must have made pretty good progress at the piano, for I recollect that already at the age of four I was made to play to people; if I did well, I was rewarded by all sorts of good things, which were thrown to me from an adjoining room: bonbons, paper roubles, etc. This gave me great pleasure.

If I was naughty my punishment consisted in my being placed under the piano. In like disgrace other children were put in the corner. To be put under the piano seemed to me most degrading and humiliating.

When I was four years old it was decided that I should have a piano mistress. She was found in the person of a certain Anna Ornazkaya, who had just finished her studies at the St. Petersburg Conservatoire as a pupil of Professor Cross, one of the many piano teachers invited to join the first Russian College of Music by its founder, Anton Rubinstein.

Anna Ornazkaya remained with us for two or three years, but taught only the piano. As far as I can remember we had other teachers as well; probably an alternate succession of German 'Fräulein' and French 'Mademoiselles,' who were an essential feature of a Russian

THE COMPOSER'S PARENTAL GRANDPARENTS

country household. Although I have no definite recollection, I conclude that this was the case from the fact
that, as an older boy, I must have had a fairly good
mastery of the French language. After I was able to
read and write, one of the punishments for a crime
committed in school hours was that I had to write out
upon a slate, which was then in fashion, the entire
conjugation of a French irregular verb. This punishment,
however, was soon abolished as being too light; consequently I must have learned French from somebody, for
with our parents we always spoke Russian.

Thus passed the first years of my childhood. Of my
parents, who often disagreed, we loved our father the
better. This was probably unfair to my mother; but as
the former had a very gentle, affectionate manner, was
extremely good-natured and spoiled us dreadfully, it is
natural that our childish hearts, so easily won, should
turn towards him. Our mother, on the other hand, was
exceedingly strict. As our father was generally absent, it
was she who determined the routine of the household.
From our earliest days we were taught that 'there was a
time for everything.' Besides a detailed plan for our
lessons, regular hours were set aside for piano playing,
walking, and reading, and these were never violated
except under special circumstances. This careful planning
out of the day I have now, by the way, readopted, and
appreciate its value more and more; but at the time I
was unable to realize it and disliked the constraint
imposed.

One of the arguments between my parents which
cropped up repeatedly was the one concerning the future
of my elder brother and myself; my youngest brother
Arkadi was not yet born. My father wanted us to follow
his own example and enter the army. He wished us to be
educated at one of the most distinguished and privileged

military colleges for officers of the Guards, the 'Corps of Pages' in St. Petersburg. As our grandfather on my mother's side was a general we were entitled to enter this institution, which was only open to the select few. My mother, on the other hand, insisted on my going to the College of Music in St. Petersburg, although she did not oppose my father's wishes in regard to my elder brother Vladimir. And the worthy Anna Ornazkaya supported her with great energy. For a long time my father remained inflexible, for he still adhered to the principle dictated—one must admit—by class prejudice that 'pour un gentilhomme la musique ne peut jamais être un métier, mais seulement un plaisir.' The thought that his son should become a musician was intolerable, for this 'proletarian' profession was entirely unsuited for the son of a nobleman.

But sometimes fate is stronger than all prejudices, and it was fate this time that decided my parents' quarrel. When I reached my ninth year only one of my mother's four or five beautiful estates was left in our possession. The rest had been gambled away and squandered by my father. The expensive 'Corps of Pages' was out of the question. When my father had to be content in sending my brother Vladimir to an ordinary military college, he declared himself satisfied with the idea of a musical education for me. He had to abandon all hope of the Imperial Guards' uniform shedding its lustre in his own home.

Mlle Ornazkaya now took up my preparation for the St. Petersburg College of Music with renewed zeal. She was very keen that I should eventually—that is, after finishing the junior classes of the Conservatoire—become the pupil of her former teacher, Professor Cross. But the good soul did not rest there. As our pecuniary circumstances grew worse from month to month, she took pains to procure a scholarship for me at the College of Music. To my happiness and her own satisfaction, she succeeded in both objects, for Professor Cross declared himself willing to get me a scholarship only under the condition that, on entering the so-called 'professorial division' of the College, I should join his class; in the lower division I should be suitably prepared for this by Demyansky, a former pupil of his.

Only the first half of this plan, however, was realized, for reasons to which I will return later in my narrative."

How was it possible that the Rachmaninoffs, whose property was certainly above the level of that of the average provincial Russian landowner, should be brought to complete ruin in so comparatively short a time? In order to understand this one must consider the general position of the landed proprietors at that time. The abolition of serfdom alone had placed them in a precarious pecuniary position, for it deprived them of unpaid labour. Only careful calculation and extreme thrift could possibly relieve the situation. This, however, was not to the taste of the proverbially lavish Russian nature. Still less did it suit Vassili Rachmaninoff's outlook on life; for, although the household in the country was managed by a strict and sensible woman in a nowise luxurious manner, he flung the money out of the window in handfuls. Added to this came the death of his father-in-law, Boutakov, shortly after the decease of his own father, and he was forced to manage his estates personally, although he knew nothing about agriculture and did not take the slightest interest in farming, except perhaps where it concerns horses. His agents and others holding positions of trust on the estates which were further removed stole and cheated wherever possible, and to their hearts' content; so that one after another of his beautiful estates had to be sold in order to pay his debts on the estate. The last to go was "Oneg," after a vain and desperate struggle to retain it. It was sold by public auction.

In the year 1882 the Rachmaninoffs moved to St. Petersburg. At the same time a conflict, which had been steadily brewing for years, came to a head, and Rachmaninoff's parents separated. An official divorce did not take place: this was hardly possible, as it was not in accordance with the creed of the Greek Orthodox Church, but they were never reconciled.

GRANNY BOUTAKOVA

CHAPTER TWO

THE ST. PETERSBURG CONSERVATOIRE

1882–1885

The modest home in St. Petersburg—The parents separate—
Granny Boutakova—Rachmaninoff pupil of Demyansky as a
preparation for his work under Professor Cross who had
secured him a scholarship—The two first profound musical
impressions: the singing of his sister Helena and of the
choirs in the churches and cathedrals of St. Petersburg—
Diphtheria—Death of his sister Sophie—Summer on the
estate "Borissovo," belonging to his grandmother Boutakova—
Cousin Siloti becomes a star of the first order in the musical
world of St. Petersburg—Rachmaninoff's mother consults
him about little Sergei's hopeless laziness—Siloti's answer—
The last summer in "Borissovo"

IN St. Petersburg Madame Rachmaninoff took a modest flat, where, together with her children and her mother—the widow of General Boutakov—who paid all the household expenses, she settled down as well as it was possible under the circumstances. As her eldest son, Vladimir, was being educated at the Military College, Sergei remained the only "man" in the family.

After the more or less unrestricted life in the country, where the spacious rooms and corridors of the manor-house afforded ample freedom for playing about and romping, it seemed rather hard to put up with the comparatively limited space and the quieter life of the St. Petersburg flat. Besides, the absence of their father, whom the children loved beyond everything, cast a gloom over their life in the city; nor could Mme Rachmaninoff forget her husband, whom she cherished up to her last breath with the strong, all-embracing, self-sacrificing love of which Slav women are capable. (She died only in September 1929, in Soviet Russia, without ever again seeing him.) During that time in St. Petersburg she often mingled her tears with those of her son, who lamented his father's absence with childish longing. But this mutual grief did not tend to draw mother and son closer together; the mother, contrary to her former habit, took hardly any interest in the children and devoted all her thoughts to the husband who had left her.

Thus it happened that at home the boy's closest companion was his grandmother, whose favourite he was, and, being an uncommonly bright and cheerful child, he did not fail to make the most of this advantageous position. One knows what grandmothers are! This one spoiled her grandson with all her might. She never made the slightest attempt to bring him up, either mildly or strictly, overlooked all his failings, and shut her eyes to the mischievous tricks which he invented all too often, while she revelled in his precocious and affectionate ways.

One may well imagine that under these circumstances his studies and, unfortunately, the music as well, did not exactly flourish. In the comfortable knowledge that, even if he did not practice, his efforts were more successful than those of his classmates, young Sergei grew lazier and lazier. In the end he did nothing at all, showed a marked preference for shirking his lessons, and relied on his talent and on the inspiration of the moment which, as he now says, was merely a way of expressing his laziness. Thus he gradually developed into a little rogue—the terror of the backyards and streets of St. Petersburg. Instead of going to the College of Music he visited the ice rink, which delighted him, and soon developed a skill in skating which he was far from attaining at the piano. Another favourite sport of his was to jump on and off the running trams, which in those days were drawn by horses along the seven-kilometre stretch of the Nevsky Prospect; a very suitable pastime, one will admit, for a budding famous pianist, especially in the winter, when the pavements were glazed over with ice!

But this life, lacking, as it did, all supervision, may have had its advantages; it certainly developed a sense of responsibility and an independence of spirit in the boy, which were to come to his assistance during the most difficult periods of his later life.

In spite of his laziness young Rachmaninoff was made to perform at all the pupils' concerts given by the St. Petersburg Conservatoire, which were frequently attended by the President of the Imperial Russian Musical Society, the Grand Duke Konstantin, and other social and musical celebrities. This, however, did not cause him a moment's trouble.

At this time the famous 'cellist, Karl Davydov, was director of the St. Petersburg Conservatoire, founded by Anton Rubinstein in 1862. The latter for some years past had been travelling all over the world, giving concerts, and did not resume his position as director of this College of Music till 1887, after Davydov's death. Had Rubinstein returned to St. Petersburg three years earlier, it is highly probable that the musical development of the boy Rachmaninoff would have taken a different course. Davydov evidently did not recognize and value the musical abilities of the child, although he frequently paraded him as a pianist.

Outside his life at the Conservatoire there were two musical events which deeply impressed Rachmaninoff and left their indelible mark on his soul. Let us hear what he himself has to say about it:

"I have to thank my sister Helena for the most beautiful

and profound musical impressions I received at that time, and even during my whole childhood. She was five years my senior and fourteen years old when we moved to St. Petersburg. She was an unusual girl: beautiful, clever, original, and, in spite of her slight figure, of Herculean physical strength. The fact that she could bend a silver rouble with the fingers of one hand impressed us boys tremendously. At the same time she was gifted with a glorious voice, which, even now, seems to me the most beautiful I have ever heard. Although she took no lessons she could sing everything, for nature herself had seen to the training of her wonderful contralto voice. My enjoyment in hearing her sing can hardly be described. It happened that, just at that time, Tchaikovsky, who later played such a significant part in my musical development, became known and popular in Russia. It was through my sister Helena that I was first introduced to his music, which touched me to the heart. She used to sing *None but the Weary Heart*, and this as well as some other songs which she rendered magnificently, in spite, or, perhaps because, of her youth, pleased me beyond words. She usually accompanied herself, but sometimes I had to take my place at the piano and the result was not very satisfactory, for I was far too self-willed to consider the feelings of the singer; I simply played as it pleased me and left the singer to follow as best she could. These attempts to perform together often ended in my sister exclaiming, 'Oh, get out!' and boxing my ears.

Although we were poor, my sister's beauty and her unusual qualities attracted many suitors to our house. I remember that this greatly occupied my grandmother's thoughts. She used to take me—a mere hop o' my thumb—into her confidence, and we spent many evening hours discussing the good and the bad qualities of these young

THE COMPOSER'S MOTHER, MADAME LYOUBOV
RACHMANINOFF (NÉE BUTAKOVA)

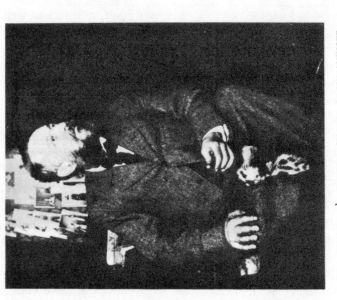

THE COMPOSER'S FATHER, VASSILI RACHMANINOFF

men, carefully weighing up their chances against one another.

'But those whom thé gods love . . .' This saying came true in my sister's case, for when she was seventeen she developed pernicious anaemia, which grew more and more threatening. I remember the uncanny feeling I had when she pricked her finger and I saw water instead of blood. She was not destined to see the spring of her eighteenth year. Six months before her death she had begun to study under the famous singing master, Pryanishnikov, of St. Petersburg. These lessons were chiefly limited to the learning of a few operatic parts. Pryanishnikov insisted upon her taking part in the singing audition held at the Imperial 'Marien' Theatre, where her voice and rendering caused almost a sensation. She was immediately engaged as one of the select members of the troupe at this theatre, an honour which previously can hardly have been bestowed upon so youthful a singer. But, as I have said, she died before she had an opportunity to appear before the footlights.

The second group of strong musical impressions which I received at that time I owe to my grandmother, whose kindly hand almost imperceptibly guided my fate during the St. Petersburg years. My grandmother was very religious and attended regularly the services held in the different churches of the city. She always took me—her favourite—with her. We spent hours standing in the beautiful St. Petersburg churches: St. Isaac's Cathedral, the Kasan Cathedral, and other old places of worship in all quarters of the town. Being only a young greenhorn, I took less interest in God and religious worship than in the singing, which was of unrivalled beauty, especially in the cathedrals, where one frequently heard the best choirs of St. Petersburg. I usually took pains to find room underneath the gallery and never missed a single note. Thanks to my good memory, I also remembered most of what I heard. This I turned into capital—literally—by sitting down at the piano when I came home, and playing all I had heard. For this performance my grandmother never failed to reward me with twenty-five kopeks, and, naturally, I was not loath to exert my memory for such a consideration, as twenty-five kopeks meant a large sum to an urchin of ten or eleven."

These musical pastimes were not only remunerative but definitely useful in that they laid the foundation of Rachmaninoff's knowledge of, and exceptional command over, the technique of phrasing in Russian church singing, to which we owe some of his most beautiful compositions in that genre; but they had, unfortunately, no connection whatever with his studies at the St. Petersburg Conservatoire. His teacher, Demyansky, must have been an unusually bad master, for he failed to rouse even so promising a pupil. Altogether, the staff of teachers in the preparatory "lower division" of St. Petersburg College of Music of that time could hardly be called remarkable. The lessons in musical theory were given by a certain Roubetz. When the nine years old Rachmaninoff entered the College and this man recognized the perfect ear of the boy, who was able, promptly and unfailingly, to name every note in the most complicated chord structures, he decided that the child did not need any teaching in elementary theory (which, it is true, included solfeggio classes, oral training, musical dictation, choir singing, etc.) and sent him straight into the harmony classes held by Professor Liberius Sachetti, a sound theorist, and teacher of aesthetics and musical history at the St. Petersburg Conservatoire. Now the nine years old Rachmaninoff sat in the harmony classes of this learned pedagogue, blinked his eyes, and did not understand a word of the lectures, as he lacked the most elementary knowledge of theory; nor was he in a position to make good this lack of knowledge, for Sachetti's method of teaching was based on an abhorrence of all books, and he expected his pupils to take notes from his lectures. The diligent ones did— but not Rachmaninoff. It was hardly fair to expect this of a child of nine years. Thus passed lesson after lesson without adding one whit to his knowledge, which was nil. The first time he was called up, his ignorance was brought to light in the most dreadful manner; he could not answer a single question put to him. Little Rachmaninoff defended himself, protesting that he was far too small for such wisdom and, would they, please, leave him in peace. To his joy this scene resulted in Sachetti promptly sending him back into the theory classes of the worthy Monsieur Roubetz. And there he remained, confident in the knowledge of this master's high opinion of his "talent," and idled away the time until he left the St. Petersburg College of Music.

During their third year in St. Petersburg the Rachmaninoff family were visited by great trouble. A diphtheria epidemic broke out in the town and all the Rachmaninoff children fell victims to this malicious disease, which in those days was still extremely dangerous, as the Behring Serum had not yet been discovered. The boys recovered, but Sergei lost his second sister.

Towards the end of this disastrous year in St. Petersburg, 1884-85, it became apparent that Rachmaninoff's mother had not been as blind and indifferent to the activities of her younger son as might have been imagined.

A new and brilliant star had then made its appearance on the St. Petersburg horizon, namely, Alexander Siloti. Siloti was twenty-two years old. He came from an aristocratic family of landed proprietors, had studied under Nikolai Rubinstein and Tchaikovsky at the Moscow

College of Music in the year 1881, and had been a pupil—
and, as rumour would have it, a favourite one—of Liszt
from 1883-84. In 1883 he had reaped great honours at
the Musical Congress in Leipzig. In the eyes of the social
and musical world of St. Petersburg all this surrounded
him with a glamour which, by the way, shone un-
diminished up to the catastrophe that resulted in the great
Russian breakdown. Siloti was closely connected with
the Rachmaninoff family, as his mother was a sister of
Vassili Rachmaninoff, so that he and Sergei were first
cousins.

It was to Siloti that Mme Rachmaninoff decided to
turn in her trouble. She brought her son to his great,
and already famous, cousin. To him she related her
difficulties, and asked what she could possibly do to
drive the nonsense out of her boy's head, as he was
doubtless gifted with a very great talent, but was also
an incredibly lazy little ne'er-do-well. Siloti's concise
answer was as follows:

"There is only one person who can help; it is my
former teacher, Sverev, in Moscow. The boy must come
under his discipline."

Mme Rachmaninoff meekly accepted this oracular sentence. She decided to place the boy under Sverev's rod
of correction at the Moscow Conservatoire at the beginning
of the new school year, that is, the following autumn.

Now it was for the boy to see how he could make the
most of his freedom during the last summer holidays,
before the beginning of a presumably serious epoch in his
life.

Since the Rachmaninoff family had moved to St.
Petersburg it was arranged that Sergei should spend the
three months' summer holidays, so generously granted to
Russian school children and equally freely given to the
pupils of the Conservatoire, with his grandmother in the

district of Novgorod. Mme Boutakova had yielded to the fervent requests of her favourite grandson and bought the small-holding "Borissovo" as a compensation for the four or five estates so gaily wasted by her son-in-law.

These three months of unhampered freedom in "God's own world," which the boy Rachmaninoff loved more than anything, were naturally the most enjoyable months during his St. Petersburg years and, without doubt, the happiest of his childhood. "Borissovo," embedded in endless meadows, fields, and woods, lay by the River Volchov which flows into the lake Ilmen. There the boy led a glorious life of absolute freedom: sheltered and surrounded by his grandmother's infinite love, yet restrained in nothing. In the river one could fish and bathe, and it was not long before Sergei had established himself as the hero of the village children by his excellence in the art of swimming. Or he took the boat and floated downstream, into the greenish-red glimmer of twilight; from the high water-reeds came the chattering of wild-duck, while slim-necked herons crossed the pale northern night sky like slow, black shadows. Vesper bells from neighbouring Novgorod drifted over the peaceful country-side. These bells . . . they were lovelier than all else. The boy would spend hours in the boat, listening to their strange, compelling, utterly unearthly voices.

Did he dream then that he would, one day, immortalize the peal of Russian church bells in his music?

The dog-cart was frequently got ready and the grandson drove his grandmother to the service held at the convent near by. There, as in the whole neighbourhood, the old lady was held in high respect. But the grandson also was known to all; from the Mother Superior down to the humblest nun, from the peasant behind the plough to the bell-ringer who, with his two hands and every joint of his arms and legs, manipulated so ingeniously the ropes attached to the numberless tongues, uniting the sounds in such strange rhythms.

But music, although not practised methodically, was by no means forgotten at "Borissovo." Whenever they had visitors from the neighbourhood, or if they themselves paid a call, Her Excellency took a natural delight in astonishing the appreciative neighbours with her grandson's talent, and was eager to show them that the boy, although a little scoundrel, knew how to play the piano.

This was the time, according to Rachmaninoff's own recollection, that he made his first attempts at improvising. He found it far too dull, and not consistent with his dignity, to play the Sonatinas by Kuhlau and Diabelli, or the Studies by Cramer, Kullack, and others, which he had learnt at the College of Music; so he took matters into his own hands and improvised persistently, and, relying on his listeners' rather low standard of musical education, introduced what he had played as masterpieces by Chopin or works of some fashionable composers unknown in the neighbourhood. He was always rewarded by great applause, and this harmless deception has never yet been discovered.

The last summer which the boy Sergei spent at "Borissovo" was overshadowed by the thought of his imminent removal to Moscow. In order to instil into him the necessary respect, his future mentor, Professor Sverev, had been represented to the boy as a kind of tamer of wild beasts, whose uncontrollable temper only equalled his strictness, and who thrashed his pupils at every possible opportunity, so that they lived in a state of fear and trembling. Such a prospect seemed uncomfortable even to a brave boy like Rachmaninoff. With a troubled mind he roamed through the fields and woods of his grandmother's estate, and many a deep sigh escaped him when he listened to the bells of the St. Sophia Cathedral

38

of Novgorod, and thought of the Kremlin bells which he was so soon to hear.

When the fateful day arrived he drove his grandmother to the convent for the last time, to attend a solemn farewell service which was held there.

Then his grandmother hung a small bag, containing a hundred rouble notes, around his neck, made the sign of the cross over her beloved grandson, and took him to the station. It was with a heavy heart that she sent him on his long journey to Moscow.

Since then he has only seen the kind old lady—the only friend of his childhood—once again.

Soon after his departure Mme Boutakova sold the estate, which she had purchased solely for her grandson.

CHAPTER THREE

MOSCOW. SVEREV AND ARENSKY

1885–1889

Strict discipline under Sverev in Moscow—Sverev and "his boys"—The Moscow Conservatoire—Taneyev and the teachers—Rubinstein's visit to Moscow—The "Historical Concerts" and the hundredth performance of Demon*—First meeting with Tchaikovsky—Musical antagonism between Moscow and St. Petersburg—Rachmaninoff's arrangement of* Manfred *for two pianos—Summer in the Crimea—Arensky's harmony class—First attempt at composition. Finishing examination in harmony (Tchaikovsky's attitude)—Taneyev's counterpoint class—Siloti as a Professor of pianoforte—Last pianoforte examination—"The Art of the fugue" with Arensky—Scriabin—Last examination in the fugue class*

ON a rainy day in August 1885 Rachmaninoff, who was then twelve years old, arrived in Moscow. The boy could hardly guess that this city which he dreaded so much would soon become his second home and provide such a rich field for his artistic development. It was arranged not only that he should have lessons from Sverev, a figure who loomed in his imagination as a terrifying spectre, but also that he should live with him. He did not, however, have to present himself immediately on his arrival, but was given a respite of three days which were to be spent with his aunt, Mme Siloti, who always passed the winter in Moscow.

In the meantime it will be worth our while to take a closer look at his future teacher. Nikolai Sverev—a man of about sixty—was one of the most original characters in the social and musical world of Moscow towards the end of the nineteenth century. A mere accident had settled his musical career. His story in many ways resembled that of Rachmaninoff's father. Like him he descended from a distinguished family of the Russian landed aristocracy, squandered a few beautiful estates which he had inherited from his father, and was unusually musical. But Nikolai Sverev's talent had received better training. He had been a pupil of Dubuque who, besides Villoing—teacher of the brothers Rubinstein during the thirties and forties of the nineteenth century— was considered the best pianoforte teacher in Moscow. After selling his last estate Sverev accepted a Government post in St. Petersburg. On his journey through Moscow he met his former teacher, Dubuque. The latter was pleased to see his pupil, whom he liked principally for his great social talents.

"Where are you going?" he inquired.

"To St. Petersburg."

"What for?"

"I have accepted a post at the Ministry."

"Why?"

"Because I have to earn my living."

"What is your salary in St. Petersburg?"

"One hundred roubles per month."

"You had better stay here. I could get you piano lessons for the same sum."

Sverev remained in Moscow and was soon the most sought after and the best-paid pianoforte teacher in the ancient city. He got introductions to the great merchant families—the plutocracy of Moscow—who formed a set of their own and lived in rich mansions in the quarter of the town which lies beyond the River Moscow. There Sverev flourished, partly through his musical abilities, but principally through his social talents. His presence was a *sine qua non* at all the sumptuous dinner-parties and other elaborate entertainments for which the representatives of the Moscow business world were famous. He was particularly appreciated at the card table, which never failed to appear after the meals of these Moscow parties. Sverev had a flair for all the—so-called—"commercial" card games, such as Whist, Boston, and Preference, but he was most popular at the gambling table, when his distinguished manners, which were after all natural to him, often made a deeper impression than the millions of the caviar kings. As his numerous lessons brought him a good income, which was well supplemented by his winnings at cards, he always lived in grand style and this gave him a peculiar prestige. But no one ever heard him play the piano after he began his extraordinary successful career as a teacher. He preferred theory to practice. Judging by the number of his famous pupils he must have been a good teacher. To increase his reputation as an instructor, and no doubt for his own pleasure, Sverev always took a few pupils into his house. He preferred them to be as inexperienced as possible, so that he could himself supervise and influence their mental and musical development. As he delighted in parading his pupils and appeared everywhere in their company, he made it a rule that those who lived with him should either be talented or possess exceptional moral qualities, such as diligence, ambition, etc.

When, in the year 1866, Nikolai Rubinstein founded the Moscow Conservatoire, he proposed that Sverev should join him as one of the first pianoforte teachers there, but only in the lower division. Sverev accepted the offer without, however, greatly reducing the number of his far more remunerative private lessons.

This, then, was the man who became Rachmaninoff's teacher. With him two other boys, Maximov and Pressmann, entered Sverev's house. The former and Rachmaninoff satisfied the above-mentioned conditions by possessing talent in the highest possible degree, while Pressmann qualified more on account of his moral qualities. Maximov, who promised to be one of the most brilliant Russian pianists, died of typhoid fever when he was barely twenty; Pressmann, who developed into a good teacher, ended his career as Director of the Conservatoire founded by the Imperial Musical Society in Rostov on the Don, where he achieved excellent results.

But we will let Rachmaninoff himself describe his first impressions of Sverev's household, to which his aunt, Mme Siloti, brought him after the three days he had spent with her.

He says:

"I entered Sverev's house with a faint heart, having heard a great deal about his unbridled severity and his 'loose wrist,' which was in evidence not only at the piano. I felt that my golden days of youth and freedom had come to an end.

Now began a life full of discipline and serious study. Sverev's 'family' consisted of himself and an old sister who, like himself, was unmarried and managed the household. On weekdays we hardly ever saw Sverev, for he gave lessons from nine in the morning till nine o'clock at night, and always away from home. As he led a very social life he hardly ever returned home when his work was done, and when he did arrive it was at such a late hour that we boys had gone to bed long ago. We shared a bedroom and a piano (this terminated in a little tragedy). Each of us had to practise three hours daily, which must have been a nuisance to our neighbours. Sverev's sister, who in his absence had full authority in the house, turned out to be a rather disagreeable and spiteful person. She supervised us with the utmost strictness, and woe to him who began practising five minutes too late, or left the piano five minutes too early! He was reported to her brother without mercy.

The rumours of Sverev's excessive strictness with which I had been frightened proved to be utter nonsense. He was a man of rare intelligence and great kindliness, qualities that earned him the highest respect from the best of his contemporaries. He was an enthusiastic admirer of Dostoyevski, whom he had known personally and whose works he had closely studied. Yet his irritability was as great as his kindliness. When he lost his temper he was capable of attacking his victim with his fists and throwing at him any object within his reach; in some cases he might not have hesitated even to kill his opponent. We boys had many a chance to test his 'loose wrist.' I was chastised by him four or five times, but never, as the others, for any 'musical' sin. In my case they always said: 'To-day the boy's laziness has got him into trouble again.' But on the whole Sverev was an unusually humane, fine, and noble-thinking man. Amongst the Professors at the College of Music, who—with the exception of two or three outstanding artists teaching in the higher 'virtuoso' classes—were ordinary, uninteresting people of a mediocre mentality, Sverev was by far the most original character and distinguished himself through his vivacious and sparkling intellect, which lifted him high above his environment.

It looked almost as if he were making a fool of himself over us boys. I hardly dare decide whether or no his exceptional treatment of us was unconsciously prompted by vague practical considerations. It is a fact, however, that outside our lessons, which always took place at the Conservatoire, he treated us as if we were his equals. I ought to mention that he never accepted a penny from us for board or lessons. We got our living and teaching

44

absolutely free of charge, and never, under any circumstances, did he let us want for anything. Our clothes, which were the same as the uniform that had been made compulsory in all the Russian secondary schools and consisted of a tunic with a high military collar and long trousers, were ordered from the most expensive tailor in the town, the same who supplied Sverev's own clothes. There was no first night, no interesting or outstanding performance at the Little Theatre, no opera at the Grand Theatre which we did not attend. We saw all performances given by foreign theatrical stars who visited Moscow. At that time I had the good fortune to admire such celebrities as Salvini, Rossi, Barnay, and Eleonora Duse, as well as many other actors of international fame. The four of us always occupied the most expensive box in the *bel étage*. Out of principle Sverev never took anything cheaper than a seat in the *bel étage*, for Sverev and his 'boys' were well-known figures amongst first-night audiences. I need not emphasize how greatly this education tended to develop our artistic outlook. We stored up unforgettable memories, at the Little Theatre in particular, where we saw Yermolova and the magnificent actors who made up the rest of the cast, such as the Sadovskys, Jushin, Lensky, and others. It goes without saying that we visited every good concert in Moscow.

Sverev ordered our lives with the same strict discipline as our piano playing. He laid the greatest stress on tidiness of execution and was quite capable of sending a pupil out of the room for the first wrong, or even blurred, note. On the other hand, he exhibited real joy over a technically faultless rendering. In spite of the wholesome fear which we felt for him, he inspired us with respect and even enthusiasm for his personality. We vied with one another as to who should first jump up and bring him an ash-tray, light his cigarette, help him into his overcoat, or render

to his skill as a teacher. It frequently happened that when, during the week, he dined at the house of some wealthy Moscow merchant, one of us was sent for by special messenger. The choice usually fell on me. After arriving at my destination and peeling off my heavy winter garments, I had to sit down at the piano and play a Study by Cramer or Czerny, a Study by Reinecke (the first piece which, on my arrival from St. Petersburg, I had played to Sverev and his particular favourite), a Sonata by Mozart, or other pieces. When I had finished, it was Sverev's habit to say in my presence: 'You see, *this* is how one plays the piano!' and turning to me: 'You can go home now'; whereas during a lesson that very same morning he had shouted at the first wrong note: 'Is *this* how one plays the piano? Get out at once!' I am sure that these evening performances in other people's houses, given by his boarders, must have tended to increase the number of his pupils, though certainly Sverev had not arranged them for this purpose.

During my first year with Sverev, Anton Rubinstein visited Moscow. One may imagine the feverish excitement and the impatience with which we boys, who regarded ourselves as future pianists, looked forward to this event.

At that time Sergei Ivanovitch Taneyev, who was barely thirty years old, had followed Nikolai Rubinstein—after an interval of several years—as Director of the Moscow Conservatoire. He asked Anton Rubinstein to honour the college by coming to hear some of the pupils play. Rubinstein came, and with great solemnity, in the presence of all the teachers and pupils, the little concert took place. A young man and a girl student sang, and Joseph Lhévinne and I, who were both the same age— either twelve or thirteen—played the piano. My piece was Bach's English Suite in A minor. When the concert was finished Taneyev rose and begged Rubinstein in the

name of all present to play us something, so that the
numerous pupils assembled should at least once in their
lives enjoy the experience of hearing him play. Rubinstein
had not come to Moscow to give concerts, but to conduct
the hundredth performance of his opera *Demon* at the
Grand Theatre. But he actually sat down and played
Beethoven's Sonata in F sharp, Op. 78. I presume he
chose this piece, which is by no means Beethoven's
happiest, because it lasts only ten minutes. His playing,
at that time, did not impress me as deeply as it did only a
year later, when it gripped my whole imagination and
had a marked influence on my ambition as a pianist.
This may have been due to the piece he had chosen,
which was then unknown to me; or perhaps the inward
excitement caused by my own playing dulled my sense
of appreciation.

In the evening there was the customary banquet at
Sverev's house. About twenty people sat down to table,
amongst them we three boys. As a reward for my 'good
playing' in the morning I was allowed to lead the great
Rubinstein to the table by holding on to his coat tails,
a distinction that swelled me with pride. Afterwards
I sat silent, taking no interest in the food, and
hung upon every word that fell from Rubinstein's
mouth. I remember one of his remarks, which made
me very thoughtful. A pianist of growing reputation
—I believe it must have been young d'Albert—had
recently given concerts in Moscow and St. Petersburg
and was being hailed by the over-enthusiastic Press as the
one and only worthy successor to Rubinstein. Someone
asked Rubinstein whether he had heard him. 'Yes,' was
the laconic answer. But the questioner persisted and
inquired how he liked the playing of this young pianist.
Rubinstein leaned back and, eyeing him sharply from
beneath his bushy brows, said, as it seemed to me, with

a touch of bitterness and irony: 'Oh, well, everyone can play the piano nowadays. . . .'

At the festival performance of *Demon* at the Grand Theatre, given for the benefit of the stage decorator and mechanician, Walz, whose fame had spread far beyond the borders of Russia, Sverev and his 'Three Musketeers' were naturally present, occupying their usual box in the *bel étage*. One incident which took place during this performance I shall never forget. Rubinstein conducted. The house was sold out and the most brilliant audience that Moscow could command filled the boxes and stalls and crowded right up to the galleries. As the curtain rose upon the second scene and the orchestra played the well-known passage in C minor, to which the audience listened with critical attention, one noticed that the stage was not too well lighted. A few short, dry taps with the conductor's baton plunged the orchestra into immediate silence, and through the sudden stillness that hung over the whole theatre one heard Rubinstein's disagreeably grating voice:

'I have already asked for better stage lighting at the rehearsal!'

There was some hurried movement behind the scenes, and suddenly the stage was flooded with brightness almost as strong as daylight. Rubinstein calmly picked up his baton, which he had placed on the score, and began conducting the scene all over again.

This autocratic attitude in front of an audience numbering two thousand people made an indelible impression on me.

In the following year Rubinstein gave his famous historical concerts. In these he presented a complete survey of the works of Bach, the old Italians, Mozart, Beethoven, and Chopin, up to Liszt and the Russian Moderns. These concerts took place on seven Tuesday evenings, in the large hall of the Moscow Union of Noblemen, a magnificent white-columned building, which must be one of the finest concert-halls in Europe. On Wednesday mornings he repeated the whole programme in the concert-hall of the German Club for the benefit of students, who had free admission. Naturally Sverev, with his three boys in tow, was present at both series of performances. In this way I heard the programme of these historical concerts twice, and was able every Wednesday morning to re-examine my impressions of the previous evening. I stored up wonderful memories, with which no others in my experience can compare.

It was not so much his magnificent technique that held one spellbound as the profound, spiritually refined musicianship, which spoke from every note and every bar he played, and singled him out as the most original and unequalled pianist in the world. Naturally I never missed a note, and I remember how deeply affected I was by his rendering of the *Appassionata*, or Chopin's Sonata in B minor.

Once he repeated the whole finale of the Sonata in B minor, perhaps because he had not succeeded in the short crescendo at the end as he would have wished. One listened entranced, and could have heard the passage over and over again, so unique was the beauty of tone which his magic touch drew from the keys. I have never heard the virtuoso piece *Islamey*, by Balakirev, as Rubinstein played it, and his interpretation of Schumann's little fantasy *The Bird as Prophet* was inimitable in poetic refinement: to describe the diminuendo of the pianissimo at the end as the 'fluttering away of the little bird' would be hopelessly inadequate. Inimitable, too, was the soul-stirring imagery in the *Kreisleriana*, the last (G minor) passage of which I have never heard anyone play in the same manner. One of Rubinstein's greatest secrets was his use of the pedal. He himself has very happily expressed his ideas on the subject when he said: 'The pedal is the soul of the piano.' No pianist should ever forget this.

Although Rubinstein lived for another ten years, I never again heard him play except once at a concert in Moscow given by the singer, Mme Lavrovskaya, and then he only accompanied her in two songs of his own composition. I noticed that he did not keep strictly to the music before him, but seemed at times to improvise, illustrating the two rather weak compositions *Open the Prison Gate* and *Night* with such striking flashes of tone colour that one was unable ever to forget them again."

Although Rachmaninoff made astonishing progress at the piano, even during his first year under Sverev's strict guidance, nothing whatever was done to enlarge his knowledge of theory. Here, as at the Conservatoire in St. Petersburg, he was exempted from attending solfeggio classes or studying anything connected with this subject. It was Sverev's wish that his pupils should first enlarge their musical horizon from their taste, and then add to their knowledge of musical literature. For this purpose he engaged an elderly and dignified lady, Mme Belopolskaya, who was a sound pianist and came to the house once a week in order to spend several hours playing on two pianos with all the three boys. In this pleasant and stimulating manner they became acquainted with the whole bulk of classical and post-classical music, for they played all the chamber music and the Symphonies of Haydn, Mozart, Schubert, and Schumann.

When they had been with him a year and the summer approached, Sverev decided to do even more for them. He always spent his summers in the Crimea, on the estate "Oleis," the property of the Moscow millionaire Tokmakov, whose children he instructed in piano playing.

This year he took a little house in the near neighbourhood, where he installed his three boys, not by themselves but in the care of Ladoukhin, who was a professor of theory and harmony at the Moscow Conservatoire. It was his task to teach the boys in two and a half months what, according to the curriculum of the Moscow Conservatoire, took two to three years' study, namely, the whole bulk of elementary theory and the first harmony course (thorough bass).

Towards the end of May the party started on their journey to the most southerly point of Russia, that charming spot in the Crimea which would surely outrival the Côte d'Azur if it were within easier reach. One unusual feature characterized this journey; while Sverev travelled first-class, the boys and Ladoukhin occupied a third-class compartment. This leads one to suspect that of late the card tables had not been yielding quite so freely.

So as to leave ample time for theoretical studies as well as for the bathing and idling which was rendered necessary by the infernal heat of the Crimean summer, the practising of the little pianists was reduced to one hour only. Ladoukhin, helped by the keenness and interest of his pupils, proved excellent in carrying out his task. When, in the early autumn, the three boys returned to Moscow, they passed their examination at the College of Music brilliantly and were immediately promoted to the second harmony course, directed by the well-known composer, Anton Arensky.

One of Sverev's conditions in taking exceptionally talented pupils into his house was that the boys should not go home for their holidays and that they should see as little as possible of their relations in Moscow. In making these rules he probably intended to keep the future artists away from the softening atmosphere of exaggerated tenderness and sentimentality and to shield them from the dangerous influence of premature admiration. As far as Rachmaninoff was concerned, this scheme worked admirably. His character and his whole manner changed considerably, even during his first year in Sverev's house. From a boisterous, lazy little ne'er-do-well, ready for any foolish prank, he turned into a quiet, reserved, and sober boy who worked hard. Coming from the seclusion of Sverev's house into the democratic world of mixed classes at the Conservatoire, he was noticeable for his calm indifference to any form of rowdiness or insubordination. There was only one idiosyncrasy that he made no attempt to subdue, and which is characteristic of him even now— his easy, infectious, and quite uncontrollable laughter. His classmates soon discovered this and did their utmost to make him laugh at every possible opportunity, with the result that his mirth affected the whole class, and he was made the scapegoat.

*　　*　　*

Arensky, a composer of good taste, with an unusually delicate sense of harmony, was, unfortunately, not a good master. He was a poor teacher, showed little interest in his pupils, and was lazy and hot-tempered. He seemed to imagine that vociferous outbursts of abuse were sufficient in themselves, and never made any further attempt to influence or help his pupils. But towards Rachmaninoff, who was .his pronounced favourite, he behaved in a markedly different manner. He soon recognized the great talent which the boy showed in his own particular subject, and took a deep and affectionate interest in him. This, it is true, was an easy task, for little Sergei from the very beginning showed a lively interest in harmony and its alluring intricacies and did not need to be pushed, as he always worked harder and with better results than his master had expected. Although he hardly ever found fault with Rachmaninoff's work, Arensky pointed out to him innumerable different ways in which his melodies might be harmonized.

While instructing and, at the same time, stimulating the natural invention of his eager pupil he poured out to him the whole wealth of his gift for harmonic combinations and showed him patiently over and over again how to extract himself from harmonic entanglements of his own making.

In later years Rachmaninoff readily admitted that Arensky's harmony lessons were of great help to him. At the end of the college year Rachmaninoff was the only one in his class to solve the problem of the last lessons. This consisted in altering simple melodies harmonized in two parts into four- or five-part harmonies. At his last lesson Rachmaninoff showed ten of these little songs, which greatly delighted Arensky. The boy was very quick to notice the different marks which his master gave him for his work in harmony and which fluctuated between "good," "very good," and "excellent." His ten songs were all marked "excellent," and it was hard to say who was better pleased, the boy or his master.

During that year also Rachmaninoff made his first attempt at composition. So far neither he nor his two companions at Sverev's had thought of it. But one evening when the lamp was lit, and the three boys were sitting at the large round table in the living-room busy with their usual occupations, one of them—it was not Rachmaninoff—made a suggestion. "How would it be if we composed something?" he exclaimed. This proposition was made in the same childish spirit as if the talker had said: "Let's all hide under the table!" or "What about a game of 'Old Maid'?" They found some manuscript paper and each took a sheet. Pressmann wrote an Oriental march in eight bars, and Maximov the beginning of a song; but Rachmaninoff filled nearly two pages with his neat writing. It was a Study in F sharp and without doubt the Composer's Opus 1!

Sverev, as might be expected, got wind of this new game. He made Rachmaninoff play his Study to him, and although it was a trivial little piano piece and showed no glimpse of his talent, it had one or two passages which must have struck the experienced teacher as unusual and left him with the suspicion that the boy might one day become a real composer. It is possible that he communicated this presentiment to one of his best friends, who, from that moment, took a particular interest in the boy's development. This friend was no other than Tchaikovsky.

Tchaikovsky frequently met the boy in Sverev's house. Sverev, who, as we already know, discouraged all display, loved nevertheless to show off his three boys to his friends and intimates. It was not to be expected that he would hide the brilliantly gifted Rachmaninoff from Tchaikovsky, who was then rightly considered the highest musical authority in Moscow. Tchaikovsky was a frequent guest at Sverev's house, and here, on an occasion when Rachmaninoff played the composer's *Nocturne* in a manner that delighted him, began the friendship between the boy and this generally idolized musician.

Soon afterwards, when he was already Arensky's pupil, Rachmaninoff gave Sverev a surprise that was as unexpected as it was gratifying. During the season Tchaikovsky's *Manfred* Symphony was first performed at one of the Symphony concerts given by the Imperial Russian Musical Society. The orchestral score had just been published. How great was his surprise when, one day, he was asked into the music-room and Rachmaninoff and Pressmann played to him the former's arrangement for two pianofortes of the *Manfred* Symphony! Very soon Tchaikovsky himself had to hear this achievement, which was rather noticeable for a boy of thirteen, and did not withhold the highest praise, which was mixed with surprise and pleasure. Without any guidance whatever young Rachmaninoff had made himself acquainted with the problems and secrets of score reading and had immediately applied his newly acquired knowledge in this very practical fashion. In order to understand Rachmaninoff's tremendous admiration for Tchaikovsky, which began during his first years in Moscow and never diminished but grew stronger as the years advanced, it is necessary to be acquainted with the relationship of the Russian musicians to one another and realize the competition which existed between the two great cities, St. Petersburg and Moscow.

A strange antagonism had always divided these two. It extended to all conditions of life, but was more noticeable where art, and particularly music, was concerned. The division was, in itself, easily comprehensible. Moscow was the home of the ultra-conservative landed aristocracy and the old-established business classes; the stronghold of the typically "Russian spirit" voiced by Katkov in the notoriously reactionary paper *Moskovskiya Vyedomosty* (*Moscow News*). St. Petersburg had rapidly developed into a bureaucratic capital. It was the home of the Imperial Court, the heads of services, the Guards, and ambitious officialdom. It flirted with "enlightenment" in the shape of Western European internationalism. In Moscow kindly manners and a comfortable life were the general aim. One grew a long beard and wore a heavy bearskin or sable coat; one called the Emperor "father Tsar" and never questioned his doings; whereas in St. Petersburg one shaved, wore a glittering uniform with gold-encrusted collars, and tightened one's belt instead

57

of dining, so as to afford a new pair of gloves, and spoke of the Tsar as "His Majesty." It is easy to understand how St. Petersburg looked down contemptuously on the reactionary Muscovites and how the latter had but an ironic smile for the puffed-up superficiality and empty-headedness shown by the inhabitants of the capital on the Neva. In all spiritual matters these two cities waged a secret war for superiority. The rivalry was carried on more or less openly and sometimes developed into an almost passionate hatred. For a parallel—and if we bear in mind the respective circumstances—we might take the jealousy and the competition shown in Germany in certain directions between Berlin and Munich.

It was the same in regard to music, and all would have been well if Moscow had championed an ultra-national musical attitude based on the foundation of the Russian spirit and tradition and if St. Petersburg had played the part of mediator between East and West. But the contrary was the case. It is hard to find a reason for this, but the fact remains, and it explains many incidents in the musical life of Russia. A great deal of it may be traced to reasons of a purely personal character, such as the temperaments and characteristics of the great Russian composers who lived in these two cities.

Moscow recognized only one of all the musical gods, Tchaikovsky, who, although a pupil of the St. Petersburg Conservatoire, became a Professor in Moscow and settled down there immediately after he had finished his studies. It was very guarded in its attitude towards the great musicians of St. Petersburg. On the other hand, Tchaikovsky had a hard fight to win appreciation in St. Petersburg, and even his Sixth Symphony, the famous *Pathétique*, had only a moderate success when it was first performed there a few days before his death. The musical world of St. Petersburg continued to treat their

Moscow colleague with patronizing condescension. But the Muscovites took their revenge in withholding their admiration from Rimsky-Korsakov and Borodin and by simply laughing at Moussorgsky, whom they considered unlearned, coarse, and verging on madness.

These conditions, however much they are to be deplored, unquestionably existed and explain many episodes in Rachmaninoff's life and in his musical development. Even while they lived with Sverev the three boys were taught not only to underrate the significance of the "small group of great ones" in St. Petersburg, but they were encouraged to misinterpret them and to bow solely and unconditionally before the musical idol of Moscow, Tchaikovsky and his few prophets, amongst whom were the two Professors of the Moscow Conservatoire, Taneyev and Arensky. Thus from his childhood upwards Rachmaninoff was taught to regard Tchaikovsky as the only musical authority, the only worthy ideal for an aspiring composer, and in this belief he grew up.

The college year 1886–87 held a double significance for Rachmaninoff's future as a musician. In the first place he had finished his pianoforte training in the lower division of the college, and one of the Professors in the High School was now to replace Sverev as his teacher. Secondly, his fate as a composer was to be decided at the opening of the new college year. According to the rules of the college, students who had finished the second harmony course were allowed a choice between two lines of study: they could either decide to go in for a general musical education—a course which was termed "Musical Encyclopædia," and included a little of everything: counterpoint, instrumentation, musical history, etc., but each in homœopathic doses—or they were free to enter the special "Composers' Division." This course was reckoned to take not less than five years, which were divided up as follows: counterpoint one year, fugue two years, and free composition two years. Students, however, were only allowed to enter this division on the special recommendation of the board of teachers and after they had passed the last examination of the second harmony course.

Let us hear what Rachmaninoff himself has to say about it:

"At the last examination of the harmony course the pupils were separated and given two problems which they had to solve without the help of a piano. These were (1) harmonizing a melody in four parts. This time, I think, it was one of Haydn's, and the tune is still fresh in my memory. (2) Writing a prélude of sixteen to thirty bars, in a certain key and modulation, which had to include two pedals, the dominant and the tonic. These pedals could, of course, be prepared in good time and transcribed into the desired key afterwards.

The examination began at nine o'clock in the morning and had no fixed time-limit. I still remember vividly Arensky's excitement about me. As this year Tchaikovsky was an honorary member of the committee the examination bore rather a special character. My classmates one after another showed their papers, and each time Arensky glanced at the first page and frowned discontentedly, after which he gave an imploring look in my direction. When all candidates had given in their work I alone was still left, sitting over my paper. I had got entangled in a daring modulation of the prélude and could not find a solution that would help me out. At last—it was already five o'clock in the afternoon—I had finished. I handed my two pages of manuscript to Arensky. As with the other papers, he sent a quick glance over the first page, but without frowning. I took the risk of asking him what this meant. Arensky smiled. 'You are the only one,' he said, 'to grasp the sense of the correct harmonic change.'

After this comforting information I went home, full of hope.

On the following day was the decisive meeting of the board of examiners to whom we were to play our own work. Amongst the Professors at the green table sat Tchaikovsky. The highest mark given was a five, which could, in exceptional cases, be supplemented by a plus sign. I knew already that I had been given this mark. When it was my turn to play and I had finished, Arensky drew Tchaikovsky's attention to the fact that I had been the only pupil who, during the last lesson, had written two-part 'songs without words,' and asked whether he would like to hear them. Tchaikovsky nodded his assent, and as I knew my songs by heart I sat down and played them. When I had finished Tchaikovsky rose and busied himself with the examination journal. It was only after a fortnight that I heard what he had been doing with it: he had added three more plus signs to my mark, one on top, one below, and one behind. This five with four plus marks—a unique occurrence in the annals of the Conservatoire—was naturally much discussed, and the story made the round of all Moscow. But, as already said, I only heard of it a fortnight later. I was probably kept in ignorance so that I should not grow vain, but Arensky eventually betrayed the secret.

Directly after the examination it was decided that in the early autumn I should enter Taneyev's first counterpoint class as a student of composition. Thus my fate as a composer was, as it were, officially sealed."

The question in regard to Rachmaninoff's piano lessons

was solved this way. At that time the pianoforte teachers in the High School division of the Conservatoire were Paul Pabst—a former pupil of Liszt—and Vassili Safonoff, who had finished the St. Petersburg Conservatoire as a pupil of Leshetitsky. Both were not only excellent pianists but exceptional teachers, as is proved by the long succession of brilliant pianists whom, between the years 1890–1914, they launched into the world. In the autumn of 1887 these two Professors were to be joined by a third, Alexander Siloti, whom the Conservatoire had engaged on the recommendation of his former teacher, Sverev. According to the rules and traditions of the college, the students were free to chose the teacher who was to continue their education as pianists. Sverev, who was keen that Siloti should get some talented pupils, persuaded his three boys to trust their fate into the hands of Liszt's "favourite" pupil, whose record as a teacher was less distinguished, for the simple reason that it did not exist.

Safonoff, who knew of Rachmaninoff's magnificent talent, and who would have been only too happy to count him amongst his pupils, exhibited little joy over his decision. From now on his attitude towards the boy's development as a pianist was anything but benevolent. As, shortly afterwards, Safonoff was appointed Director of the Moscow Conservatoire and consequently became a powerful influence in the musical life of Moscow, this circumstance had an effect on Rachmaninoff's career which can hardly be underrated. It is true that his genius was too great to be seriously hindered in its triumphal progress by any outside influence, but a different attitude on Safonoff's part would certainly have helped to remove many difficulties from his path.

Taneyev, into whose hands passed the responsibility for Rachmaninoff's education as a composer, was one of the most prominent characters in the musical world of Moscow during the last decades of the nineteenth century. He was not only an exceedingly good composer whose worth, it is true, was recognized in Russia and abroad only after his death, but he represented a great deal more in the musical life of Moscow. He was the teacher of several generations of composers as well as their shining example in musicianship and manhood; a veritable high priest of his art of a perfection rarely to be matched even in a history so rich in noble personalities as that of Music. Taneyev was not only endowed with the restless spirit of an investigator and gifted with pronounced philosophic tendencies, but he was also a man of fastidious purity and practised a touching modesty and chastity in his way of living. With it all he was typically "Russian" in all the manifestations of his character.

As I have already pointed out, the Moscow musicians, led by Tchaikovsky, were jealously eager to preserve the tradition of the great epochs in Western musical history. Ever since, in 1866, the Moscow Conservatoire had been founded by Nikolai Rubinstein, who was the younger, less famous—though not, perhaps, less gifted—brother of Anton, this had become a sort of unwritten canon, which was naturally respected and encouraged by the many German teachers, such as Huber, Hrymali, and others, whom Nikolai Rubinstein had called to the Moscow College of Music. Taneyev was one of the keenest champions of this musical ideology influenced by the West. In his opinion Music started with the Dutch contrapuntists and proceeded by way of Palestrina, Orlando di Lasso, and Bach (whom he worshipped, and whose works he knew note by note) through Mozart and Beethoven, and the German masters, Schubert and Schumann, straight on to Tchaikovsky. Until shortly before his death he thought very little of Wagner, and nothing at all of the so-called "Russian School" in St. Petersburg to whom belonged Rimsky-Korsakov, Balakirev, Borodin, and Moussorgsky. Seen from his superstrict and expert point of view, they were amateurs; very talented, one had to admit, but still dilettanti who had never received the consecration of the true musical grace which is counterpoint. It took him a long time to alter his rather hard judgment in favour of at least Rimsky-Korsakov and Borodin. His attitude towards Moussorgsky remained unchanged, and he attributed the world-wide success of *Boris Godounov* largely to Rimsky-Korsakov's revision.

Taneyev, like most great musicians in Russia, descended from an aristocratic family of landowners. An uncle of his, Alexander Taneyev, was Marshal of the Imperial Court, Controller of the Tsar's petition office, and the father of Anna Wyrubowa, the Empress's last lady-in-waiting. As a musician Sergei Taneyev was the follower of N. Rubinstein and Tchaikovsky. It was not long before his relations with Tchaikovsky became changed, for the latter soon recognized the vast superiority of his pupil in all questions of musical science and counterpoint. Taneyev was of the opinion that free mastery over musical expression depended upon a thorough knowledge of counterpoint in the strict style, such as the old Dutch masters and their Italian followers had written. This he preached to his pupils and demanded of them long years of study and an exhausting search into the mysteries and intricacies of counterpoint in the strict style. Judging alone from Taneyev's own compositions, which hardly ever bore striking evidence of his condition, one would never suppose that he had mastered the most intricate forms of counterpoint and could easily have competed with an Okeghem or a Josquin de Près; or that he was the author of a book on the "horizontally movable counterpoint," numbering a thousand pages, and of another, still longer, on Canon in all its forms, which up to this day has not been published; for what use are the strict laws of a strict art to the gentlemen of modern music who do not recognize these laws?

When Rachmaninoff finished his harmony course, Taneyev had already handed over the management of the Moscow Conservatoire to Safonoff and had reserved for himself only the direction of the special counterpoint classes.

There entered at the same time as Rachmaninoff, who was then fourteen years of age, Alexander Scriabin, who was but a little older and who became Safonoff's pianoforte pupil at the Conservatoire.

Rachmaninoff tells us:

"In the autumn of 1887, after a summer spent with my relatives in the country, I returned to Moscow. I took up my quarters at Sverev's house again, for although I was his pupil no longer he still supervised my musical education. Sverev was as severe as ever and his discipline never gave way in regard to my two companions; but in my own case he frequently exercised great indulgence, and I felt the reins begin to slacken. Unfortunately, I could not take the faintest interest in counterpoint in the strict style, in all these imitations and reversions, these augmentations and diminutions and other embellishments of an ugly cantus. I found it all dreadfully dull, and none of the rapturous praises and most eloquent sermons of the highly esteemed Taneyev could convince me to the contrary. Scriabin, who was my classmate, felt exactly the same. Our class was made up of five: two Germans, Lidack and Weinberg, whose respective instruments were the trombone and the bassoon, Scriabin and myself, and another whose name has escaped my memory.

The two Germans were tremendously worthy and diligent and always handed in elaborately prepared work. Not so myself or—I must confess it—Scriabin. We shirked our lessons more and more often, and when we did make an appearance at the Conservatoire we had seldom prepared any work. As an excuse we made out that our piano practice had left us no time for studying counterpoint. Taneyev was greatly worried by our laziness. As he was incapable of being angry and still less able to scold, he appealed to our conscience and begged and implored us to turn over a new leaf. But nothing helped. The canti firmi remained untouched and the motets uncomposed. At last the kindly Taneyev decided to employ another measure. He appealed for help to Safonoff. It is possible that Safonoff himself did not recognize the necessity and the importance of counterpoint in the strict style, or he may have relied on our better sense; the fact is that he treated us far too gently. Instead of thoroughly scolding us and threatening us with severe punishment, he clothed his admonitions in a gentle and fatherly manner that lacked all impressiveness and consequently left us in-different. Later on, when I moved from Sverev to my relations the Satins, Taneyev himself invented a strange, but entirely effective, measure, which was to bring us to our senses and get the lessons done. He wrote the theme on a piece of note-paper and sent his cook to our house with it. The cook had strict injunctions not to leave until we had handed over to her the accomplished task. I do not know what effect this measure—which could only have been invented by Taneyev—had on Scriabin; with me it certainly had the desired success; if for no other reason, I was persuaded by the beseeching requests of our own servants to do my lessons so that Taneyev's cook should be removed from their kitchen. But I am afraid he often had to wait for his supper.

MOSCOW. SVEREV AND ARENSKY

Another circumstance influenced my mental condition and awakened my diligence. I heard for the first time of the 'Great Gold Medal,' the highest distinction available to a student of the Conservatoire. It was only awarded to those who passed the final examination with the highest marks in two special subjects. As I was very ambitious I decided to earn this 'Great Gold Medal.' This decision was of immediate benefit to my work in counterpoint in the strict style. In the spring of 1890 I succeeded in passing with honours the examination into the fugue class. In order to do this I had to spend two days in isolation, from nine to nine, and write a six-part motet with canonic modulations on a given cantus firmus, to a Latin text. Here again I was rewarded with a five, and in the following year Safonoff had the little work performed by the choir of the Conservatoire, which I myself conducted.

Scriabin, also, and the two Germans must have acquitted themselves well at this examination, for in the autumn of 1890 the four of us met again in Arensky's fugue class. Arensky, who was most stimulating when he taught harmony, a subject which was no doubt especially congenial to him, failed completely in the art of the fugue. Without giving us a single explanation he constantly referred us to the fugues of Bach, whose construction we were unable to understand. As we were never given an explanation, the writing of fugues bored me stiff, and I soon left off altogether and returned to my former laziness. My classmates felt the same. This year the mark that crowned my efforts in composition was a miserable 'three,' which showed that my work was only just satisfactory. Never before had this happened to me at the Conservatoire.

But fate came to my assistance. Arensky fell ill, and Taneyev was asked to take on his class.

Thus it happened that shortly before the end of the term Taneyev appeared in the fugue class. I regret the fact that he only gave me two lessons; but in these I learned more than I did during the whole year. Taneyev began the lesson with the surprising question, 'Do you know what a fugue is?' Still more surprising was the silence that answered him. So he sat down, not at the lecturing desk but at a school desk in our midst, and covered two large pages of note-paper with innumerable examples of fugue subjects and their answers, his own as well as some taken from the classics. It came to me as a sudden revelation. Then, for the first time, did I begin to understand what a fugue really meant and what was required in order to write one. The subject began to fascinate me so much that I started working at it with great enjoyment.

At that time violent differences broke out between Safonoff and Siloti. The quarrel became more and more acute and ended with Siloti's request for his dismissal and his decision not to return to Moscow in the following autumn. The course for pianoforte covered four years, so that I had at least one more year before me. As I had no desire to continue my pianoforte lessons under another professor and accustom myself to new methods, I made a heroic decision. I went to Safonoff and told him that I intended to take the finishing examination for pianists that year. To my great satisfaction he agreed; as I was not his pupil he had no interest in me as a pianist, and he even tried to persuade me that I was not really born to be one.

'I know,' he said to me more than once, 'that your interest lies somewhere else,' by which he indicated the wider field of composition.

However this may be, I was given the task of the final examination: Beethoven's *Waldstein* Sonata and the first movement of Chopin's Sonata in B minor, and, to my own and Siloti's surprise, I passed the examination with honours. Thus the first landmark on the road to the 'Great Gold Medal' had been reached.

Unfortunately, the examination from the fugue class into the free composition class took place on the same day as the pianoforte examination. But here also I was met half-way in overcoming a difficulty. I was allowed to do the examination a day later, and my three classmates went into isolation without me. The subject of the fugue was very intricate. There was a doubt as to the answer, that is, whether the fugue was to be treated as a fuga reale or a fuga de tono. According to Arensky, all candidates had treated the answer wrongly. Here again I was lucky. When, after the pianoforte examination, I left the Conservatoire, I saw Arensky and Safonoff walking in front of me, engaged in a violent dispute. As I had very nearly reached them I heard that their discussion centred around the subject of the fugue, and at that very moment Safonoff whistled what he considered to be the right composition of the answer on which the fugue was to be built up. At the examination on the following day I surprised Arensky by handing in the fugue in its right composition. The result was similar to that of the pianoforte examination: a five with a small 'plus.'

All this happened in the spring of 1891."

It may be interesting to hear that Alexander Scriabin did not pass the remove examination from the fugue into the free-composition class. He was ploughed, but was given permission to attend the free-composition class in the autumn on the condition that he showed the examination board six faultless fugues, which were to be written during the summer holidays. This incident illustrates the very strict demands which were put upon students of the Moscow and St. Petersburg Conservatoires. One could be sure that every student leaving either of these institutions with the Diploma of the "Free Artist" was a real musician and knew his subject.

CHAPTER FOUR

A DRAMATIC INCIDENT
THE MOSCOW CONSERVATOIRE

1889–1892

The break with Sverev—Life with the Satins, with inter-ruptions—Slonov—Summer on the Satins' estate in the government of Tambov—Serious illness in Moscow in the autumn 1891—Consequences of the illness—The First Concerto for pianoforte—Premature termination of studies at the Conservatoire—The examination and Rachmaninoff's sensational success—Reconciliation with Sverev—The "Great Gold Medal"—Gutheil, the publisher, makes his appearance —First performance of the examination opera Aleko *at the Moscow Grand Theatre*

LET Rachmaninoff continue his story in his own words:

"I must speak of a very painful occurrence," he says, "which had taken place over a year previously, but which constantly oppressed my mind.

My relations with Nikolai Sverev had never been seriously troubled. I always treated him with great respect and felt for him only the highest admiration which the years I had spent in his house did nothing to lessen. I realized, of course, that owing to his quick temper he had to be tactfully treated. He, in return, seemed to like me, and had given proof of this on more than one occasion by showing an indulgence towards me which was contrary to his usual practice.

As long as I was a small boy I did not resent his chastisements, especially as in my case they were infre-

71

quent and never in connection with any musical sins. But my sensitiveness grew in proportion to my size and physical strength, and one day—I was sixteen years old—there was a terrible row between us, which resulted in a definite break.

The deeper I penetrated into the mysteries of creation, harmony, and all the other subjects that belong to the technique of composition, the greater became their attraction for me, and my pleasure in studying them. Study, however, was not always easy, for the music-room was often occupied by someone practising the piano. So I made a bold resolution, and one evening—it was in October 1889—I took the bull by the horns and, without considering the possible consequences, I approached Sverev with a request. I told him that I would like to have a room of my own and a piano to myself, so that I could pursue my studies in counterpoint and composition whenever and as long as I wished, and asked him whether he would help me to hire a piano. Our talk began calmly and proceeded in a perfectly peaceful manner until I must have said something that infuriated him. He flared up in an instant, screamed, and flung at me every article he could lay hands on. I remained quite calm, but added fuel to the fire by remarking that, as I was no longer a child, the tone he adopted towards me did not seem very suitable. The whole scene ended disgracefully.

I lived with him for another month, but did not meet him half-way as I usually did, in order to seek a reconciliation. We never exchanged a word during that month; but one day he approached me in a manner that I knew from experience would stand no contradiction. He told me to meet him after his lessons that evening at a certain boulevard in Moscow. His authority was still so great that the thought of disobeying him never occurred to me. At the appointed hour I went to the place he had indicated. Sverev arrived, and, without exchanging a single word, we walked in a direction that rather puzzled me. At last we reached the house of my relations, the Satins, whom, following Sverev's principles, I had only visited twice during the four years I lived with him. It looked as if they expected us, for a regular family council had assembled there and the sitting-room was pervaded by an atmosphere of solemnity. When we had seated ourselves, Sverev made a little speech, which he delivered in a dignified and almost business-like manner, and which amounted to this:

He had found that our respective temperaments were not compatible and that, at the moment, it was impossible for him and myself to live together. But he naturally did not wish to leave me alone and unsupported, and had, therefore, brought me here in the hope that someone present might be ready to take me in and look after me. He begged my relations to make up their minds as soon as possible. For the rest, I could naturally do as I liked.

After this we rose, and, without even mentioning the details of the matter or arriving at any decision, we walked home as silently as we had come.

The following morning I rose with the dawn, packed my belongings, and went to one of my friends at the Conservatoire who was a little older than I and lived by himself. There I intended to stay for the present. I then earned fifteen roubles a month by giving piano lessons, and that was all I possessed; but on the very next day my aunt, Mme Satina—a sister of my father and my aunt Siloti—came to me in a state of great agitation: they had searched for me in vain all the previous day, and would I come and live with them? I accepted this invitation without any demonstrations of great joy, for at that time I hardly knew my relations. But what else could I do? In the years that followed I lived with them—with a few interruptions—and was always sure of a most affectionate welcome. In later years my life became more closely associated with theirs and their house became my real home, in the true sense of the word. But of that I will speak later.

During the time immediately after our quarrel I did not see Sverev except at the Conservatoire or in the street. I always greeted him politely, but my greeting was never acknowledged."

The incident described above had a deep and decisive influence on Rachmaninoff's further development, both mental and artistic.

In the interest of his musical education, Rachmaninoff has, in later years, regretted that he did not accept his mother's invitation to go to St. Petersburg. After the incident with Sverev the ageing and lonely woman had written to her son and made this proposal. At that time Anton Rubinstein had again resumed his lessons at the St. Petersburg Conservatoire, while the composition classes were under the direction of Rimsky-Korsakov, who had already become a great master of his art and was admired and recognized by the whole world. But Rachmaninoff, with his strong sympathies for Moscow, still regarded Rimsky-Korsakov with indifference and even aversion, and it was long before he changed his attitude towards the creator of the Russian fairy-tale opera. Thus, even the tempting prospect of becoming Anton Rubinstein's pupil did not persuade young Rachmaninoff to take up life in St. Petersburg; this would have looked almost like a betrayal of Tchaikovsky and Taneyev, and would, in any case, have meant his giving up all the old and cherished Moscow traditions. The boy refused his mother's suggestion and her pathetic entreaties to live with her, since it would prevent the continuance of his studies at Moscow.

That he should live with his father was out of the question, for Vassili Rachmaninoff led a very unsettled life, wandering from place to place, and would have been at a loss to know what to do with this son of his.

Under these somewhat dramatic circumstances, Rachmaninoff, as described in the previous chapter, finished his studies as a pianist, and was transferred from the fugue class into the class for free composition.

The alluring title of "Free Artist" was gradually drawing nearer, and with it the "Great Gold Medal," which the youth still dreamed of as the most desirable and appropriate reward for his steadily increasing diligence. Two more years were necessary to complete the course for free composition at the Conservatoire.

Rachmaninoff spent the summer of 1891 with his grandmother on his father's side in the government of Tambov. This visit was attended with serious consequences, for, after a bathe in the river on a cold September day, he developed a severe attack of malaria which broke out on his return to Moscow and very nearly ended disastrously.

*   *   *

We can return to Rachmaninoff's own account of himself.

"After the summer holidays I returned to Moscow in the autumn of 1891 and continued my lessons in free composition with Arensky. We had already reached the stage of free forms of composition and their mastery: sonatas, quartettes, and symphonies. My only other classmate was Scriabin, for Lidack and Weinberg had been dropped in the last fugue class. In their place in the upper division of the free composition class we found two prospective

75

composers: Leo Conus and Nikita Morosov. Both were sound and talented musicians, but not shining lights in composition.

From the very beginning of the college year I was worried by symptoms of an intermittent fever, which I had caught during the summer holidays. In the morning my temperature was normal and I felt quite well and went out, but every evening I had a high fever and collapsed completely.

At that time I did not live with the Satins, but shared rooms with Slonov, a friend at the Conservatoire. Slonov was a singer and pianist and was as passionately devoted to music as I was myself. At least once a week we spent several hours together, singing and playing whatever came to hand. By then I had already started to compose and had finished my first concerto for pianoforte, a trio (which has never been published), and several songs. I wrote with great ease and composition did not cost me the slightest effort: I composed as I spoke, and often my hand could hardly follow the swift flight of my musical ideas. Slonov was the only person towards whom I exercised no restraint, and I showed him everything I wrote, so that he got acquainted with my work as it progressed.

My illness grew steadily worse, and soon I was unable to get up. Another college friend took the matter in hand by moving me into his house. This friend was Youri Sakhnovsky, the composer and, later, well-known music-critic of the *Russkoye Slovo*. His father was a wealthy merchant who ran a large racing establishment. In his flat in a house richly decorated with wood carving, situated on the 'Tverskaya Zastava' and well known to all men of the world because the road to the race-courses and fashionable night clubs led past it, I lay in a state of delirium and soon became quite unconscious.

THE MOSCOW CONSERVATOIRE

It was Siloti who saved my life. He did everything in his power to help me and called in one of the most famous doctors in Moscow, Professor Mitropolsky. The latter diagnosed brain fever and ordered the most careful nursing without giving much hope of my recovery. But my strong constitution triumphed and, although I lay in bed until shortly before Christmas, I did eventually recover.

This illness, however, was not without consequences. The worst of them was that I lost half my facility for composing.

But this condition did not prevent me from coming to another decision about my work at the Conservatoire, which was nearly as bold as the one I had carried out two years ago. I had barely recovered from my illness when I went to Arensky and informed him that I had no intention of staying at the college for another year and wished to take the final examination in the spring. I asked him to assist me in this plan and he promised his help, and actually succeeded in obtaining for me the permission to carry it out, although it was against all the college rules.

My example had a stimulating effect on Scriabin, who immediately approached Arensky with a similar request. But it is the early bird that catches the worm. Scriabin's request was not granted. This annoyed and worried him so much that he left the composition division at the Conservatoire and only continued his study of the pianoforte under Safonoff. Thus it happened that one of the most prominent Russian composers remained without the official sanction of a diploma.

In return for the privileges granted to me, Arensky demanded several compositions: a symphony, a number of vocal recitatives, and an opera. I began working on the symphony at once, but it progressed with difficulty;

I literally had to force out each bar, and the result was accordingly poor. I saw and felt that Arensky, to whom I showed the different movements as I completed them, was not pleased. They satisfied me even less. From Taneyev also, whom Arensky had invited to judge my work as an expert, I had to swallow some rather bitter criticism. In spite of this I finished the work, and handed in the demanded recitatives as well. I had made up my mind to finish my studies at the Conservatoire during the college year, and was determined to achieve this, if for no other than pecuniary reasons. Besides myself, Leo Conus and Nikita Morosov were expected to finish their course at the Conservatoire this year.

The great day on which we were given the examination problem fell in April. Our task consisted in composing a one-act opera, *Aleko*. The libretto, which was handed over to us, had been adapted from Poushkin's well-known poem, *The Gipsies*, by the writer Vassili Nemirovitch-Dantshenko.

At that time I had rejoined my father, after being separated from him for several years. Through my friend, the above-mentioned Sakhnovsky, I had been able to procure him employment at the business belonging to the latter's father. We had taken a small flat in the outlying suburbs, beyond the 'Tverskaya Zastava,' not far from the race-courses, where lived the three of us: my father, my friend Slonov, and I.

As soon as I had been given the libretto of *Aleko* I ran home as fast as my legs would carry me. I was afraid to lose a minute, for the time allotted to us was short. Burning with impatience, I felt already the music to Poushkin's verses beginning to stir and bubble within me. If only I could go to the piano I knew that I was ready to improvise half the opera.

But on arriving home I found visitors there. Some men

had come to see my father on business, and they occupied the room in which the piano stood. Their discussion seemed to have no end—they stayed the whole afternoon, and the evening passed without my being able to go near the piano. I flung myself on my bed and wept with fury and disappointment because I was not able to start working at once. My father, who found me there, was very surprised to see a big youth of my age in this condition; but when he learnt the reason he shook his head and promised never again to place me in such an agonizing situation, and he faithfully kept his word. Evidently he fully understood the seething impatience to create which possessed me.

On the following morning I began my work, which I found very easy. I took the libretto as it stood, and the idea that it might be improved never even entered my head. I composed, as it were, under high pressure. Slonov and I sat at my writing-desk, facing one another. I wrote without once looking up, and only passed the completed sheets across the table, when the kindly Slonov immediately proceeded to make fair copies of them in his neat hand.

A fortnight later Arensky asked the examination committee whether he might have a look at the work of his three candidates. He was granted permission to do so and sent for us. It was exactly seventeen days since we had been given the work. In order that we should not get a glimpse of one another's compositions, two of us were sent into the garden, while the third stayed with Arensky. The first to go in was Morosov. As he had composed but little so far, his session lasted only three-quarters of an hour. Conus's fragment did not occupy much more time. Then came my turn. I had a surprise up my sleeve. Arensky began by asking: 'Well, how far have you got with your opera?'

'I have finished it.'

'In the pianoforte score?'

'No, in the orchestral score.'

He looked at me incredulously, and it took me a long time to convince him of the truth of my statement and make him believe that the packets of music which I drew out of my case really represented the completed score of *Aleko*.

'If you continue at that rate,' he said, 'you might write twenty-four acts in one year! This is pretty good.'

I sat down to the piano and began to play. The work pleased Arensky, but he naturally found some faults in it. At that time I, being full of youthful arrogance, did not agree with his criticism; but now, when it is too late, I feel convinced that every objection of his was justified. I did not alter a single bar.

The examination took place thirteen days later, so the time allowed for our work had been exactly one month. This examination was attended not only by a high official from the Ministry of Education but luckily also by a few people with musical understanding, such as Altani, chief musical conductor at the Moscow Grand Theatre, and, of course, Taneyev and all the Professors of the Conservatoire."

Neither Morosov nor Conus had quite succeeded in finishing the work. But Rachmaninoff had prepared another little sensation. When his turn came he produced the score, beautifully bound in leather with gold lettering, and placed it on the examiners' table. He had spent the last of his money on the binding. But he was compensated with success. Probably it was the greatest success Rachmaninoff has ever had without playing a single note. A loud "Oh!" accompanied by a general shaking of heads, passed round the table with the green cloth.

Then Rachmaninoff played his opera. It found favour, and he was given a "five" with a plus sign. Altani murmured something about performing it.

All this was very gratifying, but the greatest joy was still ahead. Amongst the Professors of the committee sat Sverev. When Rachmaninoff had received the handshakes and congratulations of all present, Sverev came up to him and led him towards a window recess in the corridor, where he embraced and kissed the young boy, saying that he was very happy and expected great things of him. Then he took his gold watch from his waistcoat pocket and presented it to him. Since then Rachmaninoff has never been without it, and is wearing it even now.

A more perfect ending to his years at the Conservatoire could not have been planned, and it made Rachmaninoff extremely happy.

Young Rachmaninoff's long-cherished wish was realized. The board of teachers at the college unanimously agreed to award him the "Great Gold Medal," and his name was added to the Roll of Honour and inscribed on the marble tablet which hung in the vestibule of the Conservatoire. He was the third pupil, since the foundation of the college, to be awarded this honour. One of his predecessors was his teacher, S. I. Taneyev.

But fate intended to compensate him even more generously for many wrongs—especially pecuniary ones—which he had suffered. It was only natural that rumours of the brilliance with which young Rachmaninoff had solved his examination problem—the opera *Aleko* which he had written in fourteen days—spread like wildfire through Moscow, and penetrated into all circles interested in music.

There was a prominent music publisher in Moscow who was on the look out for a composer whose works would be able to give a new and brilliant lustre to his house. This publisher was called Gutheil. By diligently reprinting German editions of classical music, publishing and selling dance and gipsy music—for the latter was always in great demand in Russia—he had accumulated a fortune which increased rapidly. Soon he was enabled to buy the operas by Glinka and Dargomyshsky through the liquidation of a Petersburg publishing firm. This fact was an unexpected stimulus for his wealth, and gave his firm an excellent name. Therefore the publishing firm Gutheil in Moscow became an element not to be overlooked in Russian music life. But that did not satisfy the ambitious M. Gutheil. "Now," he thought, "is the moment to make a bid for immortality." What he needed was the name of a great living composer to put his firm in the topmost ranks of Russian publishing undertakings.

All the great Russian composers were already in firm hands: Tchaikovsky favoured Jurgenson, the masters of the St. Petersburg group Bessel. So one had to explore amongst the younger generation. Now this young Rachmaninoff, whose examination opera had drawn such enthusiastic comments from all the musicians at the Conservatoire, might turn out a good investment. One had heard of him already a few years ago when, at a pupils' concert at the Conservatoire, he had played a concerto of his own for pianoforte, and a little later when, at a concert in the Vostriakov hall, he had achieved an almost sensational success with a trio of his own composition. Then, shortly before this year's examination for composers at the College of Music, the great Moscow violinist Besekirsky had called on Gutheil, pressed his hand, and, casting his eyes heavenwards in the most significant manner, had said: "M. Gutheil, a new Mozart has been born in our midst." All this looked really worth while. In short, Gutheil decided to capture young Rachmaninoff for his business.

Gutheil planned his campaign with great strategic skill. He did not attack from the front, but made a detour around the position by going to Sverev.

"You have a bit of luck, my boy," said Sverev to Rachmaninoff one day, "you have no sooner started composing than publishers come running after you. Of course you must go to Gutheil, but I should advise you to talk it over with Tchaikovsky. He has experience in such matters."

Rachmaninoff naturally followed this good advice. He did not have long to wait, for soon after Sverev asked him to come to his house and play the opera *Aleko* to Tchaikovsky, who had just returned to Moscow. Tchaikovsky was charmed with the little opera, for in it he recognized his own influence to a much higher degree than in any other work written at that time by young composers.

When Rachmaninoff inquired about Gutheil, he answered:

"You are lucky, Sergei" (he always addressed young Rachmaninoff in this familiarly affectionate manner when they were alone or in an intimate circle of friends; otherwise he never failed to use the correct and polite "Sergei Vassilyevitch"), "you are really fortunate! What did I not do until I found a publisher, even when I was a good deal older than you? I did not receive a penny for my first composition and considered myself fortunate that I did not have to pay in order to see myself published. I think it is almost a miracle that Gutheil not only offers you fees but asks you to state your own terms. Now, this is my advice: make no conditions whatever, but tell him that you leave it to him to fix a price. In this way you avoid all sorts of future annoyances and keep a free hand for yourself."

When, during his first discussion with Gutheil, Rachmaninoff adopted the attitude suggested by Tchaikovsky, the publisher believed that he was setting a trap for him. He thought it over a long time, hummed and hawed, and could not make up his mind to a definite offer. The works in question were the opera, six songs (Op. 4), and two pieces for violoncello and piano (Op. 2). At last he named a sum: five hundred roubles. Rachmaninoff nearly fell from his chair. He was still earning no more than fifteen roubles per month for one weekly piano lesson, and five hundred seemed to him an almost fantastic sum, a capital fit for a duke. He accepted without hesitation. From now until his death M. Gutheil was for Rachmaninoff not only an ever ready and generous publisher, but also a true and devoted friend; and, certainly, he was one of the most eager admirers of the composer's muse.

Altani, the austere principal conductor at the Grand Theatre, had already spoken of his intention of having *Aleko* performed, but this was forgotten during the summer holidays. Only the dances from the opera were played by Safonoff at a Symphony concert in Moscow given by the Imperial Russian Musical Society, and had a great success.

The first performance of Rachmaninoff's first opera did not take place till a year later, that is, in the spring of 1893, at the Grand Theatre in Moscow. Let us hear what he himself has to say about it:

"It is strange how none of my memories of more recent periods are nearly so vivid and clear as the memories of my childhood and my years at the College of Music. It seems that there is less and less to tell. One of my last and most particularly vivid impressions of that time is the performance of my opera *Aleko* and everything connected with it.

84

I think that the honour of having this work performed was due not so much to its merit as to the influence of Tchaikovsky, who liked the opera. There is also another circumstance that may have helped, and I mention it because it was the first and the last time in my life that I used other than purely artistic means to reach an artistic goal.

I entered for a short time into the life of society, but not of my own accord nor for my own pleasure. I was persuaded to do so by one of my relations who held a very prominent position in the St. Petersburg bureaucracy and had connections which reached as high as the 'Spheres,' as the Court circles were then nicknamed. When he heard of my rising fame in Moscow he left me no peace until I had travelled to St. Petersburg, where he wished to introduce me into society, for, in his opinion, this was essential for my artistic career. He also dragged me to Napravnik, who was Musical Conductor at the Court and whose word was law at the Imperial Opera Theatre. This visit, however, had no further consequences. It was not Napravnik who helped me in getting my opera performed but a man who professionally had nothing to do with music or the theatre, a certain K. who was Director of the Seal Office and the right-hand of the almost omnipotent Court Minister. Musical evenings were sometimes given at his house in Krassnoye Selo. One of these coincided with my visit to St. Petersburg. The occasion was the birthday of our hostess, and the best artists from the Imperial Theatres of St. Petersburg and Moscow vied with one another in the effort to entertain her guests.

I was taken there by my relative, and have never regretted it. During the evening I made the acquaintance of the leading members of the company at the St. Petersburg Dramatic Theatre, Davydov and Varlamov, who

were probably the two cleverest comedians that Russia
has ever produced. Both wished to appear on the stage
at the same time. One was usually sufficient to reduce
the audience to fits of laughter. Now they appeared
together, playing a scene between Tshitshikov and
Petrishtshev from Gogol's novel *Dead Souls*, which they
had made up themselves. When they had finished it took
the audience a long time to calm down their almost
hysterical mirth. Then Figner, the famous tenor of the
St. Petersburg Opera, sang, and I finished the performance by playing my two dances from *Aleko*. ('No more,
on any account!' had been my relative's instructions.)
Amongst the guests was the Manager of the Chancery
Office of the Imperial Theatres, His Excellency Monsieur P. In the midst of the applause which followed my
playing the hostess rose, approached His Excellency, and
said with her enchanting smile:

'Really, what charming music! You will have it performed in Moscow, won't you? I promise you I will come
over for the first night.'

A refusal was out of the question. This was her gratitude.

In the spring of 1893 my opera was actually performed
at the Grand Theatre, and this, even though the lady
of Krassnoye Selo did not honour the evening with her
presence, made me inexpressibly happy.

No effort was spared to make it a success. The best
singers which the Moscow Grand Theatre could produce
took part in it. Altani conducted.

I cannot describe how thrilled I was at the orchestral
sound of my own music. I was in the seventh heaven.
Tchaikovsky attended the last three rehearsals. We sat
together in a corner of the darkened house. Altani's
conception of some parts did not please me. I remember
the following dialogue between Tchaikovsky and myself:

Tchaikovsky: 'Do you like this tempo?'

Myself: 'No.'

Tchaikovsky: 'Why don't you tell them?'

Myself: 'I am afraid.'

But Tchaikovsky could not stand it for long, and during an interval he cleared his throat and said:

'Mr. Rachmaninoff and I think that the tempo here might be taken a little quicker.'

He was always scrupulously polite in making such suggestions.

On the same occasion he said to me:

'I have just finished an opera in two acts, *Yolanthe*, which is not long enough to fill an evening. Would you object if it was performed together with yours?'

This was exactly how he put it: 'Would you object?' He was fifty-three and a celebrated musician and I only a beginner of twenty-one.

At the first performance of *Aleko* Tchaikovsky was naturally present, and on his recommendation the General Superintendent of the Imperial Theatres, Vsevoloshky, had come over from St. Petersburg. When the opera was over, Tchaikovsky leaned out of the Superintendent's box and applauded for all he was worth. In his kindness he realized how much this would help a beginner in Moscow. Under such circumstances the opera naturally had a great success. Several numbers were encored, and this, in Moscow, was the one indispensable condition of an opera's survival. When the curtain had been lowered, everyone called for the Composer. I was dragged on to the stage, and my youth must have impressed the audience, for I was called again and again.

To my special joy and satisfaction, my grandmother Rachmaninoff had come from Tambov and watched the performance (together with my father) from a box in the *bel étage*. She was proud of her grandson, as she told me afterwards.

The first performance of *Aleko* took place towards the end of the season. The opera could only be given twice more before the holidays. The Press received the work very favourably, though every criticism, one must confess, began with the sentence: 'Considering the Composer's youth one must admit that . . .' "

Thus Rachmaninoff had achieved the sanction of the public as well as the Diploma at the Conservatoire, and had entered public life as a composer.

At about the same time he made his first appearance in Moscow as a pianist. The Electric Exhibition was opened during the summer, and there were Symphony concerts under the direction of the conductor, Voizekh Hlavatch, at which well-known soloists appeared. One of these was Rachmaninoff, who played Rubinstein's Concerto in D minor for a fee of fifty roubles!

This ended the young artist's years of study. Life lay before him like a sun-flooded garden, gay with flowers. The bitterness which no man, least of all an artist, can escape was reserved for the future. In later years Rachmaninoff was to receive his full share of sorrow and disappointment.

CHAPTER FIVE

THE "FREE ARTIST" IN MOSCOW—PERFORMANCE OF THE FIRST SYMPHONY AND ITS CONSEQUENCES

1893–1895

Rich musical harvest of the summer 1893—Settling down in rooms in "America," Moscow—Op. 3, the Prélude in C sharp minor—Last meeting with Tchaikovsky—Conducting in Kiev—Tchaikovsky's death—The Trio, Op. 9—Hard struggle for existence—The "Belayev Circle" in St. Petersburg—The First Symphony and its performance in St. Petersburg under Glazounov—Parting from Granny Boutakova in Novgorod

THE larger part of the summer of 1893 Rachmaninoff spent with Slonov on an estate in the government of Kharkov belonging to a wealthy Moscow merchant, Monsieur Lyssikov, who was a friend of Slonov. The richness of the southern "black-earth" soil, yielding an endless crop of fruit; the sweet air, laden with germinating, blossoming, and ripening life, seemed to have a stimulating effect on the young Composer. He felt quite at home with the Lyssikovs, and delighted in the joys of country life, as always when he could escape from the bricks and mortar of the town. The musical harvest garnered by his publisher Gutheil after the summer holidays was very plentiful. It consisted of a Fantasia for two pianos in four movements, an orchestral Fantasia (according to the terminology of Liszt a "Symphonic Poem") on Lermontov's poem, "The Rock," two pieces for violin (Op. 7), and a long Sacred Concerto, which was not published but was performed by the famous "Synoical Choir" of Moscow during the same autumn.

Previous to his departure for the summer holidays young Rachmaninoff had already, and for the first time in his life, set up his own establishment in furnished rooms of a second-rate order. "America" was the name painted on a pale blue signboard on the large, cream-coloured building decorated with stucco ornaments, Nomen est Omen! No one could guess the fateful significance which the combination of the two words "Rachmaninoff" and "America" would one day assume. But at that time his rooms had nothing whatever in common with the New World. They were no more modern or progressive and offered no greater comfort than any of the other second-rate establishments in Moscow inhabited by students, travellers, unmarried civil servants, and ladies and gentlemen of no fixed occupation, and christened: "Madrid," "Louvre," "Paris," "Brussels," etc. But "America" offered special advantages in being situated in one of the broadest and airiest streets of Moscow, which led up to the "Arbat" Place.

In the early spring Gutheil published the pianoforte pieces Op. 3, which were written before the journey to Charkov, and included the famous Prélude in C sharp minor, which was then, as in later years, of such decisive importance to the twenty years old Composer. The fact that this Prélude was composed in "America" has a certain prophetic interest. At the time the publication of Op. 3 inspired one of the best-known Russian journalists, A. A. Amfiteatrov—who, although not a musician, would sometimes write on music—to contribute an article in the *Novosti Dnya* (*Daily News*) under the heading "A Man of Great Promise." This, like all Amfiteatrov's articles, was widely read and caused a sensation. In his article on Rachmaninoff's Op. 3, Amfiteatrov showed better prophetic qualities than many of his journalistic colleagues. He recognized the exceptional quality of the Prélude in C sharp minor, which was soon to conquer the whole world and would now be played in Kaffir kraals, if they contained such things as pianos. In his journalistic rapture he called the pieces of Op. 3 "small master-pieces," and prophesied a most brilliant future for their composer.

Soon afterwards Rachmaninoff visited his former teacher Taneyev, and found Tchaikovsky with him. Tchaikovsky had of course read the article by Amfitea-trov. He greeted Rachmaninoff with a smile.

"Well, Sergei, what do I hear? You have already started to write 'masterpieces'! Congratulations, congratulations."

He showed great interest in all that had happened during the previous summer, and when he heard how much Rachmaninoff had written in these three months, he wrung his hands in mock despair and exclaimed:

"And I, miserable wretch, have only written one Symphony!"

This was the *Pathétique*, his last composition.

Rachmaninoff, who loved and admired Tchaikovsky beyond everything, had decided to dedicate his Fantasia for two pianos, which he considered the best work he had composed during that period, to Tchaikovsky. Tchaikovsky wished to hear it, but Rachmaninoff refused to play the work to him for fear that he would mar the first impression by playing an adaptation for one piano. It was his intention to introduce this Fantasia to the Moscow audience during the same autumn, by playing it with Paul Pabst at the latter's concert. Tchaikovsky promised to come over from St. Petersburg to hear the work. But fate decided otherwise. . . .

Instead of the Fantasia, Rachmaninoff played the

Symphonic Poem *The Rock*, which pleased Tchaikovsky very much. For the following winter Tchaikovsky had planned an extensive concert tour through Europe as a conductor, and promised Rachmaninoff, whose admiration he returned with sympathy and affectionate understanding, that he would include *The Rock* in his programme wherever he gave a concert.

Shortly afterwards Rachmaninoff was to go to Kiev in order to conduct several performances of *Aleko*. Tchaikovsky, who was always ready to chaff, parted from him with these words:

"This is how famous composers part from one another! The one goes to Kiev to conduct his opera, the other to St. Petersburg to conduct his Symphony!"

A few weeks later, while Rachmaninoff was conducting the first performance of *Aleko* in Kiev, he received a telegram from St. Petersburg with the information that Tchaikovsky had suddenly died of cholera, after suffering for only three days. A short time before this happened Tchaikovsky had conducted the first performance of his Sixth Symphony, the *Pathétique*, which had but a moderate success.

Tchaikovsky's sudden death was a great blow to Rachmaninoff. He lost not only a fatherly friend who had set him an example as a musician, which, consciously and unconsciously, he had always followed, but a helpful and energetic patron of his young but steadily growing musical activities, a loyal supporter and a faithful adviser whom he needed badly for his first faltering steps into the great world of music.

He returned to Moscow, deeply grieved. Creative artists, when affected by a sorrow so great that it defies words, usually find expression in some work of art. Tchaikovsky had done this when, in the year 1881, he wrote the Trio for pianoforte in A minor, whose tempo at the beginning is marked " 'Pezzo Elegiaco,' in memory of a great artist," his friend Nikolai Rubinstein, who died in Paris. In naïve imitation of this, Rachmaninoff composed his *Trio Elegiaque* for pianoforte, violin, and violoncello in D minor (Op. 9) during the month that followed the death of his oldest friend and dedicated it to the memory of Tchaikovsky. The Fantasia for two pianos dedicated to the living man Tchaikovsky had never heard. The *Trio Elegiaque* was first played in December, at a concert in Moscow, which was consecrated to the name of the dead composer. The performers were Rachmaninoff, the violinist Barzevitch, who in Vienna had stood sponsor to Tchaikovsky's violin Concerto and was then a Professor at the Warsaw Conservatoire, and Anatol Brandoukov, who, after Karl Davydov, was probably the most outstanding Russian violoncellist and was later to become the Director of the Moscow Philharmonic Society. He had been highly appreciated by Tchaikovsky and had benefited greatly through this circumstance.

After Tchaikovsky's death Rachmaninoff had to bury many artistic hopes which had depended on the advice and on promises given by the great composer. *Aleko* was not performed with *Yolanthe*; the opera, in fact, disappeared completely from the repertoire of the Moscow Grand Theatre. Nor did the Symphonic Poem *The Rock* gain the rapid European fame which it would, no doubt, have achieved under the baton of Tchaikovsky. Safonoff, it is true, had the piece performed at a Symphony concert given by the Conservatoire, but this was no effective substitute for the publicity lost throughout Europe.

Although Rachmaninoff already had an excellent reputation in the musical world and in the social world of Moscow, the life of the young artist was not as easy as one might imagine. Gutheil's far from meagre fees

93

did not go a very long way, and the more remunerative method of paying royalties had not, so far, been adopted by publishers in Russia. As the flow of inspiration was steady and functioned quickly and promptly, it would always have been possible for him to do emergency work and compose to order in order to keep the pot boiling; but Rachmaninoff had always felt an abhorrence for this type of work and would have preferred to go hungry rather than resort to it. Luckily it never came to that. Some additional source of income, however, had to be found. The idea of giving piano lessons was an easy one to realize, for he was always pestered with requests from all sides. Rachmaninoff adopted this measure, but it can hardly be imagined what agony it caused him. People to whom the highest standard of excellence is but a natural and easy achievement never make good teachers. They simply cannot understand that some feat of execution or spiritual conception, which in their case takes place with the ease of a natural process, may cost others a great deal of effort. Rachmaninoff's face alone, his stony features and painfully lifted eyebrows, had a paralysing effect on his boy and girl pupils, of whom the latter predominated. In his lessons he never played a note to his pupils, but merely directed their playing, and his sudden changes of tempo, the frequently forced rubati, seemed to them, when repeated by themselves, unintelligible and out of place, and they were at a loss how to deal with them. An instance of how a definite musical conception cannot be separated from the strong personality in which it originates and that once it is detached from its source and stands by itself it seems senseless or, at best, carries little conviction. However this may be, neither Rachmaninoff nor his pupils, nor their relations, extracted any pleasure from these lessons. They were, nevertheless, continued.

THE "FREE ARTIST" IN MOSCOW

It seems incredible that neither Rachmaninoff nor any of his intimates ever thought that he might use his skill as a pianist for the purpose of earning money by organizing an extensive programme of concerts. Safonoff's Machiavellian remark, "I know that your interest lies somewhere else," was to exercise its suggestive power for some time to come. Rachmaninoff felt he was a composer and nothing else, and this was the opinion held by all his circle. If he performed as a pianist he only did so in order to introduce his own compositions, although it must be admitted that on these occasions the audience and the critics invariably expressed their astonishment that a composer should play the piano so surprisingly well. This conception of his artistic personality clung to Rachmaninoff up to the time of the Great War, when he was already a man of forty. But, in spite of this, he made some efforts to turn his piano playing to financial advantage. These efforts, however, had a premature and rather surprising end, and were never repeated. The well-known impresario, Langewitz, engaged Rachmaninoff on quite favourable terms for a concert tour with the Italian violinist, Teresina Tua. On this tour they were to visit several Russian towns. The journey, which was begun in the autumn of 1894, was to last for two or three months; but, to the astonishment of all parties concerned, Rachmaninoff cut it short a considerable time before it was completed. Playing in the provinces, the troubles and discomforts of travelling and, above all, the necessity of accompanying Mlle Tua day in, day out in her rather trivial violin repertoire oppressed him very much. Under the pretext that the impresario did not pay him his fees at the appointed time (which was true) he packed his things and went back to Moscow, without a word to Langewitz or Mlle Tua. There he arrived, a little embarrassed it is true, but tremendously happy to be rid of this tiresome obligation. Thus ended the first and, for many years, the last tour of the young artist.

However comprehensible from an artistic and human point of view this episode may be, it discloses a highly irritable state of mind, which was soon aggravated in an alarming and even threatening manner. The direct cause of this was the performance in St. Petersburg of Rachmaninoff's first Symphony, in the autumn of 1897.

During the 'eighties, while Rachmaninoff was studying at the St. Petersburg Conservatoire, the so-called "Belayev Circle" was formed and became one of the most important music centres in the capital, although its attitude was one of conscious opposition to the Conservatoire, the Imperial Russian Musical Society, and Anton Rubinstein, whose rule in the capital was still supreme. The diplomatic mediator between these two musical kingdoms was Rimsky-Korsakov. He was then Professor of composition, instrumentation, and counterpoint at the College of Music and, at the same time, the undisputed leader of the "Belayev Circle." This Circle had evolved from the "Mighty group of Five"—Balakirev, Moussorgsky, Cui, Borodin, and Rimsky-Korsakov—but had, after the death of Borodin and Moussorgsky, and after the desertion of Balakirev, who deteriorated into a state of gloomy bigotry and misanthropic introspection, shrunk to two members only, one of whom, Cui, could no longer be taken quite seriously. The "Belayev Circle" centres around Belayev, a rich timber merchant and an enthusiastic music lover, who, by his magnificent bequests, had contributed considerably towards the improvement of Russian music at the end of the nineteenth century.

Apart from Rimsky-Korsakov and Glazounov, about whom Belayev seemed to be absolutely mad, the Circle consisted of several St. Petersburg composers, most of whom were pupils of Korsakov and whose names may be found in the lists of the publishing firm M. P. Belayev in Leipzig (which was one of the bequests of this generous patron). Regardless of the contempt with which, on the whole, the musicians of St. Petersburg looked upon the representatives of the Moscow musical world and the intrigues existing between the two cities, Belayev kept an eye on Moscow and captured Scriabin and Taneyev for his publishing firm. He was naturally anxious to get into contact with young Rachmaninoff as well. In this he did not succeed, because Gutheil, who was well aware of Rachmaninoff's value, always overbid Belayev's offers with gratifying generosity. Besides his publishing firm in Leipzig and the Glinka Prize, which was a yearly award for the best symphonic or chamber music work, Belayev sponsored also the so-called "Russian Symphony Concerts" in St. Petersburg. They included only works written by Russian composers and were financed by Belayev. These concerts were at first conducted by Balakirev, but later by Rimsky-Korsakov and Glazounov. When Belayev heard of young Rachmaninoff's first Symphony, he asked that the work might have its first performance at one of his Symphony Concerts.

*　　　*　　　*

Rachmaninoff's account of the episode is as follows:

"The circumstances attending the performance of my first Symphony affected me very deeply and had a decisive influence on my later development. I imagined that there was nothing I could not do and had great hopes for my future. It was in the confidence bred of this feeling that I composed my First Symphony in D minor, and the ease with which I worked encouraged my pride

G   97

and self-esteem. I had a very high opinion of my work, which was built up on themes taken from the *Oktoechos* —the choir book with the chants of the Russian Church Service—in all its eight keys. The joy of creating carried me away. I was convinced that here I had discovered and opened up entirely new paths in music. S. I. Taneyev, to whom I played the work, was not at all pleased with it. But this failure did not daunt my arrogance. I travelled to St. Petersburg filled with the highest anticipations, after having sold the work to Gutheil, who, without a murmur and without having either heard or seen it, paid five hundred roubles for it.

I do not wish to belittle the terrible failure of my Symphony in St. Petersburg. According to my present conviction this fate was not undeserved. It is true that the performance was beneath contempt and the work in parts unrecognizable, but, apart from this, its deficiencies were revealed to me with a dreadful distinctness even during the first rehearsal. Something within me snapped. All my self-confidence broke down, and the artistic satisfaction that I had looked forward to was never realized. The work made a very bad impression, too, on the St. Petersburg musicians who were present. 'Forgive me, but I do not find this music at all agreeable,' said Rimsky-Korsakov to me in his dry and unsparing manner at a rehearsal. And I, utterly disillusioned, knew that he was right, and that this harsh judgment was not only due to the general embitterment against Moscow. I 'listened in' to my own work. I found the orchestration abominable, but I knew that the music also was not up to much. There are serious illnesses and deadly blows from fate which entirely change a man's character. This was the effect of my own Symphony on myself. When the indescribable torture of this performance had at last come to an end, I was a different man.

THE FIRST SYMPHONY

During the evening I could not go into the concert-hall. I left the artists' room and hid myself, sitting on an iron fire-escape staircase which led into the gallery of the 'Nobility Hall.' There I spent the time, huddled on a step, while my Symphony, which had fanned in me such great expectations, was being played. I live through that terrible experience again: it was the most agonizing hour of my life! Sometimes I stuck my fingers in my ears to prevent myself from hearing my own music, the discords of which absolutely tortured me. Only one thought hammered in my brain—'How is it possible? What is the cause of it?' No sooner had the last chords died away than I fled, horrified, into the street. I ran to the Nevsky-Prospect, boarded one of the trams, so familiar to me from my childhood, and drove incessantly up and down the endless street, through wind and mist, martyred by the thought of my failure. At last I calmed down so far that I was able to face the supper which Belayev was giving in my honour that evening. But even there the abject misery that had taken the place of my former arrogance never left me for a moment. All the encouragement of my 'colleagues' present could not comfort me. I had thought that I knew exactly where I stood. All my hopes, all belief in myself, had been destroyed."

The failure of Rachmaninoff's Symphony at the concert was rubbed in by the critics. Cesar Cui, the augur and haruspex of the musical world in St. Petersburg, wrote a devastating article in his paper, *The St. Petersburg News.* "If there were a Conservatoire in hell," he said, "Rach-maninoff would gain the first prize for his Symphony, so devilish are the discords he has dished up before us." Then he continued by accusing the Composer—and this is the first and last time it ever happened to him—of an atrocious musical "modernism," and laughed at the secret

99

idea upon which the Symphony was founded. Those who are superstitious will not be surprised at the sad fate meted out to the work, for it bears the Opus number 13!

It is very probable that Rachmaninoff's Symphony in D minor would have met with a different fate if it had been performed under another conductor and in Moscow. There the name and the personality of the young Composer, who was so well known and liked, would at least have assured him a courteous reception for his work. Then the Symphony would have been published, the first impression could have been reconsidered in the light of several performances, and the score would have been available for study. After the performance in St. Petersburg, the young Composer, wounded to the heart, withdrew his Symphony and hid the score under seven seals. No one has ever again heard a note of it, and the alarmed Monsieur Gutheil was either too tactful or too much afraid of the young man to refer to the work or to the five hundred roubles.

Although the musical circles of St. Petersburg never expected anything good from Moscow—a prejudice which was obviously strengthened by the failure of Rachmaninoff's Symphony—the young Composer had a very friendly reception in the capital. This was probably due to his human qualities. Rimsky-Korsakov, who in his *Annals* simply mentioned the Symphony in D minor without commenting upon it, in a further passage of the same book expresses his regret that they had not succeeded in persuading "the other Moscow star, Rachmaninoff" (the first one was Scriabin), to join the "Belayev Circle."

During his stay in St. Petersburg, Rachmaninoff had attended one of the famous "Fridays" at Belayev's, where the evening began with music and ended up with drinking. There he played his Fantasia for two pianos with Felix

Blumenfeld, who played the second piano. This performance took place previous to the performance of the
Symphony. The Fantasia aroused great pleasure, especially
the fourth movement with the carillon of the Kremlin
bells chiming in with the liturgical Easter Chant, "Christ
is Risen." Rimsky-Korsakov, in his austere and school-
masterly manner, drew Rachmaninoff's attention to the
final climax, which would, in his opinion, be more
effective if the Easter Chant were first given alone and
without the bells.

"In my youthful pride I had nothing but contempt for
this suggestion," Rachmaninoff said later, "but now I
realize only too well that Rimsky-Korsakov was absolutely
right."

From St. Petersburg Rachmaninoff did not return
straight to Moscow, but visited his grandmother, Madame
Boutakova. The old lady had established herself in Novgorod after selling her small estate "Borissovo," where
Rachmaninoff had spent the happiest summers of his
childhood. He spent three days with her, during which
he did nothing but brood over the disastrous performance
of his Symphony. This time his grandmother did not
succeed in comforting her beloved grandson as she had
so often done during his childhood. He was deeply
despondent when he parted from her in order to return
to Moscow. This parting was to be their last, for they
never met again. Fourteen years before it had been
fear of Sverev that oppressed his childish heart as he left
"Borissovo"; now it seemed as if his own fate lifted a
menacing arm and stared at him with cold, relentless
eyes out of the darkness that was the future.

CHAPTER SIX

SERIOUS MENTAL SHOCK AND FINAL RECOVERY

1895–1902

*Mental change after the failure of the First Symphony—
As conductor of Mamontov's Private Opera in Moscow—
Disagreeable experiences as a beginner in conducting opera
—Envious Esposito—Fedor Chaliapine—Appearance at the
London Philharmonic Society—Relapse into his former apathy
—Princess Lieven and Leo Tolstoy—Dr. Dahl, the hypno-
tiser—The Second Concerto for pianoforte—Rachmaninoff's
marriage to Natalie Satin—The honeymoon and return
to Moscow*

RACHMANINOFF tells us:

"I returned to Moscow a changed man. My confidence in myself had received a sudden blow. Agonizing
hours spent in doubt and hard thinking had brought me
to the conclusion that I ought to give up composing.
I was obviously unfitted for it, and therefore it would be
better if I made an end to it at once.

I gave up my room in 'America' and returned to the
Satins. A paralysing apathy possessed me. I did nothing
at all and found no pleasure in anything. Half my days
were spent lying on a couch and sighing over my ruined
life. My only occupation consisted of a few piano lessons
which I was forced to give in order to keep myself alive.
This condition, which was as tiresome for myself as for
those about me, lasted more than a year. I did not live;
I vegetated, idle and hopeless. The thought of spending
my life as a piano-teacher gave me cold shudders. But
what other activity was there left for me? Once or twice
I was asked to play at concerts. I did this and had some

success. But of what use was it to me? The opportunities to appear at concerts came my way so seldom that I could not rely upon them as a material foundation for my existence. Nor could I hope that the Conservatoire would offer me a situation as a pianoforte teacher, for Safonoff's enmity towards Siloti was now transferred also to me, and as he did not consider me a pianist, or did not wish to do so, he could no more offer me a class at the Conservatoire than engage me as a soloist at the Symphony Concerts given by the Imperial Musical Society.

The following little anecdote illustrates the feeling towards me which predominated amongst the Professors at the Conservatoire.

One of the Professors for pianoforte at the Conservatoire was Paul Schlözer, a very ceremonious Pole. During one of the usual elaborate suppers at Sverev's house when many notable musicians of Moscow were present, I sat opposite Schlözer at table. The conversation turned upon my first Concerto for Pianoforte, which had just been published. Someone asked Schlözer, 'Do you know Rachmaninoff's Concerto?'

Schlözer: 'No, I haven't seen it yet.' Then, twisting his small reddish moustache, he turned to me and said in a disagreeably sharp tone, 'How much does your Concerto cost?'

Myself (very embarrassed): 'I really don't know. . . . I should think about three roubles.'

Schlözer: 'Hm . . . surely it is very strange that Rachmaninoff's Concerto should cost three roubles when one can buy a Concerto by Chopin for one and a half roubles!'

Quite a few seconds passed until I remembered that Schlözer himself had composed two Etudes for the piano—his only contribution, by the way, to the musical world—and then I in my turn asked him:

'Don't you think it odd, M. Schlözer, that one has to pay three roubles for two Etudes by Schlözer when one can buy twenty-four of Chopin's for one rouble only?'

Silence!

Then, to my surprise, someone of whom I had least expected it, as is often the way in life, came to my rescue. It was the well-known Moscow railway magnate and art patron, S. I. Mamontov, who suggested that I should join the association of his new Opera Syndicate at the Solodnikov Theatre in Moscow as a second conductor."

By means of his private opera, which he founded in 1897, S. I. Mamontov intended to instil new life into the stagnant waters of the Moscow opera, which was threatening to freeze gradually but completely in the chilly atmosphere of comfortable placidity at the Imperial Theatres. Mamontov wished, above all, to brighten up the repertoire of his theatre, as compared with those of the State Opera houses, by enriching it and bringing it up to date. A man like Rimsky-Korsakov, for instance, whom the conservative musical circles regarded as ultra-modern, had the greatest difficulty in getting his works performed at any of the Imperial Theatres in Moscow or St. Petersburg. It was S. I. Mamontov's aim also to open up opportunities for fresh and promising talent in every department, for singers, painters, and musicians, to whom the doors of the old-established Court Theatres with their atmosphere of rigid and straitlaced etiquette remained closed. Amongst the first artists whom Mamontov engaged at his theatre, besides Rachmaninoff, were Fedor Chaliapin, the painters Korovin and Seroff, and the highly gifted Wrubel and his wife, Nadéshda Zabyela-Wrubel (the unique impersonator of Rimsky-Korsakov's fairy-tale characters), as well as many others.

ONE WING OF THE HOUSE AT IVANOVKA WHERE THE COMPOSER USED TO SPEND THE SUMMER

The first conductor at the Mamontov opera, Esposito, was of little account as a musical personality but had great experience and knowledge, for he knew innumerable Italian and Russian operas by heart. Rachmaninoff accepted Mamontov's offer without hesitation, because the profession of conductor fascinated him and seemed worth striving for; he had no idea then of the thorny paths that hedge in a conductor's career on every side. It also gave him a more or less solid financial basis, which, to him, was of great importance, for some time earlier he had started to support his mother in St. Petersburg. But his first delight in the appointment lasted only for a year.

He continues:

"What could have been more welcome than Savva Ivanovitch Mamontov's suggestion to me? I felt that I was able to conduct, although I had but a hazy idea of the technique of conducting, but this my youthful optimism regarded as a negligible detail. I realized with overwhelming joy that I would be able to give up the hateful piano lessons which were as disagreeable to me as to my pupils. I would like here to express my sympathy to all my former pupils and ask their forgiveness for these lessons. I know now what they must have suffered.

As I had never before conducted an opera, Esposito advised them to give me one that was well known to the orchestra, the chorus, and the soloists. Glinka's *Life for the Tsar* was selected. To-day I am able to say that, from the conductor's point of view, it is one of the most difficult operas I know. It contains more than one dangerous trap—such as, for instance, the Forest Scene, where the chorus of Poles never changes its Mazurka rhythm and sings three beats, while the orchestra must be conducted in four. Even an experienced conductor will find this passage difficult. How, then, was I to deal with it? Every opera, as is well known, suffers from a lack of rehearsals. Here also Esposito, who did not like me because he saw in me an unwelcome rival, decreed that one rehearsal would suffice. I can safely say that I knew the work as well as Esposito. I had prepared myself for it conscientiously and actually knew every single note of the score. All went well with the orchestra, but as soon as the singers joined in there was a catastrophe and everything dissolved into chaos. I was quite helpless. Esposito sat in the stalls and smiled ironically without saying a word. Mamontov ran up and down in great excitement, now and then offering a useful hint prompted by his wholesome common sense. But it was of little use to me. Full of despair and horror, I carried on the rehearsal to the end. To all my other disappointments was now added the one that I was not fit to be a conductor.

But Mamontov had more confidence in my talent than I. *Life for the Tsar*, it is true, had to be abandoned. The opera was handed over to Esposito, who actually conducted it without a hitch after ostentatiously refusing all rehearsals. But Mamontov decided to try me again, this time with a Symphonic opera, which contained fewer stumbling-blocks in the shape of complex vocal passages, recitatives, and similar difficulties. Naturally, when *Life for the Tsar* was conducted by Esposito, I watched the performance eagerly, with my eyes glued to the conductor's baton, noticing every single movement. It was only then that I realized why I had failed. I had not given a cue to any singer. In my ignorance and innocence I had imagined that an artist who walks on the stage to sing an opera is bound to know it as well as the conductor. Why should I give him a cue? I had no idea of the astonishing lack of musical understanding that characterizes most singers, who know nothing of an opera except their own part. During this memorable performance I noticed amongst other things that Esposito obviously and purposely ignored all the musical improvements which I had tried to introduce into the interpretation of Glinka's score; every fermato that I had eliminated he restored; he drifted back into the old slackness of tempo, and, when the performance was over, shouted at the tenor, with whom I had taken special trouble, 'What on earth have you been trying to sing? Have you an idea what tradition means?'

The experience I was able to gather during this performance conducted by Esposito enabled me to rehearse the opera *Samson and Delila* without difficulty and to perform it without a hitch. The audience and the Press seemed satisfied with me, for they always greeted my appearance at the conductor's desk with demonstrations of friendliness. At that time I conducted *Roussalka* (*The Mermaid*), by Dargomyshkty, *Carmen*, and *The May Night*, by Rimsky-Korsakov.

It was then Chaliapin's first season in Moscow. He was only a little older than myself. In *Roussalka*, which I conducted, he sang the part of the miller and interpreted it in his inimitable and inspired manner. Everything went well, and I realized that conducting would no longer constitute a problem for me. I was only annoyed that I had to conduct also the Sunday morning performances for school-children, when frequently some antiquated opera, such as, for instance, *Askold's Grave*, by Verstovsky—a mediocre forerunner of Glinka—was unearthed and performed. This, according to my own opinion, was beneath my dignity.

All the same, I gratefully acknowledge the fact that my one year's conducting at Mamontov's opera meant a good deal to me, for I acquired a first-hand knowledge of conducting in the true sense of the word which, soon afterwards and under different circumstances, was to prove very useful. But even apart from that, I could never consider this one year as lost, for it brought me into contact with Fedor Chaliapin, and this I count amongst the most important and the finest artistic experiences I have ever known. I can hardly think of another artist who had given me such deep and purely artistic enjoyment. To accompany him when he sang, to admire the facility of his musical conception, the quickness and naturalness with which he responded to musical and artistic stimuli and assimilated and transformed them in his own inimitable way—these experiences rank without doubt amongst the greatest artistic joys of my life. Fortunately, they were frequent and repeated over and over again. In Moscow, as well as in other places, we played and sang together, either in the quiet intimacy of the study or before large audiences. But I will refer to this later."

In the summer of the year 1898 Rachmaninoff accepted an invitation from the singer, Madame Lyubatovitch, to spend the holidays at her country house, not far from Moscow. Among the guests there was Chaliapin, as well as the ballet-dancer, Mlle Tornaghi. Savva Mamontov, the painters Korovin and Seroff, and innumerable opera singers of both sexes came down from town to spend the evenings and Sundays at the hospitable house of Mme Lyubatovitch. Thus the summer passed, riotously and swiftly.

The most important event during that summer was the marriage between Fedor Chaliapin and the beautiful and talented ballerina, Mlle Tornaghi. A tale told by Chaliapin in his *Memoirs* gives an idea of the innocently happy freedom of personal relations that prevailed among the party of artists assembled at Mme Lyubatovitch's house. He tells how, on the morning after his wedding, at about half-past six, he was suddenly awakened by the most atrocious tin-kettle music underneath his window. He jumped out of bed, and, peeping through the closed blind with one eye, saw the whole Mamontov crowd grouped in front of the house. Whoever was able, sang, while the rest accompanied on pots and pans and empty bottles, their urgent request that the young couple should get up immediately and join them in a mushroom hunt in the woods. This "hell chorus" (as Chaliapin calls it) was conducted by Rachmaninoff with much swing and emphasis.

When autumn approached and preparations for the next opera season began, Rachmaninoff gave everyone a surprise by announcing that he would not return to his former post as conductor. He was a little tired of the theatre and felt that he was not made to be the average conductor of opera. The constant repetition of old, hackneyed works which, for the greater part, were preceded by an insufficient number of rehearsals was a nuisance. No opportunity was given to work out musical and technical refinements or to produce a serious artistic creation in general and in detail. Nor, indeed, would the quality of the orchestra and the chorus of the private opera have been equal to this. Moreover, Rachmaninoff began again to feel a faint inclination to compose. At this period he wrote the songs Op. 14, the choruses Op. 15, and the *Moments Musicaux* for Pianoforte, Op. 16. After a disagreement with Gutheil, he handed over the last two works to the old-established Moscow publishing firm of Jurgenson, whose founder, Peter Jurgenson, had been a personal friend of Tchaikovsky and had published all his works.

At this juncture Rachmaninoff received in the autumn

of 1898 an invitation from the London Philharmonic Society to perform at one of their Symphony Concerts. During one of his previous seasons Siloti had played Rachmaninoff's Prélude in C sharp minor from his Opus 3 at one of his pianoforte recitals, and this had an almost triumphal success. A London publisher immediately printed copies of it, which were distributed all over the British Isles. From there they reached the Continent and America and created a popularity for the name of the young Composer that astonished no one more than himself. At that time Sir Alexander Campbell Mackenzie conducted the Philharmonic Concerts in London. The "mad" success of the Prélude in C sharp minor had the highly gratifying result that the young Composer was received with regal honours by the orchestra and the audience and, last but not least, by the Press. Rachmaninoff conducted his Fantasy for orchestra, *The Rock*, and played a group of pianoforte pieces, which naturally included the Prélude in C flat minor, for this had been one of the chief conditions of his engagement. The success was tremendous. The famous Secretary of the London Philharmonic Society, Francesco Berger, immediately approached Rachmaninoff with an invitation for the following year: he was to play his First Concerto for pianoforte in London. All this was like balm poured on the Moscow wounds. The young artist gained new courage and, under the influence of his London reception, promised Berger to write a second Concerto for England, as, in his opinion, the first one was not good enough to be played in London.

But no sooner had Rachmaninoff returned to Russia than he relapsed into his former apathy. He seldom left the couch in his room and preferred the company of his faithful dog Levko to all human intercourse. This condition lasted altogether for two years, including the

London episode. It is easy to understand how worried all his friends, and especially the Satins, with whom he lived, became over his future. They invented the strangest tactics in order to restore in him the self-confidence which he had lost.

Princess Alexandra Lieven, a friend of Mme Satin, who took a motherly interest in Rachmaninoff and was well known in Moscow for her magnificent work in social reform and philanthropy, approached even Leo Tolstoy, the all-powerful one at Yasnaya Polyana, with the request to help young Rachmaninoff by giving him a few words of encouragement. Rachmaninoff, to whom the name of Tolstoy was sacred, could be persuaded only with great difficulty to visit the "Great and Lonely One" of Yasnaya Polyana in the company of Princess Lieven. He was, of course, ignorant of the plot between her and Tolstoy which was intended to result in his renewed happiness. But the visit was unsuccessful. Tolstoy's admonishments, his appeal to the young man's human and artistic conscience, had no effect on Rachmaninoff's unconquerable indifference.

At last the young people at the Satins' house invented a new plan which was to dispel his despondency and his mental depression. This was destined to meet with a success for which they had hardly dared to hope. At that time a doctor by the name of Dahl aroused much discussion because of his "magic" cures. He achieved his miraculous results with the aid of suggestion and auto-suggestion, and was, in this respect, the forerunner of Coué. The Satins were able to persuade Rachmaninoff to consult Dr. Dahl about his apathy, which naturally worried himself as much as the people round him. Meanwhile the year 1900 had arrived. From January till April Rachmaninoff paid daily visits to Dr. Dahl. Here is his own account of them.

"My relations had told Dr. Dahl that he must at all costs cure me of my apathetic condition and achieve such results that I would again begin to compose. Dahl had asked what manner of composition they desired and had received the answer, 'A Concerto for pianoforte,' for this I had promised to the people in London and had given it up in despair. Consequently I heard the same hypnotic formula repeated day after day while I lay half asleep in an armchair in Dahl's study. 'You will begin to write your Concerto. . . . You will work with great facility. . . . The Concerto will be of an excellent quality. . . .' It was always the same, without interruption. Although it may sound incredible, this cure really helped me. Already at the beginning of the summer I began again to compose. The material grew in bulk, and new musical ideas began to stir within me—far more than I needed for my Concerto. By the autumn I had finished two movements of the Concerto—the Andante and the Finale—and a sketch for a Suite for two pianofortes whose Opus number 17 is explained by the fact that I finished the Concerto later by adding the first movement. The two movements of the Concerto (Op. 18) I played during the same autumn at a charity concert directed by Siloti. It was one of the so-called 'Prison Concerts' which were arranged with great splendour by Princess Lieven, who was Chairman of the Committee for the alleviation of suffering to prisoners, and took place in the Moscow 'Nobility Hall.' At these concerts they usually engaged the most popular artists in Moscow, because they drew the largest audience. I remember that Ysaye, Casals, and the Moscow artists, Chaliapin, Brandoukov, and I, performed on these occasions. I usually played my latest compositions. The two movements of my Concerto had a gratifying success. This buoyed up my self-confidence so much that I began to

S. RACHMANINOFF IN THE COUNTRY AT IVANOVKA (1900)

compose again with great keenness. By the spring I had already finished the first movement of the Concerto and the Suite for two pianofortes. I had regained belief in myself and could dare to think of realizing a favourite wish of mine, namely, to devote two years to composition only. For this two conditions would have to be satisfied: I must be free from all other duties, particularly piano lessons, and I must have enough money to keep body and soul together. Money was, of course, the chief problem, for it would solve the other. To achieve this I turned to Siloti, who was my only wealthy relation, and asked whether he believed sufficiently in my future as a composer to support me for two years. Siloti granted my request without hesitation, and during the next two years sent me regular quarterly sums for my support.

I felt that Dr. Dahl's treatment had strengthened my nervous system to a miraculous degree. Out of gratitude I dedicated my second Concerto to him. As the piece had had a great success in Moscow, everyone began to wonder what possible connection it could have with Dr. Dahl. The truth, however, was known only to Dahl, the Satins, and myself.

The joy of creating lasted during the next two years, and I wrote a number of large and small pieces: the Sonata for Violoncello (Op. 19), which I dedicated to Brandoukov, the Cantata *Spring* to the words by Nekrassov (Op. 20), the twelve songs (Op. 21), the Variations for Pianoforte on a theme by Chopin (Op. 22), and the Préludes for Pianoforte (Op. 23). The Cantata was first performed at a Symphony Concert given by the Moscow Philharmonic Society. All the other works I played for the first time at the 'Prison Concerts' which I have already mentioned. The first song of Op. 21 was *Fate*, on words by Apuchtin; for the music I used the first theme of four notes in Beethoven's Fifth (the *Fate*) Symphony.

I dedicated the song to Chaliapin, and he sang it for the first time at one of Princess Lieven's concerts (in 1900). This song, which he interpreted magnificently and which, for many years, was one of the 'star numbers' in his repertoire, we have played and sung together innumerable times in Moscow as well as in other towns.

Gutheil paid me fees which in those days were considered very high and were unequalled in Russia. He paid me two hundred and fifty roubles for one song, whereas the price fixed by Belayev's publishing firm was, without exception, one hundred roubles. The following story in connection with this amused me very much. One relation of mine, who was in the Government and whom I have already mentioned in connection with the first performance of my opera *Aleko*, was not only clever but very fond of music, and, being an ardent admirer of 'Gipsy Songs', had even composed two 'Romances,' which had been published. One day he managed to say:

'Not so bad, Sergei. You get more money for your music than any other Russian composer. Now, I shall be the next by getting one hundred and seventy roubles for each piece!'

I liked this cousin who, at times, showed a great sense of humour. If he was late for dinner, which was usually the case, he answered the gentle reproofs of his wife by saying jokingly:

'What do you want? Russia is large and I am alone.'

But to return to my composition, which I mentioned above. My songs Op. 21 were written for a special purpose. I needed a fairly large sum of money, and decided to write twelve songs, which Gutheil bought from me with real or simulated pleasure. The three thousand roubles he paid me I wanted for my honeymoon, which materialized in the spring of 1902."

SERIOUS MENTAL SHOCK AND FINAL RECOVERY

Rachmaninoff's marriage to Natalie Satin took place in Moscow on the 29th of April 1902, and was celebrated in an army chapel in one of the outlying suburbs of Moscow. Alexander Siloti and Anatol Brandoukov figured as best men.

The young couple left for a journey to Bayreuth, via Vienna and Italy, to attend the Wagner Festival. The music dramas by Wagner, of which only *Lohengrin* and *Tannhäuser* were reasonably well known in Russia, made a deep impression on young Rachmaninoff, who has ever since considered *Die Meistersinger* in particular the greatest achievement in music, and was never parted from his pocket-score of this work for many years.

When they returned, the young couple spent the rest of the summer at "Ivanovka," the Satins' estate in the district of Tambov. In the autumn they moved to Moscow, where they took a flat in the house which harboured the first girls' grammar school in Moscow, close to the Strastnoy Convent. Rachmaninoff lived in this flat until he left Russia and Moscow for good.

CHAPTER SEVEN

GROWING POPULARITY AS COMPOSER AND CONDUCTOR

1902–1906

Growth of his fame as a composer in Moscow—Concert activities—Concert in Vienna—The new general manager of the Imperial Theatres in Moscow—Rachmaninoff first conductor at the Moscow Grand Theatre—A Tchaikovsky week—The revolution, 1905—Pan Voyevod, by Rimski-Korsakov, and beginnings of a closer friendship with the St. Petersburg composers—Rachmaninoff's two operas: The Miser Knight and Francesca da Rimini—Decision to leave Moscow for a time to escape the enervating musical activities

DURING the first decade of the twentieth century Rachmaninoff's fame in Moscow as a composer grew rapidly and was steadily enhanced by new works. He enjoyed an unexampled popularity which bordered on idolatry and spread through all classes of society in the old Kremlin city. Although St. Petersburg felt kindlier towards him than towards most other Moscow composers, it preserved, on the whole, an attitude of aloofness far removed from the unrestrained enthusiasm with which the Muscovites greeted each public appearance of Rachmaninoff. His songs in particular scored success after success, and could be heard in all the Moscow concert-halls as well as in every household that had a piano and a member of the family able to sing them. It is no exaggeration to say that Rachmaninoff was very nearly as popular in Moscow as Tchaikovsky had been in his time. The public, at any rate, did not hesitate to award him the crown of musical sovereignty which had been held by no one but Tchaikovsky. Only a certain set at the Conservatoire, led by Safonoff who could not forgive the Composer of the Prélude in C sharp minor for not having been his own pupil, regarded this hero-worship with mixed feelings. The Dictator of the Conservatoire, who had induced the Moscow plutocracy to provide the funds for the magnificent and monumental new building of the Conservatoire, erected there under his supervision, had managed to persuade public opinion into admiring Rachmaninoff as composer of the Second Concerto for pianoforte, and other works of that period rather than as their interpreter. In the year 1908 Rachmaninoff began again to give concerts abroad. Since his brilliant début in London, which, owing to his nervous depression, had led no further, the young artist had not played in foreign countries. Now he received an invitation to play his Second Concerto at a concert in Vienna given by the Vienna Philharmonic Society. His success was satisfactory but by no means sensational. As in the case of many other first-rate artists, such as Caruso, Paderevsky, Kreisler, and others, he had to be labelled by America before he found the appreciation he deserved in Europe. Unfortunately, this did not happen till later in his life. The pianists of Europe could breathe again, for Rachmaninoff returned to Moscow, quite unaware of his importance as a pianist.

At home, however, his fame as a composer and the steadily growing influence of his artistic authority in the musical world attracted the attention of official circles. The directors of the Imperial Theatres began to put out feelers for him. A new spirit was already beginning to make itself felt there, under the influence of the new Director of the Imperial Theatres in Moscow. These were the Grand Theatre (opera and ballet), the Little Theatre (problem plays), and the New Theatre (modern comedy and occasional light comic opera). The new Director, who soon attained to the position of General Manager of all Imperial Theatres in Moscow and St. Petersburg, was a retired colonel of the Cavalry Guards, called Telyakovsky—a name of no particular distinction. A mere accident had led him to adopt the career of Administrator of the Imperial Theatres, where, thanks to his sharp intelligence and extraordinary energy (qualities not frequently met with in this position), he achieved remarkable results, which brought him not only professional satisfaction but titles and decorations of distinction.

"New birds—new songs" goes a Russian saying, and this proved true the moment Telyakovsky took up his position in Moscow. He had to fight down the most stubborn prejudice before he was able to carry out his artistic ideas. His first step consisted in demanding the dismissal of all artists who were no longer in their prime and kept their engagements on the Moscow stage only through the indolence and apathy of the management, and to call in new and promising actors. He wanted, above all, to clear the way for fresh talent. His first great coup of engaging Chaliapin, who joined the company of the Grand Theatre in 1898, had proved a tremendous success. Now he prepared for the second, which promised to be of far greater importance, and concerned Rachmaninoff. Who were the conductors at the Moscow Grand Theatre? The first and only important one was Hypolit Altani, a Jew of Italian origin. He was intensely musical, sound, and reliable, but could not be described as an exceptional musical personality blowing like a March wind through the Grand Theatre and sweeping up the dusty corners of the stage and orchestra. There was, however, a young musician, already the hero of several stories and the talk of the town, of whose musical gifts one heard remarkable accounts, and who was not only a wonderful pianist but had proved during his short engagement at Mamontov's opera house that he was capable of achieving good results as a conductor. His name was Rachmaninoff. Telyakovsky sent his delegates to him. "Highly placed officials," as Rachmaninoff put it, came to his house, or tried to meet him elsewhere, and made inquiries about his work, describing to him in the most glowing terms all the social and artistic advantages attaching to a post at the Imperial Theatres. The young Composer resisted for a long time, but was eventually persuaded to accept the offer. He was not attracted by the material advantages, but solely by the artistic opportunities which the new post opened up for him and by the prospect that he would be working with Chaliapin for the glory of Russian art. So at the beginning of the season 1905–6, Rachmaninoff entered the Union of the Imperial Grand Theatre of Moscow as a conductor. It had taken Telyakovsky and his helpers one and a half years to persuade him into taking this step. Rachmaninoff found it hard to part from the unrestrained freedom of private life. He feared that in spite of the long summer holidays (over three months) given by the Imperial Theatres his work as a composer would suffer from the strenuous and exhausting routine of a conductor of opera. Although officially, and to spare Altani's feelings, he was not placed above the latter, he was given unusual and almost unlimited administrative power, which made his position exceptional—much like that of Eduard Napravnik at the St. Petersburg Imperial Opera House. But, instead of signing a contract for five years, he only agreed to tie himself for the five months of that year's season, from October till March.

Moscow looked forward to Rachmaninoff's first appearance at the conductor's desk at the Grand Theatre with

tremendous excitement; for was he not their elected
favourite? It proved an intoxicating and entirely undisputed victory. For his first performance Rachmaninoff
had chosen Dargomyshky's opera *Roussalka* (*The Mermaid*),
one of the few standard works amongst Russian operas.
This he probably did because it contained one of
Chaliapin's star parts, that of the old miller who goes
mad after his daughter commits suicide and staggers
across the stage thinking he is a raven. That particular
scene was full of possibilities and gave Chaliapin ample
scope for displaying his dramatic genius. But this by no
means exciting work did not offer a single number
in which the conductor was able to shine. In spite of
this fact, and quite apart from Chaliapin's triumph,
Rachmaninoff had a sensational success. Perhaps he owed
it to the well-known fact that an audience always craving
for new sensations was excited merely by the fact that he
was appearing for the first time as a conductor at the
Grand Theatre. At first he could not be found anywhere,
because everyone looked for him in the wrong place,
immediately behind the prompter's box, from where, up
till now, opera had always been conducted, not only at
the Grand but at all the other Russian theatres. Ignoring the warnings of old Maestro Altani, who, like all
routineers, declared that there was only one position from
which one could conduct an opera—facing the singers
and turning one's back to the orchestra—Rachmaninoff
broke with an old tradition and, following the example
of Richard Wagner, had the conductor's desk placed in
that part of the orchestra which was nearest the stalls.
His success proved him to be right, but he found great
difficulty in persuading Altani—who, by the way, died
soon afterwards—that this was really an improvement and
in getting his permission for the desk to remain there
permanently. Until he and the other conductors could be

convinced of the value of this new arrangement, the conductor's desk, and those of most members of the orchestra, had to be moved each time that Rachmaninoff conducted. This naturally caused a great deal of inconvenience and must have inspired much profanity among the stage hands on the subject of the fads of the new conductor.

Rachmaninoff, however, was not the man to give in when, after careful thinking, he had come to the conclusion that he was right. He never compromised in questions concerning art. This fidelity to his convictions, which some considered to amount to obstinacy—unjustly, for Rachmaninoff always gave in to arguments more convincing than his own—made his friends look forward to his career as a conductor of opera with some apprehension. They expected terrible conflicts between him and some celebrated singers, amongst whom Chaliapin could be counted as one of the most hot-tempered and dogmatic. He had quarrelled with almost every conductor at the St. Petersburg and Moscow theatres. But these gloomy forebodings were not realized, and the dreaded catastrophes never occurred. Rachmaninoff's musical authority was so great, his superiority during each rehearsal so convincingly obvious, defying all contradiction, that no one dared rebel against it.

Rachmaninoff's position was strengthened by his attitude; he avoided all personal intrigues and suppressed the prima donna worship which corrupts the atmosphere of most opera theatres. The favouritism that usually surrounds great conductors of opera was never allowed to take root under Rachmaninoff's influence. His calm and dignified bearing, his cool judgment, ignoring all but artistic motives, his unchanging manner and just treatment defied all attempts on the part of the prima donnas to gain personal preference. It is not surprising that in this

^cleaner atmosphere the artistic life of Moscow began to breathe anew.

Unfortunately, the external circumstances of Russian life did not encourage Rachmaninoff's endeavours to reform the Grand Theatre. On the contrary, outside the theatre everything tended to destroy the artistic achievement prepared and carried out within, and to curtail its influence on Moscow society and the wider circles of the opera audiences.

Everyone knows that in the autumn of 1905, directly after the Japanese War, which proved so disastrous for Russia, and as a result of Count Witte's October Manifesto proclaiming the Tsar's renunciation of absolute autocracy, a revolution broke out in St. Petersburg and Moscow. Unfortunately, it was not taken seriously enough by the Government and failed to teach them a lesson for the future. This revolutionary upheaval was termed "Agrarian Unrest" and was only suppressed with difficulty by the so-called "penal expeditions." It affected also the country districts and spread its terror of destruction and murder through entire provinces. The position in Moscow during November and December of that year looked grave. It began with a general strike. The lighting, the waterworks, the postal and telegraph services, and the electric trams ceased to function. The inhabitants were forced to stand in endless queues (*Polonaises* or "Tails" as they were called in Moscow), armed with pails and jugs, waiting their turn to draw enough water for daily use from the few wells in the town. After five o'clock in the evening the whole city was plunged into impenetrable darkness. The streets were patrolled by police, strike pickets, and private gangs of thieves who posed as protectors and searched everyone they met, with the result that the unfortunate victims went home with empty pockets. No wonder that hardly anyone dared to go out into the street! At first the theatres remained open, playing to empty houses; but later they also had to be closed, as the musicians, the stage hands, and all employees joined in the strike. In December there was street fighting; barricades were erected and shot down, and even the Guards and Cossacks, called in from St. Petersburg, had trouble in mastering the situation and restoring life to a reasonably normal course. The Tsarist Government at that time was less than ever inclined to give in.

One must admit that these circumstances were not favourable to the development of a successful career as an opera conductor, especially at a theatre whose name, "Imperial Theatre," was enough to excite the unthinking mob to fits of insane fury. These events, particularly the outrages perpetrated by the blind instinct of destruction in the country districts, made a deep impression on Rachmaninoff. They definitely influenced his attitude towards the "Great" Russian Revolution twelve years later, and drove him across the borders of his native country. He loathed nothing more than the plebeian abuse of the most beautiful of human ideals, that of personal freedom. As he himself practised the strictest self-discipline and felt the greatest admiration for every achievement won by hard work, he was incapable of showing any tolerance of what he termed "lack of discipline."

An amusing episode was to disclose the opinion of their young conductor on all such matters to the musicians of his orchestra. All Russians love smoking. Rachmaninoff himself enjoyed it as much as any of his musicians. Altani, who was short-sighted and not over-energetic, had allowed a bad habit to grow up in the orchestra. Players who had to pause for several bars (the third trombone, the harp, or one of the drums) used to creep through the orchestra and disappear through the door at the back in order to

have a little smoke. This, of course, could be seen from
the house, and many a devoted music lover must have
been seriously disturbed by the crouching black figures
in the orchestra creeping soundlessly to and fro. Rachmaninoff prohibited these little escapades and inflicted
severe punishments when his orders were disobeyed. At a
time when everyone was full of ideas of "freedom" and
swore destruction to all tyrants, this upset the gentlemen
in the orchestra. They formed a deputation and sent it
to Rachmaninoff to show this young greenhorn of a
conductor, whose head was obviously swollen with an
exaggerated sense of his authority, that they would not
stand such treatment. The deputies held passionate
speeches on "freedom and human dignity" and ended up
by saying that they resented his treatment and would in
future oppose it. Rachmaninoff listened to them with a
stony calm; not a muscle in his face twitched. "May I
ask the gentlemen to hand in their resignations; they will
be accepted without fail," he said, turned his back on
the deputation, and left them standing in dumb
amazement.

Of course no one sent in a resignation, and never again
did it happen that a musician stole away to have a smoke.
Common sense triumphed and, strange as it may seem,
from that moment Rachmaninoff's popularity with the
members of his orchestra knew no bounds. His upright-
ness, his unswerving sense of justice checked even the
most wicked and spiteful tongues.

After *Roussalka* he rehearsed *Life for the Tsar*. This still
lingered in his memory as an ugly nightmare from his
experience with it at Mamontov's opera house. This time,
however, it was the means of his achieving a sensational
success. It was considered an old-fashioned opera, and
was performed only out of a sense of duty on official feast
days, such as the Tsar's birthday, the Anniversary of his

Saint, the Borki Memorial Day, etc., and in general served as a convenient stopgap. But under Rachmaninoff's handling it was hardly recognizable. Glinka's imperishable but slightly worn melodies seemed to have acquired a new glamour; the magnificent choruses were sung with precision and had an enchanting swing that contrasted gloriously with their old hurdy-gurdy rhythm. Here the old chorus-master, Avranek, was an invaluable support to Rachmaninoff. This man, a genuine artist, who only lacked creative vision to make an outstanding conductor, was quick to recognize the new spirit invading the stuffiness of the Grand Theatre in the person of this young conductor, and with it the possibility of instilling fresh life into the old machine, worn out by routine. The chorus and the orchestra of the Grand Theatre, the best in Europe, have never sung and played as they did under Rachmaninoff. And here I should like to place it on record that, in my opinion, the Moscow Grand Theatre at that time achieved an artistic perfection which has rarely, if ever, been equalled by any other opera house, with the possible exception of the Scala Theatre in Milan, and later, perhaps, the Metropolitan Opera House in New York. I am anxious to emphasize this fact, as it seems otherwise likely to be forgotten.

Amongst other old operas to which Rachmaninoff gave a new vitality were *Carmen* and, of course, the two favourite works by Tchaikovsky, *Eugene Onegin* and *The Queen of Spades*. Rachmaninoff, who considered no honour too great for his beloved master, made the hundredth performance of *The Queen of Spades* an occasion for a whole "Tchaikovsky week" at the Grand Theatre, during which he presented only operas and ballets composed by Tchaikovsky. He conducted the operas *Eugene Onegin, The Queen of Spades, The Opritchniki, Yolanthe*. At the performance of *The Queen of Spades* the smaller parts were taken by stars who usually made no appearance in this opera. Thus Chaliapin impersonated Tomski and the Turk in the Intermezzo, and the magnificent coloratura singer, Madame Neshdanova, the hepherdess, etc.

During his two years at the Grand Theatre Rachmaninoff conducted only three first performances. These were *Pan Voyevoda*, by Rimsky-Korsakov, and his own operas *The Miserly Knight* and *Francesca da Rimini*.

Pan Voyevoda is one of Rimsky-Korsakov's weakest operas, and even Rachmaninoff's careful rehearsals, during which he worked out the smallest details, and his inspiring direction could not win a lasting success for it in Moscow. The performance took place on September 5, 1905. On the previous day all the printers had gone on strike, and consequently all printing works in the town had suspended their work in preparation for the impending general strike and the "revolution" to which we have already referred. On the day of the first performance no notices were sent out, and this resulted in a half-empty theatre. The scanty audience gave the composer, who was present, only a lukewarm reception. Rimsky-Korsakov himself mentions it in his *Chronicles*:

"In the early autumn I was called to Moscow to attend the first performance of my opera *Pan Voyevoda* at the Grand Theatre. Rachmaninoff, who is very talented, conducted. The performance was excellent, except for one or two singers who were rather weak; chorus and orchestra were magnificent. . . . One could not have wished for anything more beautiful than the beginning of the opera, the Nocturne, the scene with the fortune-teller, the Mazurka, the Krakoviak, and the Pianissimo of the Polonaise in the scene between Yadviga and Pan Duiba."

The close study of this opera and Rimsky-Korsakov's music as well as his frequent personal contact with the composer during his stay in Moscow brought about a complete change in Rachmaninoff's attitude towards the creator of *Sadko*, *Snegourotchka* (*Snow-white*), and numerous other masterpieces of Russian opera. We know that during his years of study Rachmaninoff swore only by Tchaikovsky and refused even to consider the composers of St. Petersburg. He had clung to this point of view for a long time; now, at last, the veil of prejudice slipped from his eyes, and he admitted frankly that he was glad to be able to give way to an artistic and personal admiration for Rimsky-Korsakov, unhindered by prematurely formed opinions.

Rachmaninoff himself says:

"When *Pan Voyevoda* was being rehearsed, Rimsky-Korsakov and I became better known to one another. As if I had awoken from a nightmare, I shook off all my Muscovite prejudice against the great St. Petersburg composer. I recognized the artistic sincerity and integrity which inspired Rimsky-Korsakov and raised him high above all pettiness. His admirable mastery of the technique of composition, especially his skill in instrumentation and his sensitive control of orchestral tone-colour, could not but fill me with sincere admiration. I grew really fond of him, and this feeling deepened from day to day. I believe that as far as his music is concerned my appreciation has not yet reached its limits. My association with Rimsky-Korsakov taught me a great deal. I was given more than one opportunity of verifying his incredibly fine ear for orchestral detail. One evening after a rehearsal we went to the Solodovnikov Theatre to hear his opera *A May Night*. The performance had not yet begun. We took seats in the middle row of the stalls. The conductor and the orchestra, who must have got wind of the composer's presence, took the greatest pains and fiddled and trumpeted for all they were worth. Suddenly—Levko was just starting his aria—I saw Rimsky-Korsakov frown, as if he were in great pain: 'They are using B clarinets!' he groaned and gripped my knee. Later I verified from the score that A clarinets are indicated. A similar episode took place after the last rehearsal of *Pan Voyevoda*. I had asked Rimsky-Korsakov not to attend any previous rehearsals. In the fortune-telling scene this opera has a fortissimo beat in the dominant chord played by the whole orchestra. I wondered why the tuba remained silent. When I mentioned this to Rimsky-Korsakov he answered:

'One would not hear it, anyway, and I hate writing down superfluous notes.'

When the rehearsal was over he expressed his entire satisfaction, which made me very happy, merely adding:

'Who joins in this fortissimo beat?'

I counted all the players, one after another.

'And why is the tom-tom playing?'

'Probably because the directions say so.'

'No, they give only the triangle.'

I sent for the musician in question. He produced his part, and there the tom-tom was marked down.

Rimsky-Korsakov asked for the score. It turned out that the tom-tom was not included in the beat but had been marked down by mistake, and that the triangle alone had to play. This striking proof of his sensitive ear convinced me that the tuba would have been inaudible in this passage.

I think I may say safely and without boasting that Rimsky-Korsakov returned my love for his art and his personality with sympathy and appreciation for my work as conductor. He expressed the wish that his opera, *Kitesh*, which at the time he was just completing, should have its first performance at the Grand Theatre under my direction. To my deep regret this was not realized for when he sent in his work I had already given up my post as conductor."

Although conducting Rimsky-Korsakov's opera was an event in Rachmaninoff's life, it was even more important to him that he had an opportunity of performing his own operas, *The Miserly Knight* and *Francesca da Rimini*, at the Grand Theatre. This happened in January of 1906. The first of these operas is adapted from Poushkin's dramatic poem, which was used with hardly any cuts. The text for *Francesca da Rimini* was written by Modest Tchaikovsky, who had often supplied the libretti for the operas of his famous brother. Unfortunately, this was not to the advantage of the work. No one will deny that Modest Tchaikovsky's biography of his brother, which embraces two volumes, was a definite achievement and a valuable work of reference for the history of art; but as a dramatic poet he was not successful, although some of his plays were performed at the St. Petersburg and Moscow theatres. A literary critic, well known for his sharp tongue, used to say of Modest Tchaikovsky: "He is a good fellow and very pleasant to meet and, as it seems, hard working, but he lacks something; only, I don't know what it is." Some time later he returned from the theatre where he had attended the performance of a play by Modest Tchaikovsky. He burst into the room, full of excitement and enthusiasm, and exclaimed: "Now I know what Modest lacks. . . . Talent!" In spite of this, Rachmaninoff did not hesitate to accept Tchaikovsky's offer to supply the libretto when he intended to write a supplementary opera to *The Miserly Knight*, which had only one act. The glamour which the name of Tchaikovsky had for him may have influenced his decision.

Rachmaninoff's account of the time when the two operas were in rehearsal is as follows:

"I had already completed *The Miserly Knight* when I took up my post at the Grand Theatre in the autumn of 1905. It was Chaliapin who inspired me to write this opera. One can easily understand how the character of the old Baron, who retires into the gloomy depths of the cellar to worship his hoard of gold, would appeal to Chaliapin's dramatic instinct. I composed the opera for him.

Francesca da Rimini took shape in the summer of 1906. In the autumn, when, after my holiday at Ivanovka, I returned to Moscow, I approached Chaliapin with the suggestion that I should coach him in the bass parts of both operas. In *Francesca* he was to impersonate Malatesta. I must mention that Chaliapin's feelings towards me were those of sincere friendship. I think he must have been aware of my great admiration for him. He met my proposal with his characteristic enthusiasm and at once declared himself ready to study both parts. But the time passed, and he never again mentioned my proposal. In connection with the works of other composers, such as *Boris Godounov* Moussorgsky, *Mefistofele* by Boito, *Mozart and Salieri* by Rimsky-Korsakov, and others, I showed no mercy towards him and was positively cruel during the rehearsals of his parts. His magnificent power of conception surprised me again and again, and compelled me to fresh admiration. The smallest hint sufficed to stimulate his wealth of imagination into creating a mental picture of high perfection and of the most complicated structure, which he endeavoured at once to realize. It often happened that I kept him at the piano for two or three hours, or even longer, for I would not let him go until he knew the music of his own part and the whole opera down to the last detail of orchestration. What other singer would have made this possible? But in the case of my own operas I could not bring myself to act in the same way. A kind of pride—or was it shyness?—prevented me from doing it. I never even played my opera to him. Yet one day he surprised me by saying that the phrasing of my opera was faulty. I contradicted him, for I was not aware of having made a mistake. This was followed by a heated argument, and since then my operas have never been mentioned between us.

Then it happened that, quite by chance, Altani drew my attention to a young singer, who had just been engaged by the Grand Theatre at the modest salary of 3,000 roubles a year. It was George Baklanov, who later achieved world fame. He had an enchanting voice. I sent for him and asked whether he could learn the two parts in my operas within a month, for I had decided that I would not wait for Chaliapin, whom, by the way, I worship as much to-day as I did then. Baklanov agreed at once, and from that hour worked with me and the chorus-master like a slave. To dispel all doubts about the phrasing I asked Lensky, who was at that time the principal actor at the Imperial Little Theatre, to hear Baklanov sing and to give his opinion. Lensky came, listened to the whole part, and could not find the slightest fault with the musical phrasing. To my great joy he even suggested that he should help Baklanov to study the part from the dramatic point of view. Thanks to his coaching, the young singer surpassed himself. He was wonderful in the part of the old miser.

To-day when I recall my attempts at musical drama, I cannot help saying that I still have some regard for *The Miserly Knight*. This is not equally true of *Francesca da Rimini*. The poetic background supplied by Modest Tchaikovsky was too poor. Even while I composed it I suffered agonies over the inadequacy of the text. No sooner did I come upon a situation that was dramatically alive and demanded to be set to music (such as, for instance, the appearance of Malatesta who surprises Francesca and

Paolo) than the text would suddenly give out. In spite of my urgent requests, Modest could not be persuaded to add a few verses.

The success of these operas encouraged a thought which, from time to time, had secretly crept into my mind, to remain there with obstinate persistence. 'Solitude,' it said, 'solitude for your creative work is what you need. Leave Moscow and compose—do nothing but compose! . . .' In the autumn of 1906, when my contract with the Imperial Theatre came to an end, I did not renew it, in spite of the most tempting pecuniary and artistic promises held forth by the directors. Altani had died, and I was offered almost unlimited authority. But I remained firm and would not allow anything to interfere with my resolution."

It is comprehensible that Rachmaninoff's growing fame as a composer in Moscow and further afield and his unequalled popularity as a pianist and conductor did not allow for much "solitude and creative work." His flat on the Strastnoy Boulevard was constantly besieged by friends, admirers of both sexes, agents, and business men of all sorts. Rachmaninoff's name on a concert programme, no matter in what capacity, acted like magic in producing a full house; his participation in any kind of enterprise, whether in or out of his profession—at parties, clubs, associations—was a guarantee of their quality. But apart from his musical fame, his powerful personality, his high character, and the earnest sincerity of his nature won him a position of unequalled authority amongst the people of Moscow. No better proof could be given of his artistic integrity than his sacrifice of money and reputation in order to obtain the solitude demanded by his creative faculty.

During the first decade of the twentieth century Moscow

had reached the pinnacle of its artistic evolution. The atmosphere was so saturated with possibilities that the Muscovites, who responded with equal and untiring enthusiasm to every manifestation of true art, began almost to find it oppressive. In the "Theatre Square" two theatres, the Grand and the Little, faced one another. The former offered opera with Chaliapin, Sobinoff, Madame Neshdanova, Baklanov, and others, also ballet stars to whom all Europe was soon to pay homage. In the Little Theatre one could enjoy plays and comedies acted by the incomparable Madame Yermolova (the Russian Ristori), the magnificent artists, Pravdin and Lensky, and the unequalled comedienne, Madame Sadovskaya. Not far away rose the unpretentious building of the Moscow Art Theatre, where Stanislavsky and his marvellous cast offered fresh artistic revelations with each performance and inaugurated a new epoch in theatrical history. To these one must add the New Theatre, which specialized in light comedy from abroad, and the Korsh Theatre, the home of intimate Russian comedy, with actors of the highest standard and pronounced originality. Three different series of Symphony Concerts were in competition and vied with each other in presenting the most interesting and beautiful programmes, executed by soloists and conductors of the highest rank. These were the Philharmonic Concerts where Arthur Nikisch, who was welcomed with unfailing enthusiasm, conducted regularly each year, and also Mottl, Muck, Weingartner—in fact, all the greatest conductors Europe could produce: then there were the concerts of the Imperial Musical Society under Safonoff, where, besides himself, illustrious visitors from St. Petersburg, such as Rimsky-Korsakov, Glazounov, and many others, conducted. Thirdly, there was the New Symphony Concert Union, founded by the double bass virtuoso and con-

than any other contemporary conductor, and regarded each new performance by Nikisch as an important event in his life, every detail remaining with him for years afterwards. Nikisch's genius as a conductor was indeed supreme, especially when he interpreted Tchaikovsky, who was Rachmaninoff's ideal. His performances of Tchaikovsky have never, to this day, been surpassed, or even equalled. The reason for this may be found in Nikisch's sincere and wholehearted admiration for Russian music and its masters. Rachmaninoff's homage proves that this love was not entirely unrequited.

But the Composer was also attracted by the dignified repose of Dresden, which at that time was still the capital of the Kingdom of Saxony. Its beautiful gardens and public parks invited early morning walks along the Elbe, where one might imagine oneself back on the banks of the River Volchov.

In the autumn of 1906 Rachmaninoff and his family took a house, standing in a garden, a little way back from the quiet "Sidonienstrasse." The most important piece of furniture in his very modest establishment was a Bechstein Grand, which alone occupied a whole room. There he spent three years in close retirement, interrupted only by the summer months, when he visited "Ivanovka," the Satins' estate in his native country. This saved him and his family from the overwhelming attacks of homesickness with which they were now and then threatened. Everything in Dresden was excellent: the opera, especially the Wagner repertoire conducted by Schuch, was as brilliant as ever; the concerts at the "Gewandhaus" in Leipzig were magnificent; nothing interrupted the peace he needed for composing, and no one disturbed his unremitting concentration with unnecessary visits and superfluous questions. No one disturbed him. Perhaps this was the very thing he lacked. How he longed at times for the friends he had escaped! How pleased he would often have been to see them. For despite his very reserved character Rachmaninoff's nature was one that needed an exchange of ideas—though only, it is true, where music was concerned. In Moscow he had only to lift a finger and all the young composers flocked into his house: Medtner, Gödicke, Morosov, the brothers Edouard and Jules Conus, the violoncellist Brandoukov, and also Taneyev, as well as many others. They played their latest compositions to one another, they discussed music or had heated arguments about the latest problems connected with it, or touched at times upon more serious questions. It cannot be denied that this occupied a great deal of time; but it was very stimulating. Here, in Dresden, one had to do without it. A timidity which was partly conscious and partly unconscious made Rachmaninoff keep the strictest incognito for a considerable time after he had settled down in Dresden. Consequently he had no social intercourse and the musicians in Dresden were unaware that he was living in their midst.

But here again fate came to his rescue and brought him an ideal friend. Nikolai von Struve was studying in Dresden. He was a German–Russian of Rachmaninoff's age, well-born, well endowed with this world's goods, highly musical, and not without talent as a composer of songs. Their superficial acquaintance soon ripened into a friendship which lasted up to Struve's sudden and premature death, caused by an accident in Paris in 1921. Their isolation from the musical world of their native country, their mutual desire for an exchange of ideas on general and musical questions, their common interests, their mutual friends and, not least, their sympathy and attraction for one another, soon established a close intimacy between the two men, who had never met until they lived in Dresden. This friendship was fostered by

137

long walks, which frequently took them far beyond the walls of the town. And there was another circumstance that drew them together and gave them common ground; a matter which interested them both deeply, although they acted in different capacities.

The Russian double bass virtuoso and conductor, Koussevitsky, who, thanks to his marriage to the daughter of the Russian tea king, Kouznetsov, had come into the possession of a tremendous fortune, decided to follow the example of the St. Petersburg timber merchant and art patron, M. P. Belayev, and establish a firm of music publishers which was to differ from all others in that the profits from the works published were to go to the composers and not to the firm. A large sum was put aside for this purpose. The terms and conditions of this enterprise, which was intended as a bequest, were worked out by Dr. O. von Riesemann in conjunction with the Moscow lawyer, Kersin. The management was handed over to Nikolai von Struve, while Rachmaninoff became one of the most active members of the committee of judges who decided upon the works to be published. Rachmaninoff, who always felt deeply for the troubles of his colleagues, especially those who, despite their undoubted and great talent, could not achieve success, took up this idea with the liveliest interest. He has encouraged, amongst others, such first-class composers as Scriabin and Medtner. He could not, however, be persuaded to use this firm for his own purposes, but remained true to his first publisher, Gutheil. He pursued his work as a member of the judging committee with great energy, until the outbreak of the war and Struve's early death made an end to the business, which had flourished in Berlin for many years. To-day this enterprise, which has been considerably enlarged through the additional purchase of Gutheil's business and, above all, through Rachmaninoff's works, is carried on in Paris like any other publishing firm under the name "Grandes Editions Russes."

It is typical of Rachmaninoff that he would not use Koussevitsky's publishing firm for his own purposes. A certain feeling of moral obligation towards Gutheil prevented him from severing his connection with that publisher. It would have seemed to him like a betrayal. But it did not prevent him from showing the liveliest interest in Koussevitsky's firm and devoting to it a great deal of his time and energy.

He could have enriched the young undertaking with more than one beautiful composition, for his hope that the peaceful atmosphere of Dresden, saturated with music, would benefit his creative powers, was amply fulfilled even during the first weeks that followed his arrival. Three monumental works had their origin in Dresden. They were the Second Symphony (Op. 27), the First Sonata for Pianoforte (Op. 28), and the Symphonic Poem, *The Isle of Death* (Op. 29), as well as a collection of fifteen songs set to verses by Russian poets (Op. 26). The songs are dedicated to Monsieur and Madame Kersin as a tribute of thanks for their untiring efforts on behalf of Russian music. *The Isle of Death* was inspired by a visit to the Leipzig picture-gallery, where Rachmaninoff was deeply impressed by Böcklin's painting. The score bears the inscription, "To Nikolai Struve, in friendship." None of his previous dedications are of so affectionate a character, for, as a rule, Rachmaninoff is so reserved in his expressions of personal feeling, whether in writing or speech, that the smallest departure from his usual practice may be regarded as a distinction and an exception.

After an interval of more than ten years Rachmaninoff began again to work on a purely orchestral composition. The annihilating effect of the performance of his First Symphony in St. Petersburg over ten years ago, its paralysing influence on his creative imagination, was only just relaxing its grip. *The Isle of Death* and his First and only previous Symphonic Poem, *The Rock*, were also divided by an interval of fifteen years.

Another work of large dimensions, which Rachmaninoff began towards the close of his Dresden life, was left unfinished and will, unfortunately, remain so. This was an opera, *Monna Vanna*. The text had been written by his old college friend, Slonov, who had shown him such a touching devotion and had made the "fair copy" of the *Aleko* score. It was adapted from Maeterlinck's play of the same name. Stanislavsky personally visited the author in order to ask his permission to use the drama as an opera libretto. It was then the period of mutual admiration between Maeterlinck and the Moscow Art Theatre. Maeterlinck wrote *The Blue Bird* especially for Stanislavsky, whose production of the play was one of the greatest triumphs this theatre has ever achieved. A story told of Stanislavsky's visit to Maeterlinck's estate in Belgium caused much amusement. He had never seen Maeterlinck, who met him at the station with the car, clad in a leather coat and cap. Stanislavsky, thinking he was the chauffeur, spent the whole journey to the house questioning him about his master. Maeterlinck, who had a very keen sense of humour, never disclosed his identity, but calmly played the rôle of the chauffeur and took great delight in treating Stanislavsky to the most hair-raising tales about himself, until they arrived at the front door and he turned and welcomed his guest.

Although Maeterlinck had already given his permission to use *Monna Vanna* for musical purposes to another composer, this did not prevent Rachmaninoff from beginning at once to work out the plan for his opera, which made good progress.

Why did he not finish it? Rachmaninoff himself has

supplied the reason for this, which lies in the fact that towards the end of his stay in Dresden he gradually gave up his ascetic and almost hermit-like seclusion. He needed larger sums to support his family, which in the meantime had been increased by the birth of another little daughter, Tatyana, and was therefore obliged to accept at least some of the concert engagements offered to him from Russia, Germany, and other countries. It was only natural that the works he created in Dresden should have their first performance in Moscow, if for no other reason than to keep up his connection with this town, which he had grown to love beyond everything. He played his First Sonata for Pianoforte at a Chamber Music Concert given by the Imperial Russian Musical Society, that is, at one of the Conservatoire Concerts. By that time the liberal wave of 1905 had swept Safonoff from his post as director of the Conservatoire, and his successor showed a more friendly disposition towards Rachmaninoff's music. *The Isle of Death* and the Second Symphony were first performed at concerts given by the Moscow Philharmonic Society. Rachmaninoff himself conducted the Symphony, which had a sensational success. This was unfortunately marred by Nikisch, who soon afterwards repeated the work in Moscow. According to his usual custom, and confident of his skill as a conductor, he had the score placed on his desk without even so much as looking at it before the concert began. This method, however, did not succeed with the difficult and complicated score of Rachmaninoff's Symphony. Consequently the memorable concert was full of little incidents which passed unnoticed by the audience, but made the musicians smile and annoyed all who were acquainted with the work. If this magnificent and grandly conceived work had not been previously introduced to the public by the Composer himself, Nikisch's performance might have resulted in a first-class funeral for Rachmaninoff's Second Symphony. As it happened, the audience, who were always fascinated by Nikisch and expected wonders from a combination of his name and that of Rachmaninoff, who had gained such popularity in Moscow, swallowed their disappointment and gave the careless conductor and the mishandled composition polite and respectful applause. Since Tchaikovsky this was the first Russian Symphony of full classical dimension. It has since been given a permanent and honourable place in the programmes of the St. Petersburg and Moscow Symphony Concerts. Abroad it has not, so far, received anything like the appreciation it deserves. There are several reasons which may account for this, but we will refer to them later. Rachmaninoff's reaction to the well-intentioned but bad service which Nikisch rendered his Symphony in Moscow is characteristic of him. He bore him no grudge and even went so far as to consider it quite natural that the famous conductor should not expend much trouble on a work which was uncongenial to him. This event has not in any way diminished Rachmaninoff's admiration for Nikisch. On the other hand, the latter, who must have realized his failure in connection with the work, atoned for it by giving a splendid performance of the Symphony at the "Gewandhaus" in Leipzig.

The enthusiasm with which the public received Rachmaninoff when he conducted his Symphony in Moscow induced the Director of the Philharmonic Society, in 1907, to write to Rachmaninoff, who was still in Dresden, suggesting that he should replace Nikisch, who had suddenly fallen ill, in conducting a series of Symphony Concerts in Moscow. Rachmaninoff did not wish to accept the proposal; in the first place, because he had no programme ready for six or eight concerts (for where Nikisch might have lacked conscientiousness in regard to the scores, Rachmaninoff suffered from an overdose of it); secondly, because his modesty, which was quite unfounded, made him fear that the public would be too disappointed with this exchange. He nevertheless appeared once or twice at the conductor's desk in Moscow and was greeted by the audience with loud demonstrations of joy. Although he found great satisfaction in his activities as a concert conductor, they rendered more acute an inner conflict, which was destined to worry him considerably during the following ten years. He could not make up his mind which of the three professions he should definitely adopt. Was he a composer, a pianist, or a conductor? He was equally successful in all three branches and, what was even more important, all three gave him equal and real artistic satisfaction. Thus for the next ten years we see him constantly wavering between the three, wondering to which he should eventually turn, until, as we will explain presently, an accident solved the problem for him.

The multiplicity of his artistic talent and his overpowering wealth of musical gifts found convincing expression, while he was still living in Dresden, in an enterprise which was to prove highly important for the future of Russian music in Europe and was launched in Paris during May 1906.

Diaghilyeff, who deserves the highest praise for his European propaganda of Russian art, especially the ballet, and who died far too early (in 1929), held his first Russian Season ("Saison Russe") in Paris during the spring of 1906. He arranged a series of Symphony Concerts at the Grand Opera, for which he engaged the best musicians Russia could provide: Rimsky-Korsakov, Glazounov, Scriabin, Chaliapin, Josef Hofmann, Nikisch, and Rachmaninoff. Rachmaninoff appeared in three capacities: as a composer, as the conductor of his Cantata, *The Spring*, and as the interpreter of his Second Concerto for Pianoforte.

Rachmaninoff's own account of these concerts is as follows:

"Diaghilyeff and the Paris conductor, Chevillard, had made excellent preparations for the concerts. I did not have to do much work with the chorus and orchestra: my Cantata had been practised and the concert went off as desired. I shall never forget Rimsky-Korsakov's criticism of my work. When the performance was over he came into the artists' room:

'The music is good, but, what a pity! There is no sign of "spring" in the orchestra.

I felt at once that his remark hit the nail on the head. How I would like to touch up the orchestration of my Cantata to-day. . . . No, I would alter the whole instrumentation! When I wrote it I lacked all understanding of the connections between . . . how shall I put it? . . . orchestral sound and—meteorology, which Rimsky-Korsakov handled in such a masterly manner. In Rimsky-Korsakov's scores there is never the slightest doubt about the 'meteorological' picture the music is meant to convey. When there is a snow-storm the flakes seem to dance and drift from the wood instruments and the soundholes of the violins; when the sun is high, all instruments shine with an almost fiery glare; when there is water the waves ripple and splash audibly through the orchestra, and this effect is not achieved by the comparatively cheap means of a harp glissando; the sound is cool and glassy when he describes a calm winter night with a glittering starlit sky. He was a great master of orchestral sound-painting, and one can still learn from him. It seems strange that a man who handled the secrets of the orchestra in so masterful a fashion, down to the smallest detail, should be so helpless as a conductor. 'Conducting is a black art,' he says in his book *Chronicles*

S. RACHMANINOFF AND HIS WIFE (NÉE SATIN) AT DRESDEN (1907)

of My Musical Life. Unfortunately, this thought was not exclusively his own, but presented itself also to the audience as he stood at the conductor's desk. Things were no better in Paris when, as far as I can remember, he conducted scenes from *Sadko* and his music to *Mlada*. There was a sigh of relief when he handed over the baton to Nikisch."

It was very interesting for Rachmaninoff to meet Alexander Scriabin in Paris. Scriabin had left Moscow several years previously, partly for the same reasons which sent Rachmaninoff to Dresden, partly owing to some events of a purely personal and private character. He lived in very modest circumstances, for he was not a practising musician, and spent his time in France, Belgium, and Switzerland. His world philosophy, which inclined more and more towards a hazy Theosophic Mysticism, had at that time undergone as radical a change as his "style" in music. His first important work written since the beginning of this period was the *Poème Divin* (Third Symphony), in which he combines ideas inspired by his Theosophic Mysticism with a "harmonic" language, which was then entirely new and strange. This work was not performed during the Russian season in Paris. Nikisch conducted the Second Symphony, while Josef Hofmann played his Concerto for Pianoforte, both of which still dated from Scriabin's "classical" period.

The impression of the *Poème Divin* on his Russian colleagues to whom Scriabin played it privately was very mixed. No one would grant even a conditional recognition to his revolutionary change of ideas. The earnest and slightly pedantic Rimsky-Korsakov had little sympathy for Scriabin's world-shaking conception in which cosmo-logical and musical ideas combined to form a monstrous thought-structure.

But Scriabin's new theories added much stimulus to

the arguments which took place between the Russian composers who met in Paris. His behaviour also, which was free from all pose, but very original, offered a subject for many an eager discussion. Scriabin, for example, was the first who, "for hygienic reasons," as he himself asserted, gave up wearing a hat. He walked bareheaded across the Paris boulevards and was the forerunner of a fashion which, within the course of a few years, was to be widely adopted. The conservative Frenchmen naturally abhorred this daring exhibition which defied all prevalent notions of decency. Scriabin was constantly surrounded by hordes of screaming street urchins and newspaper boys, who followed him with the rhythmic sing-song, "le Monsieur sans chapeau." But this did not ruffle his composure.

"I remember one discussion," says Rachmaninoff, "which took place between Rimsky-Korsakov, Scriabin, and myself, while we were sitting at one of the little tables in the Café de la Paix. One of Scriabin's new discoveries was concerned with the relation existing between musical sound, that is, certain harmonies and keys, and the spectrum of the sun. If I am not mistaken he was just working out the plan of a great symphonic composition in which he was going to use this relation, and in which, together with the musical incidents, there was to be a play of light and colour. He had never reflected upon the practical possibilities of this idea, but that side of the question did not interest him very much. He said that he would limit himself to marking his score with a special system of light and colour values.[1]

To my astonishment Rimsky-Korsakov agreed on principle with Scriabin about this connection between musical keys and colour. I, who do not feel the similarity,

[1] The *Clavier à lumière* (*luce*) in the score of the Symphonic Poem *Prometheus* for orchestra and pianoforte.—O. v. R.

Moscow, on the other hand, had a hard fight for popularity in France, even in the person of its greatest representative, Tchaikovsky, and has never won the same appreciation there as in Germany, where the exact opposite is the case. This fact, which cannot be denied, must be stated without attempting an explanation, which would occupy more space than we are able to give here. Owing to this attitude shown by public opinion in Paris, the St. Petersburg composers during Diaghilyeff's "Russian Season" had a much easier success than their Moscow colleagues, as, for instance, Rachmaninoff, because he was considered a follower of Tchaikovsky, and Scriabin, because his nebulous world-philosophy was not congenial to the sharp, crystal-clear intellect and the straightforward musical hedonism of the French. Therefore the triumph Rachmaninoff reaped with the enchanting interpretation of his Concerto in C minor must be counted as all the greater. The ovation he received after he had finished playing continued until he sat down again to give an encore. At that moment, just as the audience had settled down to an expectant silence, a shrill and penetrating whistle came suddenly from the gallery. It was obviously a means by which France tried to appease her conscience. But the friendly and astonished smile with which Rachmaninoff looked up to the gallery charmed the audience into renewed demonstrations of enthusiasm, which would not cease until the first strains of the Prélude in C sharp minor calmed down their excitement.

Other concert tours broke into the uninterrupted work and the peaceful life which Rachmaninoff had hoped to lead in Dresden—too many, according to his taste. One of these took him to Berlin, where he played a trio with the Bohemian String Quartette (in those days undoubtedly the best in Europe) at the Chamber Music Concert given by the strictly conservative Academy for Singing. It was his first and—for a considerable period—his last appearance in the German capital, and, strangely enough, the Paris whistling episode was also repeated here.

The year 1908 found Rachmaninoff still in Dresden. But his periods of undisturbed work away from the "madding crowd" grew steadily shorter. The musical world of Russia and the Continent made more and more frequent demands upon him, and for artistic and pecuniary reasons they became harder to refuse.

In the spring of that year the Moscow Art Theatre celebrated the tenth anniversary of its existence. A great festival united all Moscow at the theatre. Innumerable speeches were held and the row of deputations, sent by public and artistic associations, who handed over addresses and read out messages of congratulation, seemed endless. An unforgettable impression was created when Chaliapin suddenly walked to the piano and, turning to Stanislavsky, began to sing, accompanied by the pianist, Könemann, "Dear Konstantin Sergeyevitch . . ." Then followed a short, warm address of congratulation, which was written in the form of a letter and concluded something like this: "heartiest congratulations in which my wife also joins, yours, Sergei Rachmaninoff." The public, crowding the theatre to the last corner, thrilled by the association of the three famous names, Chaliapin, Stanislavsky, and Rachmaninoff, who were then undoubtedly the most popular personalities in Moscow, was frantic with enthusiasm, and Chaliapin had to repeat this musical letter of congratulation three or four times before he was allowed any peace.

Here I should like to quote some of Rachmaninoff's reminiscences connected with the Moscow Art Theatre and the personalities associated with it. His own account is as follows:

"From the very beginning I took the greatest interest in Stanislavsky's venture and its development, for personal as well as artistic reasons. I had the greatest respect for Stanislavsky and his artistic aims which had their origin solely in his passionate love for the theatre; in this respect he had always been my example. But I felt attracted also to many of the members of the Art Theatre, most of all to the author, Anton Tchekhov, who was magnificent, and might justly be termed the 'Poet Laureate' of the Moscow Art Theatre. He was always my favourite amongst Russian poets and authors, and has remained so up to this day. I think very highly of him. Apart from his glorious talent he was one of the most charming men I have ever met, and with it all, touchingly modest. Long before the existence of the Art Theatre I counted myself amongst his most ardent admirers and knew him personally. The greatest compliment I have ever been paid came from his lips. I want to quote it, not in any spirit of self-advertisement, but to give you an idea of his personality.

Soon after I got to know Chaliapin—it was during my engagement as conductor of the Moscow Private Opera and my name was entirely unknown—he and I went on a concert tour, which took us to the Crimea. There, in Yalta, lived Anton Tchekhov. He had gone there in vain search for new health for his diseased lungs. Now, I must tell you that Tchekhov had the reputation of being a great physiognomist. Stanislavsky was fond of telling a tale to support this:

Tchekhov once met a man in Stanislavsky's dressing-room who displayed a particularly happy and lively manner and produced more jokes to the minute than fifty wise men could digest. How great was Stanislavsky's surprise when, after the man had gone, Tchekhov, who was generally rather quiet, and this time, as usual, had let the other man have his say, remarked: 'I am convinced that that man will come to a bad end.' Within a few months the man in question had committed suicide by shooting himself.

Well, we gave our concert in Yalta. We were told that Tchekhov, who was then unknown to me, had expressed the desire to attend the concert. We sent him a ticket for a seat in the director's box, close to the platform. While sitting at the piano I faced him. I did my bit, but it did not amount to much, for I was only playing the modest rôle of accompanist. When, after the concert, Tchekhov came into the artists' room, he addressed me with the following words: 'You will succeed in your career as an artist, young man.'

'What makes you think so?'

'It is written on your face.'

This I consider the most flattering criticism that has ever reached my ears, especially as it had only a very faint connection with my modest performance at the piano.

Later, Tchekhov frequently suggested that he should provide the text for one of my operas, but I regret that our combined work was never realized. Tchekhov's libretti did not lend themselves to a musical setting: their failure was due to the fact that he had no instinct for what was suitable and what unsuitable for musical purposes. This was the reason why, to my great regret, I could not use his adaptation from his own novel, *The Black Monk*, or that of Lermontov's story, *The Hero of our Time* (*Princess Béla*), which he offered me as opera libretti.

One summer, many years ago, the actors of the Art Theatre, who, without exception, were touchingly devoted to Tchekhov and included in their number his wife, Olga Knipper, came to the Crimea ostensibly in order to give a series of performances in Sebastopol and Yalta, but really for the purpose of presenting to Tchekhov his latest plays. Practically all the young writers of Russia had assembled in Yalta, in their desire to be near Tchekhov: Bounin, Jelpatyevsky, Kouprin, Tchirikov, and Gorki, who was just planning the scenario of his play *The Lower Depths*, and was introduced to Stanislavsky and his cast. I also spent the beginning of the summer in Yalta, where I occupied a country house, lent to me by a friend who took a motherly interest in me, Princess Alexandra Lieven. The hours spent in Tchekhov's company were always stimulating. . . . He never alluded to the fatal disease from which he suffered. He had studied medicine, and was much prouder of this than of his talent as a writer. 'I am a doctor,' he used to say, 'and I write a little in my spare time.'

Another of my musical reminiscences is connected with the Moscow Art Theatre. Ilya Satz was Court Composer to the Theatre, and after his early death I was asked to do something in honour of his memory. Although I did not disparage his peculiar talent, I did not count myself amongst his admirers. He was certainly a character, and this was evident in his music, but I was irritated by his lack of musical education and real skill. However, to please Stanislavsky and the Art Theatre I was ready to do all in my power to honour his memory, especially as this was associated with a scheme to support his widow, who was left in very poor circumstances. I was handed over all his musical remains and picked out what I considered the best material; but I could not bring myself to perform these works in their original form at a concert which was being planned for this purpose. I passed the selected pieces on to the composer, Reinhold Glière, who gave them a new instrumental setting. In this form I conducted the Suite, *The Blue Bird* (Maeterlinck), the waltz for *Days of our Life* (Leonid Andreyev), and a melodrama for a poem by Alexei Tolstoy, which was beautifully recited by Moskvin (the inimitable impersonator of Tsar Fedor) at a Memorial Concert for Ilya Satz, in the 'Great Nobility Hall.'

Soon afterwards Stanislavsky approached me with a request that I would compose the music for Alexander Block's drama, *The Rose and the Cross*; this I refused, although I should have enjoyed the close contact with the Art Theatre it would have brought me; but I did not share the enthusiasm of the majority of its members for this work of Block's."[1]

Now, let us return to our narrative. In the summer of 1908 Rachmaninoff made a voluntary end to his residence in Dresden. If his stay in the town by the Elbe had not justified all his hopes and expectations, this was due principally to the fact that he was unable to defend his solitude from the constant demands made upon him by the musical world of Russia and the Continent. But he will always think of this town with a feeling tinged with something akin to affection; for has it not given him many hours of deep creative satisfaction? Has he not spent many happy days there, rendered all the happier through the close proximity of his family, and through his friendly relations with Struve? In later days he visited it again and again for shorter or longer periods.

On his return to Russia he went to "Ivanovka," the Satins' estate in the government of Tambov, where he was in the habit of spending all his summers. This estate, which had been familiar to Rachmaninoff since the days of his early youth, lay about five hundred kilometres south of Moscow, in the fertile "black-earth" region. The

[1] The music for *The Rose and the Cross* was written by the young Moscow composer, Alexander Krein.—O. v. R.

main interest of all the farmers and villagers was naturally agriculture. It formed the subject of every discussion and was the centre around which everything revolved. Rachmaninoff, who had spent his childhood in entirely different surroundings, in Northern Russia where the landscape is varied and rich in natural beauty, suffered at first under the monotony and apparent desolation of the South Russian plains. He could not accustom himself to the flatness that extended to the far horizon, unbroken by forests, trees, or even a single small shrub. But gradually he grew to love these infinite distances dwindling into space, the sweet breath of blossoming meadows, the unfettered freedom around him.

From his father Rachmaninoff had inherited a passion for horses. He drove and rode like a born horseman, and took a great delight in training young horses. Every free minute he could wrest from his strictly regulated daily work he spent in the fields. No one who met him, as he trudged over fresh furrows, by the side of the plough, could have guessed that the tall farmer in riding boots with his hands stuck into the pockets of his short linen smock, and the everlasting cigarette between his lips, was one of the greatest musicians of his time. With a sigh he often envied his brother-in-law, Satin, and all who were less occupied than he, who did not have to write and read scores, much less study them, and who were not forced to play the piano and could spend their time in agricultural pursuits.

Rachmaninoff spent a good deal of money on the improvement of the estate, in purchasing agricultural machines, breeding cattle, fine horses, etc. Every little failure in the management grieved him deeply, not because of the material losses involved, but because the expected improvements did not materialize. On the other hand, every success in the sowing and cultivation of a field, or the management of the stables, filled him with joy, and a profit in the dairy put him in the best of tempers. I would like to mention here that shortly before the outbreak of the World War Rachmaninoff bought "Ivanovka" from his father-in-law, who wished to retire, and in conjunction with his brother-in-law took over the responsibility for the management of the estate.

It was then that he developed another "passion," which possesses him up to this day: the love of motoring. While in the country he frequently made long or short expeditions, visiting neighbours, friends, or relations, during which he always drove the car himself. Often his journeys into distant districts took a whole day, but he never relinquished his place at the wheel to the chauffeur who sat next to him. These journeys were his greatest recreation, and never tired him; he invariably returned happy and refreshed and in the best of tempers. As he said himself, it was only when driving the car that he could get away from the musical visions which constantly pursued him. Otherwise he never allowed himself a moment's rest, for when he was not composing he made concert tours, and when he did not happen to be on a tour he prepared himself for the next one by playing the piano or studying scores.

"A good conductor ought to be a good chauffeur," Rachmaninoff used to say humorously; "the qualities that make the one also make the other. They are concentration, an incessant control of attention, and presence of mind: the conductor only has to add a little sense of music. . . ."

While he was still in Dresden Rachmaninoff, after some slight hesitation, accepted an engagement in America for the autumn of 1909. As was frequently the case with him, the definite prospect proved a stimulant and this engagement induced him to plan one of his finest works, the

Third Concerto for Pianoforte (Op. 30), which, compared with his previous works, shows greater maturity without any loss of inventive charm and freshness.

Immediately after leaving "Ivanovka" Rachmaninoff returned to Moscow, where he settled down in his old flat on the Strastnoy Boulevard. The musical world of Moscow, who watched every step of their pronounced favourite with excited curiosity, were considerably stirred by the rumour of a Third Concerto. The few favoured ones who had heard fragments of it played on the piano were able to relate wonders, especially of the "cadenza" in which, unlike those of any previous concertos for pianoforte, the orchestra joined. But Moscow had to conquer their curiosity and wait for some time before they heard it; for the first performance of the Third Concerto for Pianoforte took place in New York.

CHAPTER NINE

THE SUMMIT OF LIFE

1909–1914

*First journey to America—Third Concerto for pianoforte—
The Boston Symphony Orchestra and Max Fiedler—
Memories of Gustav Mahler and New York—Return to
Moscow—Vice-President of the Imperial Russian Musical
Society as assistant to the Grand Duchess Helene Georgyevna
—Differences in the "Spheres"—The Kersin-Concerts in
Moscow—Rachmaninoff conductor of the Philharmonic
Concerts in Moscow—The antagonism Scriabin-Rachmani-
noff—The Bells—Sojourn in Rome*

IT was with a heavy heart that Rachmaninoff started
on his journey to America in October 1909, for during
his six years of married life he had never been separated
from his wife and family for more than a few days.
The Concert Agents, Wolfsohn Bureau, in New York
had engaged him for twenty concerts, in which he was
due to appear in two capacities: as a pianist and as a
conductor. He was to accompany the Boston Symphony
Orchestra, conducted by Max Fiedler, on a short tour,
during which they were to visit Cambridge, Baltimore,
Philadelphia, New York, and Brooklyn. Apart from this,
he had to give orchestral concerts in New York and
other towns. Let us hear what Rachmaninoff himself has
to say about his first journey into a country which was
destined to assume such great importance in his later
life.

"My Third Concerto," he tells us, "was written especially
for America, and I was to play it for the first time in
New York, under the direction of Walter Damrosch.

157

As during the previous summer I had not found much time for practising and was not familiar enough with some passages, I took a dumb piano on to the boat with me and practised during the journey. I believe it is the only time that I have resorted to this mechanical toy, which, however, at the time proved very useful.

During my tour with Fiedler and the Boston Symphony Orchestra I played my Second Concerto. Fiedler, who appeared to like both my Concerto and its composer, showed the greatest kindness and courtesy towards me during the whole journey. He offered at once to perform *The Isle of Death* with his orchestra, and I gratefully accepted this proposal. During the course of that season he also performed my Second Symphony, and I think he is the only German conductor who now and then puts my *Bells* on his programme. The success I had when I conducted my *Symphonic Poem* may have induced the Boston Symphony Orchestra to offer me an engagement as Fiedler's successor; but although it was an incomparable pleasure to work with this excellent orchestra, I refused the offer. The prospect of being absent from Moscow for any length of time, with or without my family, struck me as absurd. However, the appreciation of my work, shown by this proposal, made me very happy.

As I have already mentioned, the performance of my Third Concerto took place in New York, under the direction of Damrosch. Immediately afterwards I repeated it in New York, but under Gustav Mahler.

At that time Mahler was the only conductor whom I considered worthy to be classed with Nikisch. He touched my composer's heart straight away by devoting himself to my Concerto until the accompaniment, which is rather complicated, had been practised to the point of perfection, although he had already gone through another long rehearsal. According to Mahler, every detail of the score was important—an attitude which is unfortunately rare amongst conductors.

The rehearsal began at ten o'clock. I was to join it at eleven, and arrived in good time. But we did not begin to work until twelve, when there was only half an hour left, during which I did my utmost to play through a composition which usually lasts thirty-six minutes. We played and played. . . . Half an hour was long passed, but Mahler did not pay the slightest attention to this fact. I still remember an incident which is characteristic of him. Mahler was an unusually strict disciplinarian. This I consider an essential quality for a successful conductor. We had reached a difficult violin passage in the Third Movement which involves some rather awkward bowing. Suddenly Mahler, who had conducted this passage *a tempo*, tapped his desk:

'Stop! Don't pay any attention to the difficult bowing marked in your parts. . . . Play the passage like this," and he indicated a different method of bowing. After he had made the first violins play the passage over alone three times, the man sitting next to the leader put down his violin:

'I can't play the passage with this kind of bowing.'

Mahler (quite unruffled): 'What kind of bowing would you like to use?'

'As it is marked in the score.'

Mahler turned towards the leader with an interrogative look, and when he found the latter was of the same opinion he tapped the desk again:

'Please play as is written!'

This incident was a definite rebuff for the conductor, especially as the excellent leader of the Moscow Philharmonic Orchestra had pointed out to me this disputed method of bowing as the only possible way of playing the passage. I was curious to see how Mahler would react to this little scene. He was most dignified. Soon afterwards he wanted the double basses to tone down their playing of a passage. He interrupted the orchestra and turned to the players:

'I would beg the gentlemen to make more of a diminuendo in this passage,' then, addressing the argumentative neighbour of the leader with a hardly perceptible smile:

'I hope you don't object.'

Forty-five minutes later Mahler announced:

'Now we will repeat the first movement.'

My heart froze within me. I expected a dreadful row, or at least a heated protest from the orchestra. This would certainly have happened in any other orchestra, but here I did not notice a single sign of displeasure. The musicians played the first movement with a keen or perhaps even closer application than the previous time. At last we had finished. I went up to the conductor's desk, and together we examined the score. The musicians in the back seats began quietly to pack up their instruments and to disappear. Mahler blew up:

'What is the meaning of this?'

The leader: 'It is after half-past one, Master.'

'That makes no difference! As long as I am sitting, no musician has a right to get up!'

At the beginning of the rehearsal Mahler had practised Berlioz' Symphony, *La Vie d'Un Artiste*. He conducted it magnificently, especially the passage called 'Procession to the High Court,' where he obtained a crescendo of the brass instruments such as I have never before heard achieved in this passage: the windows shook, the very walls seemed to vibrate. . . .

During this sojourn in the United States I appeared

RACHMANINOFF READING THE PROOFS OF THE THIRD
CONCERTO (1908)

twice in the rôle of conductor: once in Chicago and the second time with the Philadelphia Symphony Orchestra in Philadelphia. Both times I played my Second Symphony."

At the beginning of February Rachmaninoff was already back in Moscow.

On his return to Russia a high honour, which was then unique in the official musical world of Russia and has never since been repeated, awaited him. A brief account of the official organization of music in Russia will help us to understand its significance.

In the year 1862 Anton Rubinstein founded the St. Petersburg Conservatoire. Four years later his brother, Nikolai, started the Conservatoire in Moscow. Almost at the same time the Russian Musical Society, inspired by Anton Rubinstein, came into existence and soon attained official status as an "Imperial Musical Society." The post of President of the Imperial Russian Musical Society was always held by a member of the reigning Imperial family. The President controlled the musical affairs of the whole country. He was not only the highest musical authority in the two Conservatoires of St. Petersburg and Moscow, but in all Colleges of Music founded by the Imperial Russian Musical Society in various other Russian towns, where the system of management was similar, although on a smaller scale. They bore the same character of Imperial Institutions. All the larger towns in Russia boasted such a College of Music, and at the time in question there must have existed more than twenty.

The first President of the Imperial Russian Musical Society was the Grand Duchess Helene Pavlovna, a Princess of Würtemberg, mother-in-law of the Duke of Mecklenburg-Strelitz, who was as great an amateur musician as the Duchess Helene. She was followed by the well-known art lover and patron, the Grand Duke Konstantin Nikolayevitch, and later by his son, the Grand Duke Konstantin Konstantinovitch—the poet "K.R."—who was a friend of Tchaikovsky.

In the year 1909 Helene Georgyevna, Duchess of Saxe-Altenburg, was called upon by an Imperial Ukase to fill the position of President of the I.R.M.S. The statutes required that the President of the I.R.M.S. should be assisted by two Vice-Presidents: one for administrative, the other for musical purposes. The latter position had so far remained vacant, and Rachmaninoff was the first person since the foundation of the I.R.M.S. to be called upon by the Duchess of Saxe-Altenburg to fill this position. It naturally carried great authority and might be compared to the post of an Assistant Minister of Education. The exceptional high standard of musical education in Russia and its unequalled uniformity were largely due to the flawless and homogeneous organization of the I.R.M.S. This statement applies only to pre-Soviet times.

The opportunity of working for the development of music in Russia, and of taking an active part in the furthering of this cause, was bound to tempt anyone endowed with sufficient love for music and the necessary energy and ability.

The Grand Duchess Helene Georgyevna was a very clever woman, whose actions were prompted by the highest motives. The fact that she called upon Rachmaninoff to assist her is a proof of her intelligence and insight.

The uniform organization of instruction in music introduced by the brothers Anton and Nikolai Rubinstein in the Conservatoires and Colleges of the I.R.M.S. actually began to loosen somewhat. Decades had passed since the death of the highly gifted brothers. Up till this time their prestige in all institutions of the Musical Society had been unimpeachable, but gradually it began to grow dim. It was high time again that some superior musical personality should take the matter in hand. That naturally referred, in the first place, to the numerous music colleges in the provinces, a fact which was immediately recognized by Rachmaninoff.

The Conservatoire in Petersburg was directed by Alexander Glazounov. The unusual musical abilities of this excellent man, the high qualities of his character, and his charming personality were highly esteemed and beloved by the Board of Teachers as well as by all the pupils. Rachmaninoff did not have to look after matters there. Also the Conservatoire in Moscow, in which the artistic level of the Board of Teachers was unusually high, had found in M. Ippolitov-Ivanov a capable successor to Safonoff. In both of these institutions where Rachmaninoff had once been an inmate his business was mainly limited to conferring with the leading personalities, to lay down the general rules for musical education, to give his opinion on the very severe programmes of study in the special divisions, in short, to build up the grand structure of the organized study of music in Russia, by adding further details to perfect it more and more.

It was different in the provinces. There were music colleges of the I.R.M.S. in Astrakhan, Kharkov, Kishinev, Kiev, Nikolaiev, Odessa, Rostov a.D., Saratov, Tambov, Tiflis, Warsaw, Ekaterindar, Ekaterinoslav, Baku, Irkutsk, Nishni Novgorod, Orel, Pensa, Stavropol, Tomsk, Wilna, and in other smaller towns. Here was great room to stimulate and to improve in all directions. Rachmaninoff used his extensive concert tours in Russia for the purpose of looking after things everywhere.

The music world of southern Russia, the "Ukraina" as this region is incorrectly called now, had for a long time looked towards the northern realm with envious eyes. Petersburg and Moscow each had one of those proud institutions, called Conservatoires, whose curriculum was placed on a par with the other universities of the Empire. On passing the examinations they were given the same rights as the universities. But Kiev, the first city of the "Ukraine," the cradle of Russia, where the base of the Empire was laid, Kiev, which had been already a large town when Moscow was still a provincial one and Petersburg did not exist, had only a music college, i.e. a second-class institute. Innumerable petitions to change the Music College of Kiev into a Conservatoire had always been met with a refusal, the reason for which was based not upon artistic but political grounds. One did not want to increase the number of universities in this troublesome and separatistic region, nor the number of students, who were known as rebellious elements against order and law. One of the first things Rachmaninoff did when he entered his new duties was that he addressed to the Grand Duchess Helene his plea to change the Kiev Music College into a Conservatoire. His reason for doing so was that, appreciating to a high degree the superiority of the Kiev Music College, he recognized the actual need of a Conservatoire for the large region of southern Russia. He met with success in his request. The result was that by attracting distinguished teachers, under the direction of the excellent composer Reinhold Glière, the new Conservatoire assumed an entirely new aspect and very soon reached a very high degree of artistic efficiency.

During the short time that Rachmaninoff held the post of Vice-President of the I.R.M.S. very great demands were made not only on his musical capabilities and his energy but also on his diplomacy and his fine tact. It could not be avoided that during his many tours

of inspection in the Russian provinces he often came
into conflict and had differences with the local celebrities,
mostly with the Boards of Control of the Music Colleges.
These were as a rule composed of rich merchants, personalities of the Municipal Administration, and other
native potentates. Rachmaninoff was, as we know,
absolutely immovable in his artistic views and decisions,
as well as in questions of a moral nature. Through the
tactlessness of the members of one of these Boards of
Control with whom he could not agree, he unfortunately
was brought to the decision to give up his post, as he
had an interest only in the artistic side of the matter, not
in its political and social side, into which, in this case, he
was drawn against his will.

Without doubt, for the musical life in Russia it was
a perceptible loss that the useful co-operation of the
Grand Duchess Helene Georgyevna with Rachmaninoff
came to such an unexpected and rapid end. Rachmaninoff closed the tale of this episode of his life with the
words:

"I parted with regret from the Grand Duchess Helene, for
whom I had grown to feel the highest respect during the
time we were working together. She had granted all my
requests for such musical improvements as I wished to
introduce, even when it involved the expenditure of large
sums of money. I shall always remember with gratitude
the period of common labours during which her generosity
enabled me to help many a poor musician."

Except for occasional concerts in Germany and England,
at which he played only his own Concertos for Orchestra
and Pianoforte, Rachmaninoff spent the years 1910–14
in Russia. He refused a brilliant offer of another American
tour, having suffered too much from the loneliness imposed

upon him during his first journey to the United States. He could not make up his mind to let himself again be separated from his family by so great a distance and for so long a time, and was even less inclined to expose his wife and the two little girls to the hardship of a journey to America.

At that time he could not possibly guess that he was destined to undertake this journey in the not very distant future and under far less favourable circumstances.

During his last years in Russia Rachmaninoff gradually gave up his activities as a pianist, for he attached a far greater importance to his profession as a conductor. At first he conducted some of the Kersin-Concerts, which played a more and more prominent part in the musical life of Moscow. As the smaller halls could not hold their steadily growing audiences, larger ones had to be taken for these concerts until at last they rented the largest concert-hall in Moscow, the "Great Nobility Hall," which the Philharmonic Society used for their concerts. These Kersin-Concerts bore a thoroughly democratic character. This, and the cheap prices of admission, at a time when democracy was gaining ground rapidly, were the chief causes for their tremendous success. No one was out to make money by them; their sole object lay in giving the poorer intellectual classes an opportunity to hear good music. Already at the beginning of the season all tickets were sold out. Rachmaninoff's appearance at the conductor's desk raised their popularity to an immeasurable degree.

The pleasure he found in conducting prompted him to accept an engagement as permanent conductor of the Philharmonic Concerts in Moscow for the seasons 1911–12 and 1912–13. Here he was given greater freedom in the choice of his programmes than at the Kersin-Concerts, which only presented works of Russian composers. His carefully prepared programmes and the charm of his personality still worked wonders with the Moscow audiences, who never failed to greet him with tumultuous applause at almost every concert.

A multiplicity of talent is more often a burden than a blessing, and so it proved in Rachmaninoff's case. He was always successful, no matter whether he played the piano, composed, or conducted. But one thing was certain: his work as a composer suffered during his activities in Moscow, in the provinces and abroad, and during his conscientious service as Vice-President of the I.R.M.S. It all took up far too much time.

Rachmaninoff's creative output during these three years was, indeed, rather meagre. Except for the Third Concerto he composed only three works, amongst which appeared his first sacred composition of any magnitude. He decided to write a *Liturgy of St. John Chrysostomos* (Op. 31), which was practised and performed by the magnificent Moscow Synodical Choir immediately after its completion. In this work he did not keep strictly to the style of Church music with which he had been so familiar from his childhood. The higher Church authorities criticized his "spirit of modernism" and excluded the *Liturgy* from the Church services. He also published two series of pianoforte pieces: the Préludes (Op. 32), which numbered thirteen and which, added to his former pieces of the same nature, formed a series of twenty-four préludes, on the model of Chopin and included the whole range of keys. Then there were six *Etudes Tableaux* (Op. 33). Henceforward Rachmaninoff published all his pianoforte pieces under this title because the inspiration to compose them was derived principally from picture-impressions of a real or visionary character. Last of all we must mention a group of thirteen songs (Op. 34), including the *Vocalise*, an air without words, which was dedicated to the famous Moscow coloratura singer, Mme Neshdanova, and soon made the round of all the concert-halls of the world. Following an old, and by then almost sacred, custom, Rachmaninoff first played his two series of pianoforte pieces at Princess Lieven's concerts in aid of her "Prison Committee."

For the first time in his life Rachmaninoff's compositions did not excite the unanimous and wholehearted admiration of the Press to which he was accustomed. The public, it is true, remained faithful to him; but the Press began to criticize his creative inspirations and objected to one thing after another. They accused him, above all, of being "out of date" and not keeping pace with the modern development of musical ideas. How different, they asserted—and here lurked the sting—how different in this respect was Scriabin!

Not long before Scriabin had returned to Moscow and been proclaimed a musical star of the first order. He had avoided this town for many years, for the Muscovites had laughed at his mania for "irrational harmonic reform" as they termed it. But Serge Koussevitsky, the former double bass virtuoso, who now conducted and managed his Symphony Concert undertaking, called the sulking composer back to Moscow and presented him to the public in the popular setting of his own concerts. At first the public manifested nothing but surprise, but soon they began to show an honest enthusiasm for Scriabin's music. This was the moment when the section of the Press which inclined towards the extreme left and professed revolutionary opinions also in regard to music began to attack the old god, Rachmaninoff, so as to overthrow him and to enthrone in his place their new idol, Scriabin. They did not, however, succeed in reversing the judgment of the concert audiences; it was still Rachmaninoff's name on a poster that overcrowded the concert-halls, while

RACHMANINOFF IN MOSCOW (1913)

Scriabin played before half-empty houses. The Press representing the Radical Left consoled itself with the old proverb about the prophet in his own country.

The Press feud over Rachmaninoff and Scriabin, which at times was carried out with intense bitterness, might have led one to suppose that the personal relations between the two composers could be none too friendly. Such, indeed, was the opinion of Moscow society and the general public, but it did not coincide with the facts. Despite the difference of their musical outlook, the two composers were united by the friendliest personal feelings; naturally, Rachmaninoff, whose well-balanced outlook on life, with its foundation of reality, could not feel at home with Scriabin's morbid philosophy, which sprang from the rather uncertain ground of mystic Theosophy; but with admirable fairness he fully recognized the great musical talent of his rival and gave many an audible proof that he was above the petty quarrels of the Press. One of the first works he performed after his return from Dresden was Scriabin's First Symphony. On visiting Leipzig the score had accidentally fallen into his hands and had immediately drawn his attention. Moscow had an almost sensational surprise when, a little later, Rachmaninoff in his capacity as the permanent conductor of the Philharmonic Concerts engaged Scriabin as a soloist for one of his first concerts. The audience was frantic with enthusiasm when it saw the two "enemies" peacefully united on the platform; the neat, nervous Scriabin at the piano, playing his own Concerto for pianoforte, and Rachmaninoff, several heads taller, at the conductor's desk, directing the performance with his characteristic calm dignity. It was not long before Rachmaninoff had an opportunity of exhibiting an even more convincing proof of his fairness and his genuinely friendly attitude towards Scriabin, which was quite unaffected by any petty personal motives. But we will tell of this in the next chapter.

However, it is not impossible that Scriabin's steadily increasing fame as a composer may have inclined Rachmaninoff to a decision which he made at the end of the season 1912–13. Scriabin had then reached the zenith of his creative energy and productivity, and Rachmaninoff felt none too happy when he examined his own creative harvest of recent years. "Perhaps people who say that I am no longer at my best are right," he may have thought, "I have hardly written anything."

Contrary to his habit of many years, he did not spend the summer in "Ivanovka." Towards the end of the winter he took his wife and children to Switzerland, where he hoped to have a thorough rest after the strain of the season's work. From there he travelled to Rome, hoping that he might once more revive the peaceful atmosphere he had enjoyed in Dresden. For the magically inspiring influence of Rome had already benefited composers of all nations, amongst them Tchaikovsky.

Rachmaninoff himself says:

"In Rome I was able to take the same flat on the Piazza di Spagna which Modest Tchaikovsky had used for a long time and which had served his brother as a temporary retreat from his numerous friends. It consisted of a few quiet, shady rooms belonging to an honest tailor. I lived, with my wife and children, at a boarding-house and went to the flat every morning in order to compose. I remained there working till the evening, and only took one meal, a frugal breakfast consisting of an undefinable stew which was called coffee.

Nothing helps me so much as solitude. In my opinion, it is possible only to compose when one is alone and there are no external disturbances to hinder the calm flow of ideas. These conditions were ideally realized in my flat on the Piazza di Spagna. All day long I spent at the piano or the writing-table, and not until the sinking sun gilded the pines on the Monte Pincio did I put away my pen. In this way I finished my Second Sonata for pianoforte and the Choral Symphony—I would rather not call it a 'Cantata'—*The Bells*, in a comparatively short time. The inspiration for *The Bells* came from an unusual source. I had already during the previous summer sketched a plan for a Symphony. Then one day I received an anonymous letter from one of these people who constantly pursue artists with their more or less welcome attentions. The sender begged me to read Balmont's wonderful translation of Edgar Allan Poe's poem, *The Bells*, saying that the verses were ideally suited for a musical setting and would particularly appeal to me. I read the enclosed verses, and decided at once to use them for a Choral Symphony. The structure of the poem demanded a Symphony in four movements. Since Tchaikovsky's example the idea of a lugubrious and slow finale, which seemed necessary, held nothing strange. This composition, on which I worked with feverish ardour, is still the one I like best of all my works; after that comes my *Vesper Mass*—then there is a long gap between it and the rest. But this is only by the way. I dedicated *The Bells* to Willem Mengelberg and his admirable Concertgebouw Orchestra in Amsterdam. I had always performed at these concerts with particular pleasure. At the same time I wrote my Second Sonata for pianoforte, which I long to revise as I am not satisfied with the setting I gave it at that time. This I dedicated to the friend of my boyhood, Pressmann.

I regret to say that my sojourn in Rome came to an unhappy and premature end. My plan to spend the winter in the 'eternal city' was not realized. Our two little girls had an attack of typhoid fever, and we moved the sick children to Berlin, where their condition, especially Tatyana's, grew very much worse. We spent long and anxious days, fearing the worst, but my confidence in the German doctors was justified. Dr. Susmann was the name of the doctor who treated my children, and it is due to his exemplary conscientiousness and unselfish care—he frequently called three times a day—that our child was saved. I will never be able to thank him sufficiently for what he has done. Our stay in Berlin lasted for over six weeks. When both the little girls had recovered we made preparations to return to Moscow, for I lacked all courage to continue my Roman idyll."

At the beginning of the season 1913-14 Rachmaninoff gave two brilliant performances of his *Bells*, one in Moscow (with the Philharmonic Orchestra) and the other in St. Petersburg (at one of the Siloti Concerts). But, despite the great success of his work at both concerts, the Composer had the impression that neither the public nor the Press gave him the appreciation which, in his opinion, he deserved. We know that he placed *The Bells* higher than all his other compositions. There is no possibility of proving whether his impression was right, for, owing to the complicated apparatus required for the performance of this work, it could not be immediately repeated, and soon the war alarm quashed all other interests in Russia, including that of Rachmaninoff's *Bells*.

In January 1914 the Composer undertook a series of concert tours in England. This time the parting from his family affected him more than ever. A day before his departure the well-known French pianist, Raoul Pugno, who had come to Moscow to give a concert, had suddenly died of a heart attack in some hotel, without friend or help. This sad incident created a very deep impression in the musical circles of Moscow, and it seemed to Rachmaninoff that a similar fate might overtake him in England. He longed to cancel his engagement, but that was impossible.

While in England he arranged a performance of *The Bells* in Sheffield for the autumn of 1914. But all the trouble spent in preparing this concert (amongst other things Edgar Allan Poe's verses had to be retranslated from Russian into English so as to adapt it to the music, a proceeding which did not tend to improve the poem of this great American poet)—all the labour proved in vain. The concert did not take place, and this was destined to be the last journey which Rachmaninoff was able to undertake for many years. For August 1914 marked the outbreak of the World War.

CHAPTER TEN

WAR AND REVOLUTION

1914–1919

The Outbreak of the World War—Wide concert activity for charitable purposes—The Vesper Mass—Death of Scriabin and Taneyev—The March and October revolutions, 1917—Decision to leave Russia—A sign of fate—The Scandinavian tour—Copenhagen—Rachmaninoff rejects an offer as permanent conductor in Boston, but decides to leave Europe and try his luck in the United States

THE outbreak of the war must have had a similar effect on all countries involved. No one realized the true meaning of a European war, or could foresee the consequences of this senseless undertaking, which was to lead some of the fighting countries—amongst them Russia—to ruin. Russia, like all the other countries, wallowed in orgies of "patriotism" encouraged by an unscrupulous Press. Those who did not join in this light-headed and superficial jingoism were marked with disfavour or even suspicion.

Rachmaninoff had always felt a great respect for German art and science, and his years in Dresden had taught him to like and understand the German character, except perhaps for one or two points which he judged with the good-natured irony of a Russian who is accustomed to face the problems of life from a broader standpoint. He could not bring himself to join in the general war-intoxication and hatred of Germany, which was fanned almost to a white heat. Moreover, many of his friends and acquaintances in Russia, such as Struve and many others, belonged to the "German-Russians," who were soon relentlessly persecuted. Rachmaninoff's great and sincere love for his native country—one of his most prominent characteristics—could not drive him to join in the political capers (of which this war was one), prompted by an unfettered chauvinism, or even to approve them. This involved him in many conflicts, internal and external, which he settled with his customary undaunted calm, consulting only his own conscience and following his inner convictions.

Compulsory military service was a question which had suddenly acquired an oppressive significance for everyone. Although Russia had universal military service, the teachers in Government service did not serve in the army and could be called to arms only as the last reserve. Rachmaninoff at the time of declaration of war was also in Government service as the Inspector of Music at the Nobility High School for Girls.

As he was not tied by contract to musical societies or any other ventures, Rachmaninoff spent the years of the war as a "free artist, without a definite profession," as he himself described it. The frontiers were closed; consequently concert tours abroad were out of the question. In spite of this, Rachmaninoff appeared more frequently as a pianist than he had done during times of peace. As he could not and would not be active in the "field of honour," he took a great delight in placing his gifts and his name at the disposal of all entertainments in aid of the sick and wounded. He gave charity concerts, or took part in those arranged by others.

Despite these strenuous activities, Rachmaninoff found time to compose, even during the war. In the winter of 1915 he wrote his *Vesper Mass*, which immediately placed him in the front rank of Russian composers of sacred music. He thought that in his *Vesper Mass* he had at last succeeded in achieving a union between the melodies of the *Oktoechos* and the Western counterpoint, a dream which had long before been cherished by Glinka. Rachmaninoff says:

"I composed my *Vesper Mass* very quickly: it was completed in less than two weeks. The impulse to compose it came to me after hearing a performance of my *Liturgy*, which, by the way, I do not like at all, for it solves the problem of Russian Church music very inadequately. Ever since my childhood I had been attracted by the magnificent melodies of the *Oktoechos*. I always felt that a special style was needed for their choral treatment, and this I hoped to have found in the *Vesper Mass*. I cannot deny that the first performance of the Mass by the Moscow Synodical Choir gave me an hour of the happiest satisfaction. This choir, which sang in the Uspenski Cathedral in the Kremlin, usually gave its rare concerts in the comparatively small hall of the Synodical School. But for the performance of my Mass, which was arranged in aid of a war relief committee, the Chief Procurator of the Holy Synod, Samarin, who had also been the Marshal of the Moscow Nobility, engaged the 'Great Nobility Hall.'[1]

The Mass is difficult in many ways: it makes great demands upon the vocal power and technique of the performers. However, the magnificent Synodical Singers produced any effect I had imagined, and even surpassed, at times, the ideal tone-picture I had had in my mind when composing this work. At that time Kastalsky, the composer of sacred music, was director of the Synodical School, whose beautiful building in the Nikitskaya street

---

[1] The composition made such a strong appeal to the music-loving Muscovites that it had to be repeated five times, before crowded houses. This was a sensation, bound to attract notice, even amongst the greater sensations provided by the war. The perfect singing of the Synodical Choir was to a large extent responsible for the success.—O. v. R.

THE COMPOSER'S TWO DAUGHTERS, IRÈNE AND TATIANA, NOW
PRINCESS WOLKONSKY (ON THE RIGHT) AND MADAME CONUS

was familiar to all in Moscow. The wealth of colour and sound for which his compositions are noted may entitle one to call him the Rimsky-Korsakov of choral music. I have learned a great deal from his works and from conversations with him. The conductor, or, to speak precisely, the 'Regent,' of the Synodical Choir was N. M. Danilin. Like Kastalsky, Danilin had been a pupil of the Synodical School and, as such, had been a member of the famous choir, which later he conducted with such incomparable delicacy of rhythmic and dynamic feeling. My Mass pleased both Kastalsky and Danilin when I played it to them on the piano, and they immediately asked my permission, granted to them with the greatest pleasure, to perform it as soon as possible. My favourite passage in this work, which I love as much as *The Bells*, is the fifth hymn, 'Lord, now lettest Thou Thy servant depart in peace . . .' (Luke ii. 29). I would like this to be sung at my funeral. Towards the end there is a passage sung by the basses—a scale climbing down to the lowest B flat in a very slow pianissimo. After I had played this passage Danilin shook his head, saying:

'Where on earth are we to find such basses? They are as rare as asparagus at Christmas.'

But he managed, nevertheless, to find them. I knew the voices of my countrymen and was well aware of the demands I could put upon Russian basses! The audiences always listened with breathless suspense to the descent of the choir into the nether regions.

I was particularly happy that my Mass pleased my old teacher, Taneyev, who was a very sharp critic, especially in the matter of counterpoint. His appreciation, expressed in almost exalted terms, was the last praise I ever had from him, for, in spite of his apparent robustness, this man of fifty died quite unexpectedly from the consequences of a severe cold which, as rumour had it, he contracted at Scriabin's funeral."

A few days after the death of Taneyev (on the 16th–29th June 1915) Rachmaninoff dedicated to his highly esteemed teacher an obituary of great warmth which was published in the columns of the *Rousskya Vedomosti*. Rachmaninoff's words picture Taneyev's personality in a concise and yet in a thorough way. They are characteristic not only of Rachmaninoff himself, but of all who mourned the revered master's death, so that it is well timed to mention them here. They run thus:

"The Master Composer, the most cultured musician of his time, Sergei Taneyev, has passed away. He was a charming personality of remarkable independence, peculiarity, and noble-mindedness. For us he was the very acme of the musical life in Moscow. He held this high post with imperturbable authority and with right to the end of his days. For all those who appealed to him he was the highest judge, full of wisdom, righteousness, affability, and simplicity. In all his doings he was a paragon of virtue for us. Whatever he did was well done. Through his personal example he taught us how to live, to work, and even to speak. Yes, even his very mode of speech was an original one: concise, to the point, and full of enlightenment. He only spoke what was absolutely necessary. No one ever heard him use superfluous or shallow talk. We all looked up to him, and there was no one who did not appreciate his counsel, direction, and advice. One appreciated him because one believed him, and one believed him because he gave advice which was truth itself and always good. He seemed to be the personification of that "Truth on Earth" which in Poushkin's drama *Mozart and Salieri* is rejected by Salieri.

Taneyev lived a simple, modest life, even, in some respects, a poor life, which fully satisfied him. As Socrates once said: 'How many things there are in this world I do not need' . . . when he saw articles of luxury, so it could have been with Taneyev. . . .

In his home, the little house well known to everyone in Moscow, all sorts of people gathered, though according to their characteristics they seemed to be a strange company, being pupils and beginners mingled with the greatest masters of the Russian Empire. But there they all felt at their ease, were happy, at home, and took a supply of life's pleasures and freshness home with them. After a visit to Taneyev's it seemed to me we all worked and lived better and happier. His relations towards mankind were unfailing, and I am firmly convinced that there neither was nor is one whom he had ever offended or hurt.

Taneyev wrote two cantatas which, so to say, were the two boundaries of his creative power. The one cantata was his first and the other his last work. The former one he wrote in the springtime of his life and the latter at sundown. In the first cantata he sang with the words of John of Damascus: 'I step out into the unknown street,' . . . in the second one he put the words in the mouth of our Lord: 'Was it not I who mounted flames upon your heads?' . . . I should like to fill up the space between these two limits of his creative powers and connect these accidentally snatched up sentences and say that Taneyev did not walk the 'Unknown Street' very long. Thanks to the strength of his mind, his heart, and his talent, he soon found the broad and right path which led him to those last heights where God had lighted the flame which shone so brightly during his whole life. This flame burned with an equal quiet light; it never flickered, never smouldered, yet it

was a guide for many who trod the 'Unknown Street.'
This flame ceased only with his life. . . ."

The death of Scriabin, that strangely iridescent genius,
in April of 1915, was the greatest blow Russian art had
suffered during the years of the war. He died of blood-
poisoning after suffering for barely three days. The
terrible tragedies caused by the war rather weakened
the impression of this sad incident; no one fully realized
what had happened. Scriabin's star was then rising
rapidly. Cruelly obscured by his death, it has never since
found its proper place in the Russian musical firmament,
which was soon to take on so very different an aspect.
We know how the Press feuds and the passionate division
of the public over Rachmaninoff and Scriabin forced the
former into rather a difficult position. A real friendship
between these two widely contrasting personalities was
impossible, despite their amiable intentions. Character-
istically, therefore, Rachmaninoff took all the more pains
to show his respect; after Scriabin's death he devoted a
large part of his concert activities to the memory of his
prematurely deceased comrade.

Rachmaninoff himself speaks in this connection as
follows:

"I am still conscious of the deep and soul-stirring impression I received at Scriabin's funeral. All the literary,
musical, and artistic celebrities of Moscow were assembled
there, and filled not only the little church situated
opposite to Scriabin's flat, but the whole vast square
in front of it. The Archbishop of Moscow gave a beautiful address extolling the divine will to freedom, which
attracted general notice. The Synodical Choir sang with
an almost unearthly beauty, for Danilin was well aware
of the public that would attend the funeral: the cream

of the Moscow musical world was united there. As
the church was not large enough to hold the whole
choir, he had chosen only the most beautiful voices and
the best singers. Apart from one or two modern works
by Kastalsky and Tchesnokov, they sang the Lord's
Prayer from the *Oktoechos*, which in reality consists
only of the D major triad and its dominant chord, but
the lovely sound of these nine- or ten-part harmonies
in all grades of strength was so indescribably beautiful
that it must have reduced the most obstinate heathen to
tears and softened the heart of the most hardened sinner.

I decided at that moment that, during the following
winter, I would make a concert tour of all the larger
Russian towns and play only pianoforte works composed
by Scriabin. All these concerts were crowded out and,
to my intense joy, proved tremendously successful. This,
however, was not the opinion of a few Moscow critics who
considered themselves Scriabin's musical disciples. They
abused me publicly and decided that my playing lacked
'the sacred consecration' which could only be expressed
by a chosen few, to whom I certainly did not belong.

The circle of friends that surrounded Scriabin during his
lifetime was composed of people who always maintained
that one could not interpret his works without a mystic
hypothesis; they had either blackguarded me in their
newspaper articles or punished me with contempt. How
great, then, was my surprise when, exactly a year after
Scriabin's death, they sent a deputation to me—to me
of all people!—announcing that they had formed a
committee for the preservation of Scriabin's memory,
and asking me not only to fill an important position in
their midst, but to arrange concerts for the performance
of his music and to take part in these either as a pianist
or conductor. This deputation consisted of some society
ladies and one of the music critics who had been par-

ticularly prominent in impressing upon his readers my futility and complete unimportance in comparison with Scriabin. When the deputation had finished their appeal, voiced in flattering terms, I expressed my great surprise at this request coming from people who had frequently shown their displeasure and mistrust of me, and said that I must refuse their advances once and for all. For the rest, I would myself decide the manner in which I would commemorate the deceased composer. I think I have proved my loyalty and keenness by the concerts I have since arranged.

It is strange how the death of a composer affects the significance of his works. I remember the following incident, which I would like to quote here; it is very instructive. When the talented Russian composer, Vassili Kalinnikov, a slightly older contemporary of mine, died at the early age of thirty-four, he left no money whatever, as he had always been badly paid. His widow, who found herself in very straitened circumstances, asked me for a small loan so that she could erect a tombstone for him. She also brought with her some of Kalinnikov's musical remains, saying:

'It is useless to take them to a publisher. I know his prices.'

I took the compositions to the publisher Jurgenson, hoping that he might buy one or the other of the pieces.

Without a word Jurgenson added up the prices I had quoted. They made a considerable sum, which was ten times larger than the loan for which I had been asked. As he went to his safe and opened it he remarked:

'Don't imagine that I pay this tremendous sum without a definite reason; I pay it because the death of the composer has multiplied the value of his works by ten.'

But to return to Scriabin: At the first Philharmonic concert of the season following his death I played his Concerto in F sharp minor, which was conducted by

Siloti. This was the first time since my days at the Conservatoire that I had played the work of another composer in public. It is a significant fact in that it marks the beginning of a new period in my artistic career which has lasted up to this day."

When, soon afterwards, Rachmaninoff was approached with the request to arrange a concert on a gigantic scale which should guarantee large profits in aid of the sick and wounded, he decided to play three concertos for pianoforte in one evening: the Concerto in E flat major by Liszt, Tchaikovsky's Concerto in B flat minor, and his own Second Concerto. So that it should bring in the required sum, the concert had to take place at the Grand Theatre. At the first rehearsal he decided that the sound of the piano in the roofed-in orchestra did not satisfy him. It was very important that at this concert the piano should sound as well as possible and as he would like it. To achieve this Rachmaninoff had a special dais erected, which fortunately fulfilled his expectations. Later he presented this to the Grand Theatre, where it has been used once or twice.

The feverish activity during the years of the war did not allow much time for composing. In the summer one had to prepare the programmes for the following winter. As, apart from a few isolated instances, Rachmaninoff still interpreted only his own works, he found it expedient to enlarge the number of his compositions in order to freshen up the programmes. In the isolation of the government of Tambov, far removed from the world, where the war was noticeable only through the medium of newspapers and where, according to his custom, Rachmaninoff spent the summer, he created the majestic alfresco pictures of the *Etudes Tableaux* (Op. 39) and the songs (Op. 38), which surprised everyone by their novel style. The concerts in Moscow at which he first played these works were the last he gave in Russia.

In March of 1917 Russia was plunged into a second catastrophe which proved far more disastrous than the war—the outbreak of the revolution. All the "subjects" of this vast country (now advanced to the status of "citizens") firmly believed that it marked the beginning of a new and splendid era and greeted the revolution with undisguised enthusiasm.

Rachmaninoff also regarded "the first bloodless revolution," which it was claimed to be, as a definitely joyful event. Many circumstances in Russia had invited the earnest criticism of all right-thinking people; here, then, was an opportunity to readjust the social organization of Russia, which was in such dire need of reform. Soon, however, he was overcome by a feeling of deep disappointment which grew from day to day with the march of events, which followed one another in rapid succession. Rachmaninoff was one of the first to realize the inevitability of the approaching collapse, and the inactivity, the indolence and weakness of the provisional government drove him to despair. He was haunted by gloomy forebodings, not so much on his own account as on that of his beloved country, which he could see being gradually overtaken. There seemed no way out of the situation, which became more and more unbearable.

Rachmaninoff himself describes this period as follows:

"Almost from the very beginning of the revolution I realized that it was mishandled. Already by March of 1917 I had decided to leave Russia, but was unable to carry out my plan, for Europe was still fighting and no one could cross the frontier. I retired to the country and spent the summer at 'Ivanovka.' This was to be my last summer in Russia. The impressions I received from my contact with the peasants, who felt themselves masters of the situation, were unpleasant. I should have preferred to leave Russia with friendlier memories.

The outbreak of the Bolshevist upheaval still found me in my old flat in Moscow. I had started to re-write my First Concerto for pianoforte, which I intended to play again, and was so engrossed with my work that I did not notice what went on around me. Consequently, life during the anarchistic upheaval, which turned the existence of a non-proletarian into hell on earth, was comparatively easy for me. I sat at the writing-table or the piano all day without troubling about the rattle of machine-guns and rifle-shots. I would have greeted any intruder with the answer that Archimedes gave the conquerors of Syracuse. In the evenings, however, I was reminded of my duties as a 'bourgeois' and had to take my turn with the other flat-owners in conscientiously guarding the house and joining in the meetings of the house 'committee,' which had been formed immediately after the Bolshevist upheaval. Together with the 'house boy' and other persons of equal rank, I discussed questions of importance to our existence, as well as other matters. You may believe me, the memories of that time are anything but agreeable. Many optimists looked upon the Bolshevists' seizure of the reins as an unpleasant but short-lived interlude of the 'Great Revolution,' and hoped that each new day would, at last, bring them the promised heaven on earth. I am not one of those people who blind themselves to reality and indulge in vague Utopian illusions. As soon as I had made a closer study of the men who handled the fate of our people and the whole country, I saw with terrible clearness that here was the beginning of the end—an end full of horrors the occurrence of which was merely a matter of time. The anarchy around me, the brutal uprooting of all the foundations of art, the senseless destruction of all means for its encouragement, left no hope of a normal life in Russia. I tried in vain to find an escape from this 'witches' Sabbath' for myself and my family.

Then an entirely unexpected event, which I can only attribute to the grace of God and which, in any case, was the happy dispensation of a well-disposed fate, came to our rescue. Three or four days after the shooting in Moscow had begun I received a telegram suggesting that I should make a tour of ten concerts in Scandinavia. The pecuniary side of this offer was more than modest, and a year earlier I would not have thought it worth my consideration. But now I did not hesitate to answer that I was satisfied and would accept the engagement. This took place in November of 1917. I had difficulty in obtaining a visa from the Bolshevists, but they were not long in granting it, for at first these new masters showed themselves fairly obliging towards artists. Later I heard that I was the last to receive permission to leave Russia in a 'legal' manner. The fact that I wanted a visa for my whole family did not appear to excite particular notice. The custom of 'hostages,' which meant keeping back relations of the traveller who, if he was unwilling to return, were either sent to the ice regions of the North or executed, had at that time not been instituted. On one of the last days in November I took a small suit-case and boarded a tram, which drove me through the dark streets of Moscow to the Nikolai station. It rained . . . a few isolated shots could be heard in the distance. The uncanny and depressing atmosphere of the town, which at that hour seemed utterly deserted, oppressed me terribly. I was aware that I was leaving Moscow, my real home, for a very, very long time . . . perhaps for ever.

I travelled to St. Petersburg by myself in order to make all the necessary preparations for the continuance of our journey. My wife, with the two girls, followed later, and together we took the train which carried us via Finland to the Swedish frontier. One circumstance brought home to me the grip of the Bolshevists: I was allowed to take with me only the most necessary articles and not more than five hundred roubles for each member of the family. This was little enough, but I kept these rules to the last letter, for fear that our departure might after all be frustrated. When we arrived at the frontier my wallet was not even searched, so that I might easily have carried my whole fortune. But at that time money seemed quite unimportant regarding the fact that we were saved.

One question only caused me much worry: Would the small sum in my possession dwindle in the exchange? In those days the word 'exchange' acquired a strange significance which can be fully understood only by those who came in direct contact with it. I remember that one day, while I was still in Moscow, I left the house of a friend greatly worried over the question of exchange. At the front door I met an acquaintance—a professor at the Moscow University—to whom I communicated my troubles.

'But, my dear sir!' he exclaimed, 'you should be the last to worry about that. Why, here you have your exchange!' and he pointed to my hands."

Apart from his fortune in actual money, his estate and his flat, Rachmaninoff left another particularly valuable heritage to the Bolshevists: all his manuscripts, published and unpublished. The revolutionary "birds of prey" have handled this unexpected possession at least with a fair amount of care. We will enlarge upon this later.

One day before Christmas Eve of 1917 Rachmaninoff and his family crossed the Finnish frontier. The journey in the overcrowded train had seemed like an endless nightmare. Their fellow-travellers were panic-stricken, fearing that they might be arrested and sent back to St. Petersburg, an occurrence which had actually taken place more than once. But this time their fears proved to be unfounded, and at the frontier the Bolshevists behaved even "very nicely," as the Composer expressed it. For the last time his name, which was on the passport, exerted its magic power in Russia.

As the trains connecting the frontiers had ceased to run, one had to cross the border in a peasant sleigh—a *reggi*, or "hen-basket," as it was called. In one of these sat Rachmaninoff with his brave wife, both little girls and their scanty luggage. A dense blizzard obscured the landscape. When Michael Glinka left Russia, where he had suffered such disappointment and sorrow, for the last time, he stopped the carriage at the frontier and spat. Rachmaninoff, despite the brutality and ruthless despotism of the Bolshevists, would have liked to kneel down and kiss the soil of his native country, which was dearer to his heart than anything in the world.

It was Christmas Eve when the travellers arrived in Stockholm. Sweden knew nothing of revolutions and war. The northern capital was celebrating Christmas with gay abandonment; every hotel, restaurant, and public-house rang with laughter and happy voices. . . . One knows how it is. But Rachmaninoff and his wife locked themselves into their hotel bedroom and wanted to cry.

Rachmaninoff played in all the principal towns of Sweden, and although he was successful everywhere, he began to realize one thing: if, in future, he played only his own compositions, he would soon be "played out" in the true sense of the words. This led him to make an immediate decision that he must become a professional concert pianist. To achieve this he had to practise, and required time and peace in order to prepare himself for the coming season, for he had already been approached with numerous offers. He decided to settle down in Copenhagen. The fact that Struve lived there persuaded Rachmaninoff, amongst other considerations, to adopt this plan. As he was a Russian subject, Struve had had to leave Berlin, where he had established himself, and now carried on the Russian music publishing business in Copenhagen, which was neutral. Rachmaninoff's decision to join him there was easier planned than realized. At last Rachmaninoff was able to secure a small house, whose principal distinction was its defective stoves, in an outlying suburb. He remembered the stoves long afterwards, because it was his daily duty to light them. Mme Rachmaninoff did the cooking and housework, and their daughters kept up the communications with the town with the aid of a bicycle.

The season 1918–19 held a lot of concerts in store for Rachmaninoff. He accepted any engagement offered to him in the three Scandinavian countries, but was able only to keep a small number of the contracts. In October alone Rachmaninoff played in fifteen concerts, but he had a good reason for breaking the other engagements.

During the previous summer Rachmaninoff had already had an offer from the concert agents, Wolfsohn Bureau, to conduct the Symphony Orchestra in Cincinnati, but he refused, as the conditions did not satisfy him. He hesitated a little longer before refusing another offer, which was wired to him from Boston, in October: the committee of the Boston Symphony Orchestra invited him to take over their world-famous orchestra, with which Nikisch, whom he worshipped, had had such an incomparable success. Up to October of that year Dr. Karl Muck had directed the Boston orchestra. But, as has been already mentioned, he refused this offer also, although the material advantages it would have brought seemed very tempting according to the ideas of that time.

These two offers from America made Rachmaninoff decide to cross the Atlantic Ocean. He realized that there, at any rate, he could be useful in one capacity or another In Europe, which still suffered from the effects of the war, his movements were limited to a few neutral countries.

Rachmaninoff really should not have had a visa, even for America, but the American Consul in Copenhagen— one of the most amiable, understanding, and thinking representatives of his office—who was convinced of his political harmlessness, gave him one.

Shortly before the departure Rachmaninoff received a second telegram from Boston, repeating the first invitation, but accompanied by a considerably larger pecuniary offer.

On the 1st of November the whole Rachmaninoff family boarded a small Norwegian steamer from Oslo and left Europe. The crossing was not entirely without danger, for the ocean harboured more mines than the captain would have wished, especially on the route to New York. Fortunately the steamer was able to avoid them, as well as other dangers of war. They sighted the British Battle Squadron, but were not molested by it.

Rachmaninoff did not know what fate held in store for him on the other side of the ocean. After all, he was sailing towards the "land of boundless possibilities" entirely at his own risk. While still on board he refused the second Boston proposal. It tied him to one hundred and ten concerts, and at that time he never imagined that he would be capable of keeping to such an agreement. Little did Rachmaninoff know then to what feats of purely physical exertion an artist can be worked up in America! But he was certain that in America he would not perish, even outside Boston, and that the career of a pianist would be easier for him.

CHAPTER ELEVEN

AMERICA

1919

Arrival in New York on November 10, 1918—"Armistice Day"—The managers Ellis and Foley—Steinway & Sons —Astonishing musical development of the American public —Advertising practices in America—The Philadelphia Symphony Orchestra and Leopold Stokovski—Reappearance in Europe after nearly ten years—The Fourth Piano Concerto—Russia boycotts Rachmaninoff's works—The Composer about himself—Final word

ON the 10th of November 1918 the little Norwegian steamer with the Rachmaninoffs on board arrived in Hoboken. The 11th of November was Armistice Day. A strange picture met the travellers whenever they went out or looked out of their hotel windows into the street below. What they heard and saw made them feel that they had entered a lunatic asylum instead of a civilized country. Upton Sinclair describes these scenes very vividly in his novel *Oil* (page 227). The passage runs as follows:

"Such a spectacle had never been witnessed since the world began; every noise-making instrument conceivable was turned loose, and men, women, and children turned out on the streets, and danced and sang and yelled until they were exhausted; pistols were shot off, and autos went flying by with tin cans bouncing behind; newsboys and stockbrokers wept on one another's shoulders, and elderly, unapproachable bank presidents danced can-can with typists and telephone girls."

But, apart from the noisy Armistice revels, everything in the New World seemed strange and unaccustomed. It was well that a few old and devoted friends—Russian as well as American—were at hand to assist the newcomers. From the first day of their sojourn in the United States these friends did everything in their power to smooth their way. They consisted mostly of artists, amongst them the former idol of the Russian public, Josef Hofmann and his wife, the Russian violinists Ephrem Zymbalist and Mischa Elman, Mr. and Mrs. Fritz Kreisler, and others. Immediate assistance was all the more necessary as, soon after their arrival, all members of the Rachmaninoff family except Mrs. Rachmaninoff fell victims to a severe attack of influenza, then called "Spanish Flu," which took a very vicious form. Their faithful friends did all in their power to secure good doctors and efficient nursing, and luckily their efforts proved successful. The illness subsided without any of the serious consequences that had been feared, particularly in Rachmaninoff's case.

Rachmaninoff was right when he presumed that in America he would be able to make a living "in one way or another." No sooner had his presence in the country become known than the concert agents approached him with the most varied suggestions. Amongst these was one of the most famous of all American managers, Charles Ellis, who so far had placed his services at the disposal of only three artists: Paderewsky, Kreisler, and Geraldine Farrar. As Paderewsky had exchanged the piano stool for the presidential throne of the newly created Polish Republic, Ellis had, as one might say, a vacancy at his disposal, which he offered to Rachmaninoff, who accepted it eagerly and has never had cause to regret it. During the first years of his American "sojourn" he worked with Ellis. But even the latter's successor (then his assistant manager), C. J. Foley, who continued his work on the same principles, has been a truly faithful friend to Rachmaninoff from the very beginning up to this day.

RACHMANINOFF AND HIS GRAND-DAUGHTER, PRINCESS SOPHIE
WOLKONSKY (1930)

Another moral and artistic support, which dates back almost to the first days of his American sojourn, came to Rachmaninoff from the firm of Steinway & Sons. They immediately recognized the importance of the Russian artist as a pianist, and his name has been constantly associated with theirs.

Thus ideal conditions for an extensive artistic activity in the United States were provided for Rachmaninoff. But what, he asked himself, will be the attitude of the public?

Nine years had passed since his first concert tour in the United States. Nine years is a long spell of time compared with the frantic rush of American life. It is possible that American audiences would have forgotten all about Rachmaninoff's existence if it had not been for the Prélude. This still made the round of all the concert-halls, cafés, drawing-rooms, and the solitary studies of elderly piano mistresses, and kept his memory alive. Consequently, as soon as Rachmaninoff's first recitals were announced, everyone remembered his name, and the audience gave him a rousing reception.

Rachmaninoff's uncommon success in the United States can be explained in various ways. One or two reasons are very obvious.

We have always referred to the pianistic brilliance of the artist. This had reached its zenith. Besides, the public of the United States recognized at once the great power of his personality, which permeated his whole manner, and did not fail to exercise a strong suggestive influence. Lastly, the choice of his programmes pleased them. He recognized the necessity of following the laws sanctified by the greatest names in the pianistic world and of submitting to a taste in music which has remained unchanged through decades. So he played the music which was in demand, and luckily the wishes of the concert-goers coincided with his own. What the public wished to hear was, in the vast majority of cases, exactly what he wished to play—the masterpieces of classical music.

Noblesse oblige . . . luckily this motto still holds good as unconditionally in art as it used to do in all other departments of life. It caused Rachmaninoff to consider only the greatest masterpieces amongst compositions for pianoforte. And these, in arranging his programmes, he found almost without exception in the past. A great master who wishes to exhibit his art through the medium of interpretation is forced to choose works which enable him to present "greatness in a great manner." The recognition of this fact led him straight back to the golden age of musical literature, and opportunities of straying on to a side-path, which would bring him nearer to the present, were very rare. Which are the works that brought Rachmaninoff his greatest successes? The *Appassionata*, by Beethoven, Chopin's Sonata in B flat minor, Schumann's *Carnival*, Liszt's Sonata in B minor, and Chopin, Chopin, and again Chopin. During the eleven years of his pianistic activity in the United States Rachmaninoff's experience was always the same. The will of the majority cannot be ignored with impunity, and this is surely proof enough that his judgment was right. Gradually he was able to introduce the music of Nikolai Medtner, whom he placed high amongst contemporary composers.

In summing up the conclusions arrived at during his long concert experience in the United States, Rachmaninoff expresses himself as follows:

"In the course of my last eleven years of concert experience in America, separated from my first visit by an absence of ten years, I have had ample opportunity of convincing myself of the great progress made by American audiences both in their power of assimilation and in their musical taste. Their artistic demands have grown to an astonishing extent. The man who exposes his art to public opinion notices this immediately. This opinion is not mine alone, but is shared by all other artists who have given concerts in U.S.A., and with whom I have discussed the subject. From this one may conclude that the remarkable efforts of American, and especially New York, society to raise the standard of musical life have not been in vain. They have used every means in their power and have not spared any money in their effort to surpass Europe in this respect. They have succeeded. No man will dare to dispute the fact."

A very welcome change for Rachmaninoff from the innumerable recitals he had to give were—and always will be—the Symphony Concerts in which he played in the large towns through which he passed on his way. He has more than once expressed the opinion that the quality of the American orchestras (which, it is true, are largely composed of European members) is incomparable. His subtle sense of sound revelled in the joy of playing with the ideal orchestras of New York, Boston, and Philadelphia. He works particularly well with Stokovsky, who, like himself, when he conducted at the Grand Theatre in Moscow, is a strict disciplinarian with the orchestra and satisfies Rachmaninoff's very particular conscience by his unequalled exactitude of accompaniment. This results in a wonderful unanimity and flexibility and mutual give-and-take when they play together. Everyone who has heard a gramophone record of Rachmaninoff's Second Concerto for Pianoforte, played by himself and the Philadelphia Symphony Orchestra, will admit the truth of this statement.

The Composer has given also a beautiful and technically perfect performance of his Symphonic Poem, *The Isle of*

Death, with Stokovsky's magnific entorchestra. Luckily this also has been recorded by a gramophone company.

As regards Rachmaninoff's private life in America during the last twelve years, we may only touch upon the most necessary details, as it brings us too close to the present and is too intimately connected with all the people concerned.

One of Rachmaninoff's first actions in America, after his pecuniary circumstances had become more favourable owing to the great success he enjoyed from the very beginning of his sojourn, was to do everything in his power to rescue his wife's nearest relations from the iron grip of the Bolshevists, for their house had been his real home since the earliest days of his manhood. After an almost endless amount of trouble he succeeded. In the spring of 1921 the Satin family were able to leave Russia. They settled down in Dresden, a town which Rachmaninoff still regards with affection and which he visits with great pleasure.

Rachmaninoff's first summers in America were spent in the United States, far away from the bustle and noise of the large towns, on a farm or in some country house whose isolation reminded him of Russia's vast and lonely plains. Very soon, however, he began to long for the old continent, where the atmosphere is so different to that of the New World. And when his daughters made their home in Paris he could hold out in the United States no longer. When meadows and trees began to blossom he was irresistibly drawn towards the happy plains of "la Belle France." There he spent a succession of summers, generally in the vicinity of Paris, in the same old country place which we have already described in the Preface. The poetry of wild and ancient parks guarded by high walls, the peaceful stillness of ponds starred by water-lilies and spanned by tumbledown bridges, the wide view over scented, sun-baked meadows shrouded by pale evening mists, brought him closer to the vanished splendour of the old Russian country estates than the rather matter-of-fact orderliness of an American farm.

But it was not until the year 1931 that he bought himself a small property on the Lake of Lucerne in Switzerland. This also—for it is the first and most important condition for his happiness—lies far removed from the main roads humming with the incessant stream of tourists. Here he established himself according to his own taste, and here—we may hope—surrounded by the almost unreal beauty of the mountains, his creative muse will find the stimulus which it has missed for so long.

The year 1918 had seen Rachmaninoff's last performance in Europe, in Scandinavia. His last concert on the Continent dated even further back—approximately to the time of his Dresden sojourn. After this long absence, in the year 1928, he reappeared in the concert-halls of Europe, and wherever he plays, whether in Berlin, Munich, Vienna, Paris, London, Prague, or Budapest, he is always greeted with the same unstinted enthusiasm. The power of his personality, the upright honesty and sincerity of his musicianship, force the public, no matter of what nationality, to come under the spell of his charm.

The great success of Rachmaninoff's European tours caused him—or his manager—in 1929 temporarily to curtail the number of his concerts on the other side of the ocean. Nowadays the great master's plan of concert activities is somewhat as follows: During the first half of the season—from October to December—he plays in Europe; during the second half—from January till April—he visits the North American towns. Sometimes the order is reversed, but this alters the fundamental principle of the plan as little as the number of concerts given in the New and the Old World.

This restless, never-ending activity in the concert-halls of the whole world, to which was added the far more strenuous work with gramophone companies, which demands the most intense concentration, has, so far, occupied all Rachmaninoff's time. It is regrettable that this should have forced him to neglect one side of his artistic personality which, in the interest of his posthumous reputation, is by far the most important, namely, his creative faculty. During the first years of his American life Rachmaninoff did not compose a single note. He himself has probably suffered for this reason as much as the innumerable admirers of his creative muse. But he had to realize that the breathless speed of American concert managers would not allow a minute of the rest and quiet which is needed for composing.

When, after his successful concert activities in America, he returned to Dresden for the first time, he was bombarded from all sides with the same question: How much had he composed? Rachmaninoff was silent. The questioners became more insistent.

"Is it possible that in all these years you have not written a single note?"

"Oh, yes" (a bitter smile played around the Composer's lips) "I have written a cadenza to Liszt's Second Rhapsody."

This ironical answer was putting the case at its worst, but it was not far from the truth. Although during the first years in America Rachmaninoff was actually unable to find much time for original composition, we have to thank him for some "revisions" which now belong to the greatest treasures of pianoforte literature. These are: The Minuet from the *Suite Arlésienne* by Bizet, the waltzes *Liebesfreud und Liebesleid* by Kreisler, a song by Schubert, lately the *Prélude Gavotte and Gigue* from the violin Sonata in E minor by Bach, and the Scherzo from the *Midsummer Night's Dream* music by Mendelssohn.

The two waltzes are perhaps the only pieces which may be placed on the same level as their great examples, the *Soirées de Vienne* by Liszt and the waltzes by Strauss- Tausig.

It was only towards the last two years of his life in America that Rachmaninoff's creative muse awakened again to independent and outstanding work. He wrote his Fourth Concerto for pianoforte in G minor (Op. 40) and a work for orchestra and choir—three Russian folk-songs (Op. 41), where the innumerable verses are sung in unison by the choir (altos and basses) while the orchestra illustrates the incidents related in the text in a very lively and humorous manner. The text and melodies of these songs, which were quite unknown outside their place of origin (the most isolated corners of Russia), had been communicated to Rachmaninoff in New York by the interpreter of Russian folk-songs, Mme Nadejda Plevitskaya, who gave a successful recital in that city, and by Feodor Chaliapin from the inexhaustible store of his memory. The first American performance of these works took place in Philadelphia under Stokovsky. In Europe, Rachmaninoff first played his Fourth Concerto for pianoforte in Berlin at a Philharmonic Concert conducted by Bruno Walter on December 8, 1931. The Russian folk-songs had not been performed in Europe up to the season 1933.

In the summer of 1932 Rachmaninoff added new wealth to pianoforte literature by an outstanding work, *Variations on a Theme by Corelli* (Op. 42), which the Composer himself has introduced at one of his pianoforte recitals in New York during the season 1931–32. In the summer he completely revised his Second Sonata for pianoforte, which was rather severe in its original setting and now wears an entirely different aspect. It will probably soon enjoy a very welcome "resurrection" in the programmes of all noted pianists.

RACHMANINOFF'S RECOLLECTIONS

There is no doubt that Rachmaninoff's position during the post-war years has grown from that of a purely national celebrity in the Russian musical world to one of international importance. The New and the Old World pay equal homage to the mature musicianship of the great Russian master in a way that is rare in both hemispheres. There is no country that does not joyfully and from the very bottom of its heart pay him its tribute of sincere admiration and enthusiasm.

It is interesting to compare the attitude of his native country to the world-wide success of the artist, who, despite America and Europe, still derives with every fibre of his being from the wide plain between the Vistula and the Volga. Our final impression is one of incredulous surprise. I will not weary my readers with an elaborate account of the situation, but content myself with a few quotations from contemporary Russian criticism; they convey more than a hundred pages of conscientious descriptions and make the position perfectly clear.

One of these documents is an article published in the official Moscow newspaper *Pravda*, and is dated March 1931. It runs as follows:

WHAT THE BELLS SAY

"Could anyone imagine that nowadays, in Moscow, in one of the principal buildings, an assembly numbering thousands should listen to a recital of Lossov, or the mystic works of the poets Balmont, Hippius, or Mereshkovsky! Such a thought seems completely mad. Yet, in spite of this, a similar—no, an even more impudent—incident has lately taken place in Moscow.

During two successive days the Great Hall of the former Conservatoire was crowded by a somewhat strange audience consisting of 'people of the past.'

RACHMANINOFF AND SOVIET RUSSIA

On the platform a Symphony Orchestra, a choir, and 'well-known' soloists. The atmosphere is restive. The famous, 'truly Russian,' *Bells* are being performed. This is not a mere Symphony—it is a whole 'mystery of jangling bells.' At first you hear small bells, then regular church bells and orthodox wedding bells, which change into a gloomy and mysterious Oratorio.

Against this background the following words:

> 'Oh, the bells, bells, bells!
> What a tale their terror tells
>   Of despair!
> How they clang and clash and roar!
> What a horror they outpour . . .'

And at last, towards the end, supported by a Church hymn, the heavy and oppressive funeral bell tolls:

> 'Hear the tolling of the bells,
>   Iron bells! . . .
> For every sound that floats
> From the rust within their throats
>   Is a groan.
> And the people—ah, the people—
> Feel a glory in so rolling
> On the human heart a stone . . .'

The faces of the listeners express emotion and enthusiasm. The ovations are never-ending.

Who staged this piously inspired liturgy in the Soviet Russian capital? And in broad daylight! Was it a 'private individual' who intruded on the platform of the Great Hall in the Conservatoire?

No. The concert was organized by the Academic Grand Theatre under governmental control.

Who is the composer of this work? *Sergei Rachmaninoff,* the former bard of the Russian wholesale merchants and the bourgeois—a composer who was played out long ago and whose music is that of an insignificant imitator and reactionary; a former estate owner, who, as recently as 1918, burned with hatred of Russia when the peasants took away his land—a sworn and active enemy of the Soviet Government.

And the author of the text (after Edgar Allan Poe) is the half-idiotic, decadent, and mystic *Balmont*, who has long ago identified himself with the 'White' emigrants.

It is not so long ago that this very same Sergei Rachmaninoff, together with Ilya Tolstoy, published an official letter in the newspaper *New York Times* (of January 1, 1931) on the occasion of Rabindranath Tagore's imminent journey to the U.S.S.R., which is unprecedented in its impudence, and in which these two 'soldiers of the White Guards' raise a volume of complaint against the tortures inflicted by the OGPU and the 'slavery' in this country and call the Soviet Government a government of murderers, criminals, and professional executioners.

Of all Rachmaninoff's works they have now chosen the most reactionary, which, more than any other, is permeated by a spirit of religious mysticism—*The Bells*! Is this a coincidence?

*   *   *

Who inspires the theatre to these enthusiastically orthodox demonstrations? In *The Bells* especially, purely musical questions are mixed up with politics in a most treasonable manner. Does the theatre realize that during the great Industrial Law Case these *Bells* were especially mentioned as a work which, in some way, symbolizes the secret aspirations of a 'White' intervention? Is it known that the pernicious Tshayanov in his book, *My Brother Alexei's Journey into the Country of Peasant Utopia*, shows a special liking for the ringing of these Rachmaninoff *Bells*? He dreams of the rebirth of a Russia of tyrants to the strains of this music.

It was for this reason that Jaroslavsky, in his article 'Tshayanov's Dreams and Soviet Reality' (*Pravda*, No. 288), wrote: 'The Tshayanovs will never live to see these times if the masses are going to attend concerts in order to hear the "Bells" of Rachmaninoff's liturgy. . . .'

We regret to state that certain 'masses' have, after all, gone through this experience.

There is no doubt that now, at a time when the class war has reached a critical point, this concert, applauded by grocers and priests (no matter whether the organizer wished it or not), has changed into a *political* mass meeting of the blackest reaction.

It was certainly not difficult to foresee that! Who might be the person interested in this experiment?"

The consequence of this article and the incident which inspired it was—it is difficult to credit—a ban on the performance of all Rachmaninoff's works in Soviet Russia and the exposure of the Composer to the "anathema," as it were, of all Bolshevistic musical authorities.

According to the Paris newspaper, *Dernières Nouvelles*, of March 21, 1931, the Conservatoire in St. Petersburg passed the following resolution:

"The Governing Body of the Leningrad Conservatoire fully agrees with the suggestion (originated in Moscow) of completely boycotting the works of Rachmaninoff, which express the decadent ideas of a bourgeois and are particularly harmful under the present circumstances when the class war on the musical front is so embittered.

The Governing Body also draws attention to the fact that one or two groups of musical specialists praise Rachmaninoff's creations under the pretence that their technique and form is perfect—that is, they carry on the class propaganda under the cover of music.

The Governing Body is obliged to oppose without compromise all teaching of Rachmaninoff's works in the Higher Colleges of Music."

As St. Petersburg and Moscow gave an example of such loyal musical-political opinions, even the Ukraina—this otherwise independent appendix to Russia—could not but follow suit. Thus the *Kharkov News*, which is the official Ukrainian organ, published the announcement of a resolution taken by the "United Ukrainian High Schools," which said amongst other things:

"The author of works which, in their emotional and mental effects are bourgeois through and through, the composer of *Liturgies*, *Vesper Masses*, and the *Bells*, the manufacturer of foxtrots [???], *Rachmaninoff*, was and is a servant and a tool of the worst enemies of the Proletariat, the world-Bourgeoisie, and world-capitalism.

We invite the Ukrainian proletariat youth and all Government Institutions to boycott Rachmaninoff's works.

Down with Rachmaninoff! Down with the whole Rachmaninoff worship!"

This is followed by four signatures of members of the above-mentioned "Governing Body."

It is useless to comment upon these unconsciously childish (but for that reason no less dangerous) expressions of obtuse musical-political stupidity.

Sapienti sat!

One sentence, however, in the first newspaper article gives one to think: "*The ovations are never-ending.*" . . . If we are to draw the obvious conclusion . . . !

But I have no intention of drawing political conclusions which may be falsified by the event.

RACHMANINOFF AND SOVIET RUSSIA

In Chapter Ten we compared the very different senti-
ments with which Rachmaninoff and Glinka said farewell
to their native country. If Rachmaninoff should ever have
occasion to leave Russia again he might well be forgiven
if he followed Glinka's example.

*   *   *

We have seen the attitude of the Old and the New
Worlds—Europe and America—towards Rachmaninoff:
they recognize in him one of the greatest contemporary
masters of his "profession." We also know how poor,
deluded, slave-driven Russia looks upon him—or is
forced to look upon him: she places a political ban on
works that abound in a wealth of music and nothing but
music. But there is still another critic whose views we
should like to hear. How does Rachmaninoff himself, in
his incorruptible integrity, regard his place and his
achievement?

On the general question of his position he is naturally
reticent, but, at the conclusion of our talk in the park of
"Le Pavillon," near Clairefontaine, he threw valuable
light on one aspect of his career:

"I don't know," he said, "whether I have succeeded in
making clear the continuous conflict that has gone on in
my mind between my musical activities and my artistic
conscience—my persistent craving to be engaged on
something other than the matter in hand.

I have never been quite able to make up my mind as
to which was my true calling—that of a composer, pianist,
or conductor. These doubts assail me to this day. There
are times when I consider myself nothing but a composer;
others when I believe myself capable only of playing the
piano. To-day, when the greater part of my life is over,
I am constantly troubled by the misgiving that, in

venturing into too many fields, I may have failed to make the best use of my life. In the old Russian phrase, I have 'hunted three hares.' Can I be sure that I have killed one of them?"

Rachmaninoff is not alone in his dilemma. These doubts must have been experienced by most great men of many-sided genius.

As a commentary on his problem and to complete the picture, I should like to close with a quotation from the Spanish philosopher, Ortega y Gasset:

"Nobility is recognized by the demands a man makes upon himself—by his sense of responsibility, not his privileges. . . .

To my mind, nobility denotes that quality in a man which leads him to choose a life of strenuous activity, striving always after higher achievements and rising with each success to ever loftier ideals, obedient only to his inspiration and his conscience."

Those who know Rachmaninoff will recognize in these words the secret of his character.

CHAPTER TWELVE

RACHMANINOFF AS COMPOSER

Rachmaninoff's musical personality as a whole—Early works (the opera Aleko and Op. 1–16)—Years of maturity (works grouped around the Second Concerto, Op. 17–23)— The two operas—Works written in Dresden (Op. 26–29)— The "third period" (Op. 30–42)—Rachmaninoff winner of the Glinka Prize—Sacred works (Liturgy and Vesper Mass)—Rachmaninoff's universal significance as a composer

EVERY genuine work of art is a reflection of its creator's personality—and not only in the limited sense that it represents his reaction to a particular external or internal stimulus. There is a general sense in which the whole quality of the artist pervades his least creation. In Buffon's phrase, "Le style c'est l'homme." It is hardly necessary to insist that in every artistic medium, and especially in the language of Music, style is as important a feature as it is in Literature. For this reason it is always possible to trace in an artist's work, and more particularly in those changes which take place in his mode of expression, the development of his personal life. These fundamental qualities which remain unchanged throughout a man's development and constitute what we call his "character" have also their counterpart in his style. The fact may be verified by a study of the output of any genuine creative artist. As for composers in particular, their style is, quite simply, the result of the way in which they "hear" the Universe, which determines the form in which they set down their impressions. Rachmaninoff is no exception to this rule.

Future historians and biographers will be able to divide

the Composer's work into the customary three or more periods. To-day, when Rachmaninoff enjoys the best of health and walks about among us in the fullness of life, obviously, after a long pause, looking forward to a renewed and vigorous blossoming of his creative genius, this method would be, to say the least of it, premature, if any definite and final classification were to be attempted. However, we may even now point to certain peaks and depressions in Rachmaninoff's life which are likely one day to provide a basis for such classification. His work presents the exciting and attractive character of a mountain tour, of continuous ascents and descents that lead us from close valleys up to radiant heights from which we are given magnificent views over the vast prospect of his musical domain.

The first pinnacle is reached, as it were, in a quick burst of youthful athleticism, with the Prélude in C sharp minor (Op. 3); this is followed by a sheer descent and a long lowland journey which threatens to lose itself in dangerous sandy plains (First Symphony, *Caprice Bohémien*, Op. 12, and others), and at last leads to a complete arrest of all creative impulse and the serious moral depression which we have described in Chapter Six. The second peak is reached with the Second Pianoforte Concerto, which is still regarded by many as Rachmaninoff's best work. Another opinion, however, which has no less authority, asserts that his creative quest led him to ever higher pinnacles of inspiration and expression when he composed the Third Concerto for Pianoforte, the Choral Symphony *The Bells*, and the *Vesper Mass*. Even the valleys that divide these pinnacles and are sown with smaller works, mostly pianoforte pieces and songs, gradually reach a higher altitude as our journey progresses. Rachmaninoff's creative muse has never again descended to such depths as preceded the Second Concerto.

S. RACHMANINOFF
(ONE OF THE MOST RECENT PORTRAITS OF THE COMPOSER)

RACHMANINOFF AS COMPOSER

If we inquire the principal elements that compose Rachmaninoff's artistic personality and consequently his "style," the answer must be: those that characterize his race; for Rachmaninoff is above all Russian—and a Russian who unites within himself all the fundamental characteristics of a people who possess a tremendous wealth of spiritual life. He is the Russian described by Keyserling in his book, *The Spectre of Europe*, in words that might have been written with Rachmaninoff especially in mind: "The Russians are a great people not because they are Slavs, but because of the strength infused by the Mongol blood, possessed by no other Slav tribe in exactly the same measure and quality. It was from this mixture that resulted the magnificent combination of tender spirituality and masterful authority, which makes the Russian people so great." This "combination of tender spirituality and masterful authority" stamps Rachmaninoff's whole personality and is evident in all his work. To it we must add another, very characteristic, feature of his temperament, which points even more strongly to his Oriental origin. I mean his pronounced fatalism, his deep consciousness of destiny. It is the same fatalism that once made the Russian people bow beneath the Tartar yoke (whence came partly the Mongol blood mentioned by Keyserling) and to-day allows them to suffer the tyranny of Bolshevism, and which, long before Rachmaninoff, marked the work of so many Russian artists of the highest rank. We need only think of Tchaikovsky and that persistent consciousness of "Fatum" which informs, not only the Symphonic Poem of that name, but also the Fourth and Fifth Symphonies and provides their philosophic content. Rachmaninoff also, with his first excursion into the province of composition, bows before this same Fate, the "Moira" of the old Greeks. He does not fight seriously against it—no, he bows before it, despite an occasional struggle; he inclines his head resignedly, for he knows that Fate is stronger than man. Consider this attitude in connection with the end of the famous Prélude in C sharp minor, which is nothing more than a "Song of Fate," or with the first of the twelve Romances, Op. 21 (*Fate*, by Apuchtin), or the Second Symphony, but above all with the Choral Symphony, *The Bells*. In all these works Fate looms inexorable and threatening before their creator ready at any moment to destroy the poor human if he should rebel. To Rachmaninoff it never brings a joyful promise of happy fulfilment, but only dark, fearful forebodings that cast their uncanny shadow not only over his own work but over the destiny of all mankind. But, as we have said, he bows humbly before the mystic force with which unknown, merciless powers drive him through life— perhaps because he recognizes them as the source of his inspiration. Death alone can conquer Fate!

Apart from these general Russian characteristics, Rachmaninoff's music naturally reveals a number of entirely personal and individual features. If the preceding life-story gives a true picture of the Composer's personality, it should be easy to find the qualities peculiar to his character revealed also in his music. I only wish to draw attention to one other characteristic of his, which superficial judgment might misinterpret as "un-Russian." It is the distinguished moderation, the tense reserve he imposes upon even the most forceful manifestations of feeling. He tightens his own reins, as it were, when the passion of his colossal temperament threatens to break loose. In his music Rachmaninoff always leaves something unsaid. It seems impossible for him to expose his deepest self to the outside world. Even in the strongest surge of emotions he always keeps back a more or less considerable measure of reserve without exhausting his powers of self-expression.

In this respect he differs vastly from his musical and spiritual progenitor, Tchaikovsky, whose excess of emotion at times carries him to the verge of hysteria. Rachmaninoff always retains some degree of self-control, despite the force of emotional excitement that breaks through his music; his intensity never reaches the final climax and he never gives us the impression of a man who could tear his hair in despair, gesticulate wildly, fling himself to the ground, and dig his nails into the earth. . . . Perhaps his music does not affect us so directly and with the same objective reality as Tchaikovsky's, but its effect is often profounder and more lasting. There is no doubt that this trait is a consequence of Rachmaninoff's general spiritual attitude towards life: his musical aristocracy, which is, of course, quite independent of his birth, for in this sense the son of a carter may be as great an aristocrat as the son of a king. It simply means that Rachmaninoff's attitude is different to that of the man in the street: essentially freer, broader, more independent and exalted, but at the same time more guarded, more reserved, and less obtrusive.

* * *

"The Muses are the daughters of memory. There is no art without recollection," said a very distinguished French author, and with these words indicated the point of view from which we ought to examine and judge all works of art. There is not a single young artist who can escape various "influences" during his years of development— unless he spends his youth on a desert island entirely cut off from the world. The young eagle, before venturing on his bold flight into unknown regions, must learn the art of unfolding and spreading his wings from the older birds.

We know the influences that surrounded Rachmaninoff's unfolding musical mind. He started his career as composer with a wholly artless, frank, and therefore disarming imitation of Tchaikovsky. And why not? It would have been unnatural if he had done anything else, for at the time when Rachmaninoff began to spread his creative wings Tchaikovsky was the undisputed king amongst Russian composers. Moscow, more than any other town in the Empire, worshipped him. The strong suggestive power which Tchaikovsky's music exercises even to-day was naturally far more compelling to a young Russian and a budding composer when the musical language of his *Pathétique* was yet new and strange. No wonder young Rachmaninoff fell a victim to this temptation, especially as, in his case, the very strong and direct charm of Tchaikovsky's personality was there to enhance the impression produced by his music. In the world of music there was no task more elevating or more honourable for a young composer than to follow in the steps of this idolized master which led, according to the general opinion in Moscow, to Olympian heights. In this young Rachmaninoff was encouraged by the undisguised Tchaikovsky-worship practised by his principal teachers, Arensky and Taneyev, while there was no cross-current to counteract their opinions. Moscow, as we know, fought tooth and nail against the new musical ideas represented by the followers of the Neo-Russian School in St. Petersburg. The importance of such men as Rimsky-Korsakov and Borodin had as yet not been recognized, and they were regarded only with tolerance; Moussorgsky was dismissed; and the question of influence from contemporary musicians abroad did not arise for several decades. Wagner was still regarded with suspicion; Brahms—after Tchaikovsky's annihilating judgment—was for many years entirely ignored by the musical world in Moscow; the French Impressionists were still unknown. Thus it happened that Moscow awarded Tchaikovsky the undisputed sovereignty over all other musicians, dead or alive, and before the radiance of his exalted position all other influences paled. Apart from Tchaikovsky and the inevitable "classics," Chopin, and perhaps Liszt, could be counted as the only other pillars of musical culture in Moscow—the latter as seen through the medium of Tchaikovsky, whose orchestral works reveal one or two colours borrowed from the palette of the creator of the "Symphonic Poems." From amongst the living composers could, perhaps, be added Anton Rubinstein, whose over-prolific muse was too near at hand to be judged in true proportion. Accordingly we can find traces of Chopin's, Liszt's, and Rubinstein's influence in young Rach-maninoff's earliest works, but at that time (we speak of the work Op. 1–15) it never gained a decisive significance. Afterwards, and from an entirely different aspect, Liszt became of much greater importance in his work. In its early stage it was wholly dominated by Tchaikovsky.

Already in his first opera in one act—*Aleko*—his examination task when he finished the Conservatoire—Rachmaninoff, as we might expect from his admiration of the creator of *Eugene Onégin*, follows his natural impulse to imitate this master. Tchaikovsky himself might have written the opera, and not even in one of his weakest moments. It is written in the simple melodic style, as Tchaikovsky favoured it in imitation of the older Romanticists of the German and French stages. The melodies are expressive and quickened by strong emotion, though they are not always particularly distinguished. The speed at which the opera was written (the score, as we know, was completed in a little over fifteen days) is noticeable, especially in the often primitive accompaniments. When young Rachmaninoff composed his *Aleko*, *Cavalleria Rusticana* had just made the round of the European stages with unprecedented success. Consequently our young composer, in imitation of this work, added an "Intermezzo" to the score of his examination task. The scenic note says: "The moon hides behind the clouds and day gradually begins to break." While the audience watch this proceeding the French horn intones a pretty harmonized melody, which unfortunately never achieved the same popularity as Mascagni's tune. The "Cavatine," frequently sung by Chaliapin, and the "Gipsy Dances" are the only tunes out of *Aleko* that were ever really taken to their hearts by the Russian public.

In this opera we can find but faint touches of that special quality, peculiar to Rachmaninoff, which he was to bring into Russian music. In its place we find a good measure of musical buoyancy and a forceful temperament, which shows in passages of high emotional tension. This quality of power has, from that time, always been apparent in the work of Rachmaninoff, both as composer and pianist, and has enabled him to achieve the majestic effects at which he aims. Despite the Composer's youth the work is conceived on the grand scale. The orchestration already gives us a hint of the future powerful "alfresco painter" of *Francesca da Rimini*.

The official Opus No. 1 of the Composer—following the opera *Aleko*, which bears no opus number—is the First Piano Concerto in F sharp minor. This work was so thoroughly revised during the machine-gun rattle of the October revolution in Moscow that hardly one note was left in its place. In its present form it may no longer be classed with the Composer's early work, but must be placed between the Third and Fourth Piano Concertos— somewhere amongst the first numbers of the fourth dozen of his compositions.

Among those works which were produced during his first period we find pieces of varying importance, with a few masterly songs and some isolated pianoforte pieces of high rank—among them the Prélude in C sharp minor

(Op. 3). All the work ranging from Op. 2 to Op. 16 bears the stamp of promise rather than fulfilment. Occasional compositions of little significance—despite one or two pretty ideas—are those of Op. 2 for violoncello and piano, the two pieces Op. 6 for violin and piano, and the six pianoforte duets, Op. 11. The only distinguished feature amongst the latter is the concluding paraphrase on the "Slava" theme, which is familiar through the work of Rimsky-Korsakov and Moussorgsky, with its ingenious harmonic changes. Otherwise these works, as well as the pianoforte pieces Op. 3 and 7, are no more than respectable drawing-room music of the kind so plentifully supplied by Tchaikovsky and A. Rubinstein. The Prélude in C sharp minor (Op. 3), which stands alone among this group, has had a fatal effect on Rachmaninoff's other compositions by absorbing the attention of the world so exclusively that little remained for his later pianoforte work. Of the other pieces in Op. 3 and 10 only the broadly emotional *Elegy* and the pleasantly rippling *Barcarole* have gained a fair measure of popularity.

Of the two larger chamber-music works which belong to this period the *Fantasia* (Op. 5) for two pianos deserves notice as being the young Composer's first attempt at programme music. It bears the sub-title *Tableaux*—a designation which Rachmaninoff later adopts for all his pianoforte compositions. The four movements are headed by verses from Lermontov, Byron, Tyoutchev, and Khomiakov. The last movement contains a wonderful carrillon—the first Rachmaninoff ever composed—which resembles the fanatic peal of Orthodox Church bells on Easter Sunday as closely as can be managed with the tones of a piano. We know that Rachmaninoff since his earliest childhood had shown the greatest interest in the musical side of the Russian Church ritual. Like many other Russian composers he was fascinated by the task of reproducing the "irrational" sound of a Russian peal and the wonderful rhythmic intricacies produced by the practised hands of the ringers, on ordinary musical nstruments, with the aid of measurable notes. He has since made several further attempts in his Symphony, *The Bells*, and in pianoforte pieces and songs.

The pianoforte trio, Op. 9 (dedicated to the memory of a great artist), is an imitation, down to the last detail, of Tchaikovsky's Trio in A minor, but here the imitation serves a special purpose. If "the great artist" in Tchaikovsky's dedication was meant to be Rubinstein, he is, in this case, Tchaikovsky himself. The whole work is a homage to the deceased master's name. The leading theme, given to the violoncello, while the piano plays a continuous melodic figure, is repeated in the finale and is a touching death-lament whose unaffected simplicity, free from all false pathos, produces an intensely moving effect. Rachmaninoff has since revised the work, which suffered from youth and lack of experience, but not so thoroughly as the first Piano Concerto and without succeeding in definitely eliminating certain structural defects.

Of the three orchestral works written in his youth, only one deserves serious attention: the Symphonic Poem, *The Rock*, after a poem by Lermontov. This early work, which contains passages open to criticism, is a convincing proof that Rachmaninoff is a born orchestral composer. He combines an unusually delicate sense of sound-colour with a natural technique for instrumental setting, astonishing in anyone so young. Already in *Aleko* the successful instrumentation, which shows decided originality in the blending of tone-colours, arrests one's attention. This quality predominates to a much greater degree in the Symphonic Poem or "Orchestral Fantasia," as the Composer himself calls the work. The lugubrious text of Lermontov's poem led him inevitably to choose a dark orchestral colouring, in which the shadows far outweigh the light. His general preference for dark orchestral shading accords well with the philosophy of fatalism which one hears in his music. It remains with him to this day. We shall come across it again and again. The two other orchestral works of that time are *Caprice Bohémien* (Op. 12) and the First Symphony, bearing the unfortunate opus number 13, of which we have spoken at length in Chapter Five. After the first performance of the Symphony in St. Petersburg no other note of it has penetrated into the world. Whether the manuscript has been preserved by the musical authorities in Moscow together with his other musical "remains" or whether it has been destroyed we are unable to ascertain. Over the orchestral *Caprice on Gipsy Themes* (Op. 12) the kindly observer had better draw the veil of oblivion, especially as it is the only one of his children which the creator would prefer to disown. It is interesting to note in this, as well as in the dances in *Aleko*, the Composer's tribute to "Gipsy music" which, as we know, played no mean part in the music of pre-revolutionary Russia and was well esteemed by the leading Russian authorities on vocal music.

For a long time it was believed that the strength of Rachmaninoff's creative talent lay in the province of song-writing. This opinion was not entirely unjustified when only his earliest works were under consideration. To-day, we should confine ourselves to saying that in song-writing *also* Rachmaninoff can take his place with the best of the Russian composers. Among his songs, especially those of his early manhood, there are undoubtedly some, any of which would have assured him the same immortality in the whole Russian-speaking world as to his predecessors, Glinka and Tchaikovsky, even if he had composed no more.

217

RACHMANINOFF'S RECOLLECTIONS

When we speak of Russian composers as song-writers, we must first of all realize that within the vast realm of the Tsar the song did not for many years take the form given to the German *Lied* in West Europe, mainly by Schubert and Schumann. In Russia flourished the so-called "Romance," carefully nursed by Glinka and his predecessors (Gurilev, Varlaamoff, and others). This was a decidedly original creation based on simple melodic laws like the folk-song and the Italian canzonet, which laid the greatest stress on the melody combined with the most primitive simplicity of accompaniment without aiming at a true musico-psychological interpretation of the poem. Moussorgsky rebelled passionately against this form of vocal composition and became the founder of a new type of Russian song. Later Nikolai Medtner attempted to solve the problem, but from a different starting-point, more after the manner of the German song-writer, Hugo Wolf. At the same time the "Romance" developed in another direction and brought forth musical blooms of the choicest beauty and unique "aroma," and led, through Glinka and Tchaikovsky, straight to Rachmaninoff, who is the last, but by no means least, representative of the school. It is only in his latest songs (Op. 38) that Rachmaninoff shows an astonishing change of style. It is true we can already find traces of this in the group of songs written since Op. 26, but it did not take a definite form until Op. 38.

The difference between the inspired and the would-be song-writer is that the former, on reading a poem, immediately conceives ready-formed melodies, musical devices, perhaps merely short phrases, which are at once recognizable as the only adequate and fitting, indeed the only possible, musical expression of the words and, once sung, simply belong to them and are indissolubly associated with them. Consequently the idea behind the words is the decisive factor in the writing of songs. Well, Rachmaninoff's songs, even those of his early days, frequently show this direct correspondence with the poet's concept, and their inspiration raises them at times to immortal heights. We can find one or more of them in each of his three groups of songs, Op. 4, Op. 8, and Op. 14.

Of the songs Op. 4 whose words, as is fitting for a youthful composer, breathe a more or less passionately expressed yearning for love, it is the setting of Poushkin's beautiful verses, *Oh, Never Sing to me Again the Songs of Georgia*, that, once heard, remains with one for ever. The whole song in its concise formal structure is a masterpiece. The melodic idea from which it is developed fits the words to perfection, as do the misty harmonies of pronounced Oriental colouring with the concluding bars altering between the major and minor keys. The song is dedicated to Natalie Satin, who later became the Composer's wife.

Of the songs Op. 8 two, *The Harvest of Sorrow* and *For a Life of Pain I Have Given my Love*, are unique in that the music recognizes the folk-lore character of the poems and conforms with it. The type of song is very rare with Rachmaninoff, and the two are beyond doubt the most Russian of all his vocal compositions. The unique melodic curves remind one of the happiest inspirations in Russian folk-song and are based on the free, unsymmetrical rhythms which constitute the fundamental principle of Russian Church singing even more than of the Russian folk-song and become so significant in Rachmaninoff's later works.

The twelve songs Op. 14, apart from one or two important numbers, contain one pearl which must be counted amongst the most valuable treasures of Russian vocal literature and certainly deserves to be ranked with the finest examples of the genius of Schubert and Schumann. It is *The Little Island*. The words in Balmont's very successful reproduction of Shelley's poem are inexpressibly tender; and equally tender, miraculously simple and impressive is the music with which Rachmaninoff clothes them. In striking contrast to this incomparable vocal poem there is another song in the same group which scored a great popular hit and won immense popularity in Russia. This song, *Spring Waters*, is inspired by an unruly temperament and breaks down all barriers with its unrestrained abandon, but no heart can resist it. Great force of expression, though used with nobler effect, is shown in the last song of Op. 14 (*'Tis Time*), a passionate call to waken and prepare, of which the world might well take heed, even in our days. This song, by the way, is based on the same motive as the Prélude in C sharp minor, the only difference being that the leading note of the dominant is taken from below and not above.

The songs written during Rachmaninoff's first period of activity convince us already that the Composer has much to contribute that is original and significant in this province. They, like his other works of this period, show certain of those idiosyncrasies in the use of the musical language which characterize every great composer and accompany him through life like certain features in his handwriting. They constitute what is commonly described as his "style," in so far as that depends on purely technical considerations. With Rachmaninoff we notice a pronounced preference for organ points that are frequently spread over the whole song or piece; a tendency towards accompaniments in chords with undulating up and down movements; the dissemination—rather difficult to define—of a harmonic twilight effect, with alterations between the major and minor keys; a preference for plagal cadences, leading over the lower dominant or its representative, and, finally and above all, a tendency to advance the melody by steps while observing the narrowest possible range with frequent repetitions of the same note in the melody. The last-named peculiarity Rachmaninoff must unconsciously have borrowed from Russian Church music, which has given him so much that is valuable and stimulating. The liturgic *canti firmi* of the Russian Church ritual move without exception in upward or downward steps in which a third is a very rare occurrence and larger intervals are simply unknown. Most of Rachmaninoff's melodies have a similar appearance, and by this means frequently achieve the greatest intensity of expression.

The last work written in the early days of his activity is *Moments Musicaux* for pianoforte, Op. 16. In one sense this still belongs to Rachmaninoff's "early works," but some of them (No. 2, E flat minor, No. 4, E minor) already show signs of maturity and, unlike the preceding piano pieces, point towards the elaborate and technically pretentious style of pianoforte movement that characterizes the period immediately following.

In the last decade of the nineteenth century there was a long, oppressive pause in Rachmaninoff's activities. It lasted through four infinitely difficult years. One held one's breath and wondered anxiously: What will happen? Is this to be the end of the wonderful promise which heralded such wealth, or will the young Composer fulfil our expectations? Then, at last, at the turn of the century, came the change so passionately longed for. A new creative spring, richer and more beautiful than one had even dared to hope for, began to blossom. Work after work flows from the never-resting pen and, strangely enough, this seems to be an entirely new Rachmaninoff who, like a phoenix, rises from the ashes of these dark years of depression. Where are the "influences," the barriers that stunted all original effort? Where the almost slavish inclination to imitate which hitherto directed all his work? They are gone—all of them—cast away like an old garment that Rachmaninoff has outgrown. Thus the years of rest have accomplished what the period of feverish activity was unable to achieve: Rachmaninoff has found himself, his own style, his own language, which from now on can be recognized among a thousand others and can never be mistaken for any but his own.

If up to that time Rachmaninoff was to be regarded as a rising star in the musical world of Moscow, or perhaps rather a provincial Moscow celebrity, Opus 17 now introduces him as a composer who demands the attention, not only of the Russian Empire but of the whole world. And, following each other in rapid succession, there appear masterpieces, any one of which would have sufficed to secure him a place among the very great men in Russian musical history and in the front rank of contemporary European composers.

We have mentioned in another part of this book how abundantly Rachmaninoff's ideas began to flow when he awakened, as it were, to new life. Soon he had far more material than he needed for the Second Piano Concerto on which he was working. Much of it had to be eliminated, and to avoid waste he had to make use of it in several other works which he completed at the same time. Thus it happened that all compositions in the vicinity of the Second Concerto (Op. 18) show a decided family likeness, which is noticeable not only in the treatment of the material but also in the similarity of the themes. To these works belong the Second Suite for two pianos (Op. 17), the Sonata for violoncello and piano (Op. 19), the Cantata, *The Spring* (Op. 20), the songs (Op. 21),

Pianoforte Variations on a theme by Chopin (Op. 22), and the Préludes for pianoforte (Op. 23).

Is it seasonable to say something in appreciation of the Second Piano Concerto? The contemporary world of music has pronounced a verdict on it which is far more important and significant than anything I could say. Within the last thirty years there is hardly a pianist of reputation who has not included in his repertoire this Concerto, which ranks with the best-known masterpieces of this kind, and it has never disappeared from the Symphony Concert programmes of the world. These facts speak more eloquently than the most extravagant praise. Practically all the thematic material in the Concerto is unique in character. It is full of happy inspirations, of a quality rare even among the greatest masters and bearing the stamp of immortality. Like a "Heavenly guest," to use Schumann's words in describing one of these inspirations, appears the second theme of the first movement as the horn announces it to the tremolo of the strings. By the side of a towering peak like the Second Concerto the other works of that time can hardly hold their own, despite many outstanding qualities. We are apt to regard them as lowland plains, an estimate which, if we saw them alone, we should recognize as unjust. In the piano pieces the pianistic style of the Composer—who, thanks to the uncommonly large stretch of his hand, easily conquers technical difficulties which others find troublesome or even impossible—predominates more and more. Among the ten Préludes (Op. 23) we find the well-known one in G minor—an effective military or quick march—that moves with tremendous energy, and contains in his middle section an exquisite melody which seems to reflect the vast horizon of the Russian landscape. It is possible, however, that some tastes may prefer to the obvious beauty of this work the more elusive but none the less insistent charm of the hymnal Prélude in D major, the Minuet in G minor, or the infinitely subtle delicacy of the Prélude in E flat major.

Very original, but unfortunately far too little known, are the piano Variations on Chopin's Prélude in C minor (probably the only Prélude that can compete in popularity with Rachmaninoff's Prélude in C sharp minor). The great impressiveness of the theme rather defeats the direct effect of the skilful and, at times, very original variations. It might have been better if the Composer had not shown his cards, so to speak, until the end—that is, if he had concluded with Chopin's theme instead of placing it at the beginning.

Immediate neighbours of the Second Concerto are the Second Suite for two pianos (Op. 17) and the Sonata for violoncello (Op. 19), both works that bubble over with an inexhaustible supply of youthful musical freshness. In the Suite the robust "Meistersingeresque" Prélude and the charming two-voiced passages of the waltz will probably exercise the greatest appeal; in the Sonata for Violoncello, where the tonal strength of the piano is rather unequally balanced against that of the string instrument, it will be the fascinating Andante with its strange harmonic half-lights.

Of the twelve songs in Op. 21 a number will always hold a distinguished place in Russian music. There is, first of all, the highly dramatic song *Fate* to Apuchtin's words and dedicated to Chaliapin, for the musical ground-colours of which the Composer has borrowed the main theme of Beethoven's Fifth Symphony, popularly known as the "Fate" theme. Of equal merit with the dreamy *Island* of Op. 14 we have *Lilacs*, fresh as dew and of a modest delicacy, yet for that reason profoundly impressive. The Composer has since written a remarkably successful piano transcription of this song which is a miniature jewel of dainty beauty and high finish. Finally, this group of songs contains one that might be described as the Composer's own confession. It is very moving and would serve as a fitting motto for his life and work. The first verse is as follows:

"No prophet I, no warrior bold,
No learned mantle wearing,
But as I go my harp I hold
The Grace of God declaring."

An exceptional position among Rachmaninoff's works is held by the Cantata *Spring*, after a poem by Nekrassov. It is his first work in which the melodic and orchestral structure reveals a faint touch of Wagner's influence. I do not mean that this circumstance in any way detracts from its value. The composition is really a solo-cantata, for the baritone solo is given equal, if not greater, importance than the choir. The story is quickly told: a peasant discovers his wife's infidelity, and during the long winter, which he spends shut up alone with her in their tiny hut, he broods in contemplation of her murder. Then comes spring with its all-conquering magnificence and, amid the singing and rejoicing all about him, the knife drops from his hand; nature awakens and surrounds him with a multitude of voices urging love, charity, and forgiveness! Rimsky-Korsakov's verdict on the work, which we quote in Chapter Seven, hits the nail on the head. Lighter, more spring-like colours in the orchestra would have made a more effective background for the beautiful musical idea. Rachmaninoff is, on the whole, not disinclined to revise older works on the basis of later experience, provided the musical value of the composition justifies such "rescue" work. Perhaps a favourable moment will one day encourage him to clothe this cantata in a more festive garment of brighter, happier orchestral colour. It is worth the trouble.

Considering the very small number of operatic works that Rachmaninoff has so far composed, it is rather difficult to answer the question whether his power in the field of music-drama is as unquestionable as in his more familiar province of pure orchestral, vocal, and pianoforte music. He still owes us a convincing proof of his ability in this direction, and the two short operas, *The Miser Knight* and *Francesca da Rimini*—the only ones in our possession besides his examination opera *Aleko*—offer no such proof. The fact that, since the publication of the two operas, Rachmaninoff has let twenty-five years go by without giving a thought to the stage makes us a little suspicious. It has always been said of opera composers, and with justice: "By their libretti shall ye know them." But even this test does not give a verdict in Rachmaninoff's favour. It is true that we cannot hold the young Composer responsible for the choice of the decidedly poor libretto of *Aleko*, thrown together at random by the Moscow dramatist, Nemirovitch-Danchenko, after Poushkin's poem. It was forced on him by the examination board of the Conservatoire. Yet he had a free choice for the libretti of his two other operas. It may be objected that no complaint can possibly be made in the case of *The Miser Knight*, for Poushkin himself . . . But that, as we shall see, is precisely the point.

The idea of setting to music the poetic drama of a great poet in its original form was not a novel one, even in the year 1905. A Russian—Dargomyshki—had originated it when he wrote the music to Poushkin's *Don Juan* without eliminating or altering a line of the dramatic poem. This led Moussorgsky a decade later to use Gogol's prose-comedy *The Marriage*, and his example was followed by Rimsky-Korsakov with *Mozart and Salieri* by Poushkin. The lack of stage success achieved by any of these three works (only the last-named was able, for a time, to hold its own in the repertory of the Russian Opera stage owing to Chaliapin's ingenious impersonation of Salieri) did not, unfortunately, prevent Rachmaninoff from converting the only dramatic poem by Poushkin which had not been used for this purpose into an opera. This was *The Miser Knight*. The idea of writing music for the work of an inspired poet rather than using the material supplied by a doubtful librettist is naturally a very tempting one; but the musicians ignore one fact, namely, that the spoken word produces an entirely different effect and occupies much less time than the same word when it is sung. They forget that the most important component of every dramatic effect is the temporal one and that incidents which ought to last for a moment are liable to be unduly drawn out through the music and lose their effect. Even apart from that, *The Miser Knight* is quite unfit for operatic purposes because it does not contain the dramatic action so necessary for a stage production. The scene in the cellar where the old miser gloats over his treasure—a psychological study of great dramatic power—alone justifies its existence on the stage. It is significant that here Rachmaninoff's music also surpasses itself and rises to great heights.

Even worse was the libretto of the other opera. The story of *Francesca da Rimini*, the beautiful sinner of Ravenna, whose memory Dante has immortalized in the *Divine Comedy*, is undoubtedly an extremely grateful dramatic subject, like every genuine tragedy that moves with inexorable rigour towards its fulfilment. *Francesca da Rimini* could make an ideal opera libretto, but Modest Tchaikovsky, Rachmaninoff's literary adviser, was unfortunately not successful in the adaptation. The verses are occasionally not so bad, but good verses do not make a drama, especially when, as here, the construction is faulty. Modest Tchaikovsky follows the example of his greater brother Peter in his Symphonic Poem on the same subject and divides his book into two parts: a framework which includes the prologue and the epilogue, and the real drama. The first leads us, with Virgil and Dante, to the Infernal Abyss, where the intoxicating storm of sinful love restlessly tosses and buffets all who have given way to it. The tragic story of Francesca and Paolo Malatesta forms only the nucleus of the opera, but it is this nucleus that interests the listener, and not Dante's and Virgil's descent into the Inferno. Owing to the faulty planning of the book the audience is not moved by a direct portrayal of the tragedy, but offered only a reflex of the impression which Dante receives from Virgil's story, described by himself in the words: "I grew faint with pity, as if I were dying."

This second-hand conception of the tragic effect doubly weakens the impression. From the musical point of view Rachmaninoff reaches a higher level with these works than with his first opera, *Aleko*, even if we disregard the fact that his purely technical mastery of his medium had, in the meantime, grown in strength. His experience as a conductor of opera, which had intervened, had made his sense of operatic effect and dramatic point considerably more acute. The journey to Bayreuth also, which he made on his honeymoon, was not without its effect on his style. In *The Miser Knight* we notice a predominance of the recitative-declamatory treatment of the voice which, in this case, is the only method suitable. Here, as in Wagner's operas, the musical centre of gravity is transferred to the orchestra. In *Francesca da Rimini* we get more melody, and some scenes even develop regular arias and a love-duet, all entirely appropriate to the character of the action and the emotions represented. Both works astonish us with their wealth of multiple shades in those deep and sombre orchestral colours, in the painting of which Rachmaninoff is unique. We picture him brooding over a painter's palette on which the colours show every conceivable shade from grey to the deepest black. In the prologue and epilogue of *Francesca da Rimini* he creates an uncanny effect of the orchestra being overshadowed by a cloud of utter hopelessness by making the invisible choir of the condemned sing the most daring chromatics with closed lips. The feeling of *lasciate ogni speranza* which overwhelms Dante in this passage through the Inferno has always been one of the most important *leitmotifs* in Rachmaninoff's work. No wonder that he is able here to give it soul-stirring utterance. Altogether both operas, despite indubitable weaknesses, offer so much that is interesting and beautiful that one cannot express sufficient regret that Rachmaninoff's creative activity in this province should have ceased. The plan of a third opera, *Monna Vanna*, after Maeterlinck, has, as we mentioned in Chapter Eight, never left the Composer's desk. Perhaps the future may bring us a surprise that will settle all our doubts.

During his years in Dresden, which, as we know, he spent in intense concentration, Rachmaninoff composed three large works: The Second Symphony (Op. 27), the Piano Sonata (Op. 28), and the Symphonic Poem, *The Isle of Death*. The songs (Op. 26), or some of them, belong to that time.

We know already that Rachmaninoff occasionally used thematic ideas taken from the so-called *Obikhod*—a collection of liturgical songs for the daily use of the Russian Church. His First Symphony was based exclusively on such themes. In these Dresden works, on the other hand, the thematic material is original, although in structure and in their austere strength and simplicity of line they closely approach the chants of the Russian

Orthodox Church, which undoubtedly supplied also one of the themes of the Piano Sonata. In the Symphonic Poem, *The Isle of Death*, he employs the Roman Catholic theme of the *dies irae* so frequently used by Liszt and other composers.

Rachmaninoff's creative imagination is most readily stimulated by impressions received outside the province of music. They can be traced either to incidents in his personal life or to the allied arts, such as poetry or painting. The greater number of his large and small works may be termed programme music. The First Symphony was admittedly founded on a programme, and I do not think I am wrong in stating that the Second Symphony also, and the First Piano Sonata (Op. 28), both of which are closely allied in idea, were built up on definite programmatic lines. If we search for models for these two compositions, we are reminded of Tchaikovsky's Fourth Symphony and Liszt's Sonata in B minor. Rachmaninoff replaces the fanfare of fate in Tchaikovsky's Symphony by threatening, heavily oppressive chords pregnant with a premonition of death, trumpets and violins swelling to a desperate groan that collapses and dies away. The words *Memento mori* would make a suitable motto for the Symphony. Whenever the work succeeds for a moment in reaching a carefree, exuberant mood, the dull, inflexible chorus cuts in with its gloomy warnings of death even in the most ecstatic moments of the lover's surrender. This is most effective at the conclusion of the Scherzo, which is almost unique in the musical literature of the last decade. In grandeur of design it can hardly find an equal, the possible exception being the Scherzo of Bruckner's Ninth Symphony.

If the Symphony with its sombre atmosphere of death premonition and death menace puts an anxious, intent question to fate, the Piano Sonata seems to give the

reassuring answer. After the pensive motive of the introduction has been repeated several times the Sonata
concludes with the return of the liturgic melody of the
first movement now transformed into a hymn of praise.
All doubts dissolve before the radiant D major, and the
Composer's meaning stands plainly expressed: that out
of all man's disquietude and dark fear of death the way
of deliverance leads to faith and God.

These two works, the Symphony and the Sonata, are
closely related, not only in the spiritual, but also in the
technical sense. In the first movements of both the scale
is used with unequalled skill as contrapuntal material—
the scale employed not as a passage but thematically.
This maze of scales which run all over the score, in every
possible direction, and with the most varied note values,
results in a contrapuntal network of extreme skill and
most original tonal charm. It shows that Rachmaninoff
is now a consummate master of his art.

When I say that Liszt's Sonata in B minor may be
taken as the model for the Sonata Op. 28, I mean that
modern pianoforte literature can show no other sonata of
such gigantic dimensions and such fresh and brilliant
exploitation of the instrument's resources. Moreover, at
the end of the Andante we get a momentary harmonic
reminiscence of the old master of Weimar—a greeting and
a gesture of homage to the great colleague.

The Symphonic Poem, *The Isle of Death*, closes the
group of Dresden works—all of which are preoccupied
with the question of life and death—with Böcklin's vision
of the rocky island overgrown with cypress-trees and
radiating eternal peace. Musical history does not show
many "pictorial" compositions. The best known are
probably the *Death Dance* by Liszt and Saint-Saëns,
modelled after Dürer, Holbein, and innumerable other
Old Masters, and Moussorgsky's *Pictures from an Exhibition*

231

after water-colours by the architect, Hartmann. It will always be a bold venture to try to reproduce the static visual impression by means of the dynamic interplay of sounds. But if anyone has ever succeeded it is Rachmaninoff with his *Isle of Death*. Already the first motive of five notes, given out on the harps and violoncelli, is full of suggestive power: it ripples as monotonously as the leaden waters stirred by Chiron's boat, and gradually and irresistibly draws and holds the listener into an imaginary world revolving about death and dissolution, tranquillity and oblivion, and surrenders him unconditionally to the uncanny, yet fascinating mood induced by such an atmosphere. It is natural that in this picture, which, like the Symphony, is masterfully orchestrated, there should be a preponderance of melancholy, oppressive, shadowy colouring which is, after all, Rachmaninoff's "speciality." Unique in effect is the passage where the old liturgic melody of the *dies irae* pierces the gloom of the orchestra in a tremolo from the violas, like a shudder of death premonition.

The fifteen songs (Op. 26) do not add any essential features to the portrait of Rachmaninoff, the song-writer, as we have come to know him through his work. In this series two songs, *Christ is Risen* and *To the Children*, are notable. The first owing to the strong moral appeal of the text, which is of topical significance, and the second through its touching simplicity that goes straight to the heart. The honour of having "discovered" this song, which up till then had led a secret existence among Rachmaninoff's vocal compositions, is due to the American tenor, Mr. McCormack.

In the works Op. 17–29 Rachmaninoff gradually reached a technical mastery that few Russian composers before him have achieved. Even apart from his thematic ideas which, as we all know, cannot be acquired by study but must, from their unique quality, be attributed to inspiration, the great technical skill shown in these works would have sufficed to give them immortality. Real mastery is lasting; it stands firmly rooted in the past, it reaches into the future and endures for ever.

Despite the high standard of the works discussed in the preceding paragraph, it is in the Third Piano Concerto that Rachmaninoff's muse rises to another of those pinnacles which form the landmarks in his career. As we have already said, conscientious historians may one day consider this Concerto as the beginning of a "third period" of the Composer's life. Rachmaninoff has never been a revolutionary, either in spirit or deed; he has not suffered any unforeseen shocks, his development did not proceed by fits and starts, in painful severing from old spiritual values and triumphant conquering of new ones, but slowly and gently with hardly noticeable transitions. The spiritual growth of this Composer offers a picture of calm, steady evolution, not one of forced and hectic renewal. Consequently it is not quite easy to fix the exact moment when a new epoch in his artistic life sets in, although there is no doubt that a change, justifying such a division, took place round about the Op. 30. This is shown in the enrichment of his store of harmonic material, in the surprising broadening of his musical conscience, which allows him to write down what, only a decade ago, would have made him turn away with a shudder. But whether we mark the beginning of a new period in his creative activity with his Third Piano Concerto, or a little later, with Op. 35 (*The Bells*), the fact remains that the Third Concerto reveals a sufficient number of new features and previously unknown technical combinations to be considered the starting-point of the new "third period." Very remarkable in this composition is the striving for strict thematic unity, thanks to which every passage with its secondary episodes is developed directly from the themes and their various rhythmic variations. Consequently the close filigree-like web of notes in this extensive work contains no mesh that is not an integral part of the work as a whole. The Specification "Piano Symphony," which may be applied also to the Second Concerto, is even more justified here. Piano and orchestra melt into one in perfect unity, and not even in the Cadenza, sanctified by tradition, is the piano left to itself, but is gradually joined by other orchestral instruments, as if to satisfy their "soloist" ambitions. I do not hesitate to assert that Rachmaninoff's Third Piano Concerto has reached a standard unsurpassed by his own previous works, or by any modern production in this province. Its themes hold us by their intense expressive power, and the mastery of its structure in general and in detail is unequalled.

A span of more than twenty years containing ten opus numbers divides the Fourth Piano Concerto in G minor (Op. 40) from the Third, but the former does not show any remarkable progress when compared with the latter. The Fourth Concerto cannot aspire to the towering quality that lifts the Third so high above the Composer's other works; but it does reveal a quality which, so far, we have not found in Rachmaninoff and which strikes us as particularly attractive. It is a complete detachment, a tranquillity of feeling and expression, with an occasional spark of humour that replaces the former grimness with innocent gaiety. In this respect the work resembles another Fourth Concerto, also in G, though in the major key: Beethoven's Fourth Concerto, which, if we bear in mind the relative proportions, occupies the same position among the works of the titan as Rachmaninoff's Fourth among his own. Once only does the dark menace of death intrude into this work: roaring trumpet blasts interrupt the contemplative calm of the middle movement; but this time the sombre call of warning is not meant too seriously. After a threefold repetition it dies away and the dispassionate, peaceful mood of the Largo is pursued until it dies away, or rather leads into the gay Rondo of the Finale. Beethoven's Fourth Concerto was followed by a Fifth, which, reverting to his usual attitude, exchanges the detached music of a mild and wise world-philosophy for the passionate struggle against the powers of Fate. What will Rachmaninoff's Fifth Concerto look like? Am I mistaken when in his Fourth I seem to hear Chopin's growing influence and a homage to Grieg, the Northern master? How I would like to have a glimpse into the future!

About half-way into the period dividing the Third from the Fourth Concerto falls the revision of the First Piano Concerto (Op. 1) in F minor. From an early work which the Composer himself considered too inferior to be played to a London audience, it has grown into a serious, mature composition that should soon be welcome in every concert-hall. It is true that the new setting has left little more of the old Concerto than a few of the most beautiful themes, which have, however, retained all the charm and freshness of their youth. The work shows no trace of the Moscow street fighting in October 1917 which took place while it was being revised; the world of imagination proved more powerful than the world of stark reality. What happiness to be an artist!

Grouped around these three Piano Concertos there are a whole number of smaller works. There are, above all, thirteen Préludes (Op. 32). The ominous number of the pieces (in Russian the number thirteen is called "the devil's dozen") can be accounted for by the fact that it completes the circle of fifths covered by these Préludes. It seems almost as if Rachmaninoff designed the bulk of his Préludes according to a plan, after the example of

235

Bach, Chopin, and Scriabin; for together with the one piece from Op. 3 and the ten from Op. 23 they now make twenty-four altogether, that is, one piece for each minor and major key of the "Well-tempered Piano." The cyclic character of the collected pieces is emphasized also by the fact that in the last Prélude (D flat major) the chief motive of the first (C sharp minor) reappears like a vision in such an obscure form, it is true, that anyone unaware of the fact must have good eyes and ears to discover it.

Rachmaninoff's style of piano-writing grows more and more involved with the advancing years. It becomes more extended and richer in carefully nursed middle voices and accompanying figures. Each piece proves the fact that he writes preferably for his own unusual hand and the infallibly rapid chord technique, which is peculiarly his own. You will not find many pianists, if any at all, who are able to compete with him in the playing of some of his own piano pieces. In substance most of his Préludes (Op. 32) shatter the notion that a prélude is an unassuming pianoforte miniature. They are magnificently planned *tone-pictures*, more suitable for the concert-hall than the home. The expression "tone-picture" has not been chosen haphazard: the Composer himself gives this designation to his next two series of piano pieces, Op. 33 and Op. 39. We have already seen Rachmaninoff as a successful "tone-painter" in the province of orchestral composition (*The Isle of Death*). He admits that even in earlier days he received musical stimuli from visual impressions. In song composition the musical outlines are more or less clearly defined by the text; in composing "absolute" piano music it is often useful to fertilize the musical imagination with ideas borrowed from one of the other arts. Thus it happened that in Rachmaninoff's case this combination of picture and sound grew, at times, into a principle of work (the terms "colour-*tone*" and "tone-*colour*" in painting and music are not used without a special reason). His new piano pieces are called *Etudes Tableaux*. Many of these take their origin from Böcklin's paintings: No. 8, Op. 39 (G minor), can be traced back to *Morning*. No. 1, Op. 39 (F minor), to *The Waves*. Sometimes the inspiration for the *Etudes Tableaux* has been taken from pictures of real life or from fairy-tales; as, for instance, No. 7, Op. 33 (E flat minor), which represents the gay bustle of a Russian fair, or No. 6, Op. 39 (A minor), the fairy-tale of *Red Riding Hood and the Wolf*. As the Composer has intentionally abstained from disclosing the source of his inspiration for each piece, we had better drop the briefly lifted curtain over the artist's workshop again, in order not to forestall the imagination of the reader or player.

The evolutionary process through which Rachmaninoff's harmony passed at that time is revealed in the *Etudes Tableaux*. Another new principle of style is shown in the free, unsymmetrical, rhythmic formation of the motives and phrases, which, as we know, follows the practice of Russian Church singing, and is here effectively and convincingly applied. In the volume of sound demanded at times by the *Etudes Tableaux* the Composer appears to have overestimated the capabilities of even the best concert piano. One gets the impression that he is impatient of the limitations imposed by the instrument. The conductor of the Boston Symphony Orchestra, S. Koussevitsky, recognizing that the difficulty could only be surmounted in one way, has commissioned the Italian composer, Ottomar Respighi, a pupil of Rimsky-Korsakov in instrumentation, to orchestrate six collected *Etudes Tableaux*. This was done by special permission of the Composer, who obviously had no desire to "paint" his own pieces. Koussevitsky has been brilliantly successful in a similar experiment with Moussorgsky's *Pictures from an Exhibition*, which Maurice Ravel has congenially orchestrated at his instigation. It is probable that the bright garment of orchestral sound will suit Rachmaninoff's tone-pictures even better than the "black-and-white" of the piano, which has only a limited range even at its best.

Between the two series of *Etudes Tableaux* falls the Second Piano Sonata (Op. 36). In style it differs but little from the First. It has the same broad treatment of piano movement in which, notwithstanding the appreciation for delicacy of detail, the main outline is, after all, the most important factor. The middle movement is very beautiful and meditative. It shows a definite relationship with the Intermezzo (Adagio) of the Third Concerto. The first and the last movement are colossal in structure and extract the utmost tonal possibilities of the piano.

Rachmaninoff's latest piano compositions are the Variations (Op. 42) on a theme of Corelli, well known through Fritz Kreisler's arrangement for violin. The work, which is of considerable proportions, may well be classed with the Chopin Variations (Op. 22), but it surpasses them in wealth of musical ideas, in maturity, and in innumerable delicacies in the variation treatment and piano phrasing. It can claim a place of honour among the best and most famous variations, such as those of Beethoven, Schumann, and Brahms.

We have drawn an analogy between Rachmaninoff's creative life and a mountain range with its heights and depths, its valleys and pinnacles. Two of these peaks we have already surveyed: the Second and Third Piano Concertos. Now we must contemplate the last and highest peak which his creative genius has so far climbed. This is lifted as high above its adjoining and surrounding neighbours as the two previous ones above theirs. It is the

Choral Symphony (for that is what we must call it rather than an Oratorio), *The Bells* (Op. 35), after a poem by Edgar Allan Poe, in a Russian version by Konstantin Balmont. Here the Composer's disposition reveals many features in common with that of the poet, a very rare occurrence. Under these conditions their artistic co-operation guaranteed a work of the highest tonal excellence. Rachmaninoff, like the poet, is not quite free from a morbid yet creative yearning for intensified dream-perceptions, due in both cases to an almost oppressive pessimism in regard to all manifestations of life. The death-knell which concludes Poe's poem is also Rachmaninoff's symbol for the summary of all human aspirations: "All joy ends in weariness" . . . The tinkling sleigh-bells in the first movement, illustrating a carefree journey into life, the wedding bells in the second movement, which contains some wonderfully happy inspirations, the fire alarm of the third, where revolt, rebellion, and ravaging fire combine in one magnificent blaze of bewilderingly splendid tone-colour, finally are subdued by the death-bell that tolls:

> "With persistent iteration
> They repeat their lamentation,
> Till each muffled monotone
> Seems a groan,
> Heavy, moaning,
> Their intoning
> Waxing sorrowful and deep . . ."

A desolate ending, unrelieved by a single glimpse of light. In this respect only Tchaikovsky, with the lugubrious finale of his Sixth Symphony, was here also Rachmaninoff's forerunner. The instrumental imitation of the last hollow, grief-stricken bells in heavy, syncopated rhythmus intoned by clarinets and horns in their lower register, harps, and strings divisi (double bass), is a

239

masterpiece of instrumentation. The whole score of *The Bells* is indisputably the best of all Rachmaninoff's orchestral works. Perhaps the people in Soviet Russia who assert that this "Song of Songs" of melancholy pessimism represents a visionary allusion to the coming revolution and its probable consequences—the funeral bells!—are not far wrong. Are we to accept this finale as the last word on the subject? There still remains the hope that a miracle may prove it false. In that case we do not doubt that the Composer will also find, and proclaim, a brighter, more optimistic outlook on life! . . .

When we discussed Rachmaninoff's creative activity as a song-writer we hinted that he had gradually freed himself from the Russian "Romance" and adopted an entirely different style in his latest work of this kind. It is marked by a far more independent form of piano accompaniment and richer, subtler harmonies. The change is noticeable in some songs of Op. 34, but takes definite form only in the six songs of Op. 38. It is highly probable that Nikolai Medtner exercised a deciding influence over him. Between these two composers we notice a process of mutual impregnation, which is the more surprising as it began at a comparatively late age. Six of the songs (Op. 34) are dedicated to the once-famous Russian tenor, Leonid Sobinoff—four to Chaliapin. This fact alone points to the different moods they represent. Among the songs dedicated to Chaliapine we find the magnificent one in ballad style, *With Holy Banner Firmly Held*, while among the Sobinoff songs the passionate *What Wealth of Rapture*, *'Tis Night and We Alone* is probably the most enchanting love-song that Rachmaninoff has ever written. The last song of the group is of unusual form. It is a "Song without Words" in the literal sense, called *Vocalise*, and dedicated to the once-famous coloratura singer of the Moscow Grand

Theatre, Mme Neshdanova. The modest and unassuming title does not do justice to this original piece, which is no mere exercise but a song—an "Aria"—of the highest emotional quality. The wonderfully curved melodic arch, with its even tranquillity, spans the song from beginning to end in one unbroken line and would be an undisputable proof of the Composer's strength as a writer of melody if any such proof were needed. We find in it a resemblance, without any similarity of notes, to Bach's *Air*, which moves in the same clarified atmosphere of divine tranquillity. The violinists have captured the piece and regard it as their property. They are probably right, for the bow of a string instrument, even of the double bass, brings out the tonal effect of this wonderful cantilena far better than the voice of the most superbly trained singer.

The new musical content of the songs (Op. 38) is indicated by the poems selected, which include no representatives of the Russian school of romantics, like Poushkin, Foeth, Tyoutchev, and others, but are gleaned from the crop of Russian lyrical poets, who were considered modern round about the year 1905—some of them, indeed, deemed decadent. They are Alexander Block, Andrey Belyi, Konstantin Balmont, Valeri Bryoussov, and even the futurist poet, Igor Severyanin. Each of these songs is a small masterpiece, but the one called *Daisies*, that concludes with the melting trill of the nightingale, is perhaps best known through Kreisler's arrangement for violin. I may disclose the secret that the Composer himself likes the last song of Op. 38, with its ingenious echo effect at the end, best of all the songs he has written. Seeing that these songs are his favourites, we may presume that in his future work he is likely to keep to the same style, while developing it still further.

A most original little work comprises the *Three Russian Folk-Songs* for chorus (unison) and orchestra (Op. 41).

The first of the three shows a sense of humour that rises, smiling, above the tragedy of incident: an attitude not often met with in Rachmaninoff. We cannot help smiling as we follow the tragic fate of the drake who leads his friend, the grey duck, over a bridge, whence she flies away and leaves him, crying. But the other two also, one of which is a melancholy love-song, while the third treats the old but eternally fresh story of the aged, jealous husband and his beautiful and probably light-minded wife, are formed by a master hand into effective little tone-pictures.

This exhausts the number of Rachmaninoff's secular compositions. How much they were appreciated in Russia, despite occasional and inevitable hostility, is seen by the fact that practically all the larger works won the Glinka Prize endowed by the St. Petersburg art patron, M. P. Belayev. This was a remarkable honour for a Muscovite, when we realize that not only the founder but all the members of the committee of judges were well-known musicians living in St. Petersburg; and we know that the attitude adopted by the musical world of St. Petersburg towards that of Moscow was anything but friendly. Rachmaninoff won the Glinka Prize (a rather considerable sum for those days) in the year 1904 for the Second Piano Concerto; in 1906 for the Cantata, *Spring*; in 1908 for the Second Symphony; in 1911 for the Symphonic Poem, *The Isle of Death*; and in 1917 for his Choral Symphony, *The Bells*.

Rachmaninoff as a composer of sacred music deserves particularly sympathetic and detailed consideration, but this would carry us too far. We can only deal with the most outstanding points. The first of Rachmaninoff's two large sacred works, the *Liturgy of Saint John Chrysostomus* (Op. 31), is to be regarded merely as an attempt to test his own ability to handle the style of chanting customary in the Russian Orthodox Church and strikes one as almost primitive in the simplicity of the means employed. There is nothing to indicate that the composer of this liturgy is soon to create a masterpiece which can hardly find an equal in the literature of Russian Church music, namely *Vesper Mass* (Op. 37). This work includes fifteen songs, nine of which are built on original liturgic chants, while six are developed from the Composer's own imagination. But these six are so well adapted to the style of the whole work that even a practised eye and ear will not be able to detect them without a previous hint. Michael Glinka had dreamt of a union between the European fugue style and the themes of the *Obikhod*—the home of Russian liturgic cantilenas—without being able to bring about this combination. When we consider a work like the *Vesper Mass* it seems doubtful whether an artificial union of two entirely heterogeneous elements would have effected the desired solution of a difficult problem in regard to style. Rachmaninoff uses imitations—and the "fugue style," as we know, is composed of such—treating them with great care and discretion. His attention is centred on the varieties of sonority to be achieved with the choir, and their resulting effects, and to these tonal demands he subordinated all the wealth of his knowledge in counterpoint. He must have known what to expect of the magnificent Synodical Singers—the first interpreters of the Mass—and how far he could tax them. As a result the *a cappella* songs of the Mass are most cunningly "instrumented" and of an extraordinarily lovely effect. At the same time they strictly preserve the austere spirit of Russian Church singing. It is rather difficult to define the qualities that go to make up this style. One would have to write a whole monograph in order to give an exhaustive answer. There is, first of all, the natural harmonization of the cantilenas, kept in the ancient Church keys; then there are the peculiar dynamics of Russian chanting with its sudden swell and diminuendo, its expiring pianissimos and sharp accentuations; and lastly the perfect chastity and austerity of the phrasing, so admirably suited to the unimpassioned voices of the choir boys; the touching simplicity and purity of sound and an absolutely unconditional subjection to a style which does not allow even one sweetly seasoned harmony to intrude. To this we must add the "free and unsymmetrical" rhythm, which we have frequently mentioned and which keeps to no time signature, following only the natural rhythm of the text. We know that Rachmaninoff handles these rhythms with perfection and has frequently used them in his secular compositions. His knowledge and skill in this field he owes mainly to a short period of eager study of the ancient Russian "kryouki" notation—a kind of neume-writing—under the direction of the greatest connoisseur in this obscure province of medieval musical history, Stepan Smolensky. The Mass is dedicated to this able man, who was an enthusiastic and steadfast champion of strict tradition in the early Russian Church music. The close connection between the work and the ritual of the Russian Church may prevent the "unitiated" hearer from enjoying it. But he cannot fail to acknowledge that this work reaches an equally high—though perhaps more remote—pinnacle in the vast realm of the Composer's activity than *The Bells*.

*   *   *

Rachmaninoff's name has long been honoured the whole world over. He himself has become world famous both as pianist and composer. Those who are familiar with the great master's work cannot help regretting that

244

his fame as a composer should rest on so few of his works: the Prélude in C sharp minor, the Second and Third Piano Concertos, the *Elegy*, and some of the later piano-forte pieces and songs, while outside Russia the majority have not yet received the appreciation they deserve. There are three reasons for this lack of general recognition of the bulk of his work.

The first is a general one. It consists of the fact that Rachmaninoff as an artist stands, as it were, on the border of two musical, and perhaps historical, eras. The change that has shaken the foundations on which music has so far been based, and out of which it has grown, has within the last two decades been so rapid that a composer of Rachmaninoff's responsibility found himself unable, or rather unwilling, to follow the fashion; especially as this so-called "development" did not follow the direct course of evolution, but consisted of side leaps and grotesque contortions in which no one who cherished his beloved art and was anxious to preserve its integrity could possibly join. Many are the gods who, within the last twenty years, have been worshipped and overthrown before our eyes! Even twenty years ago the clever young moderns were quite ready, on occasion, to snap at Rachmaninoff's life work as "old iron" and to treat the Composer as a living corpse or, even when more observant of the rules of common politeness (which do not worry the youth of our days overmuch), at best to regard him as the last surviving champion of a great but irrevocably dying musical epoch. In those days his art was criticized from the standpoint of Scriabin's musical mysticism, which was considered the only doctrine of musical evolution with a future and the one true aesthetic faith. Anyone in Russia who wanted to prove himself "advanced" waxed enthusiastic over Scriabin, whose musical mysteries and ecstasies were the fashion, while it was generally accepted that all music, including Rachmaninoff's, that moved along less adventurous lines could be disposed of by elevating the nose. The short-sightedness of this attitude is now apparent, and the false prophets of that time will fare no better than those of an earlier generation. The wheel of time has passed over Scriabin more rapidly than one would have expected, and if his art should have a renaissance, which is probable, for his purely artistic qualities are too great to fall into oblivion, it will never again be maintained that his doctrine is the only possible salvation for the future of music. Scriabin himself, who was once declared the official opposition and, as it were, the "antipode" of Rachmaninoff in Russia, would, if he were alive to-day, support him in his belief in the value of a settled musical tradition and join him in carrying on an embittered fight against all manner of "new movements"; unless he preferred, like Rachmaninoff, to follow his own path without worrying about any of these movements and fashions. What followed Scriabin? What has happened to musical "expressionism"? Where is "atonality"? Where the new intellectualism or the "Quarternote" music? All buried and done with! And only yesterday it all seemed so young and promising. . . . Yet still the development of music goes on apace and new watchwords are being invented! There are some musical temperaments—they may even belong to personalities of great power—that are never happy unless they are fighting; to whom the noise and frenzy of passionate conflict is the very essence of life. But there are others whose nobler nature forbids them to join in a street brawl for the honour of their art. They stand quietly on one side and wait until the tumult has died down. Then only, after the terms are concluded and peace restored, is their attitude proved to have been right. This is Rachmaninoff's way, and it is one of the reasons why his music at present leaves the centre of the stage to the "modernists." *Sub specie aeternitatis*—from the standpoint of posterity—it will probably be seen in a different light, and the majority will recognize its real value.

The second reason for his comparative neglect is a purely personal one. To put it shortly: Rachmaninoff the pianist stands in the light of Rachmaninoff the composer. This was for some time the case in Russia. Now it is equally true of the whole world. When, like Rachmaninoff, a man has achieved a great and almost unrivalled mastery in the practice of an art, neither his colleagues nor the public are willing to believe that this accomplishment may be but a part—and perhaps even an unimportant part—of his artistic personality as a whole. I could quote a number of examples to prove this law, so unfortunate for the person concerned but nevertheless inevitable. We need only think of the titan among pianists of all time, Franz Liszt, whose well-balanced and attractive personality reveals more than one feature in common with Rachmaninoff. During his lifetime Liszt could not win the appreciation as a composer to which, as the next generation already realized, he had a right to expect. And it was not only the shadow of Richard Wagner that darkened Liszt's fame as a composer, but his own pianistic achievements had quite as much to do with it, and perhaps to an even greater degree. In the opinion of his contemporaries the creative artist always suffers in favour of the practising artist. (When Robert Schumann was in St. Petersburg with his wife, the famous pianist, a man of high social position asked him: "Are you also musical?") This accounts for the fact that, while Rachmaninoff is recognized by the contemporary public as a pianist of genius, his importance as one of the most remarkable Russian composers of the century is apt to be overlooked.

The third reason for this regrettable fact, strange as it may sound, is a political one. The creator of *The Bells* is homeless. He is an emigrant. He misses the public for whom his works were primarily written. We do not wish here to settle the vexed question whether music is national or international. It is enough to say that music may be an international mean of mutual understanding, but that, owing to the national element present in almost all music, it is best understood by the people of the composer's own race. Similar psychological assumptions, the same cultural development under the influence of the same climatic and geographical conditions, naturally result not only in a tendency to the same reactions in art but also in the same, or at least a similar, manner of digesting and condensing the harvest of the senses and instincts for the purpose of artistic creation. Rachmaninoff lacks this most valuable of all sounding-boards for his creative activity, for everywhere, except in Russia, he must be an alien. It is true that America has offered him a second home, where he is as happy as is possible under the circumstances, but the considerable differences between the "soul" of the Russian and the American people cannot be eliminated or balanced, even by the greatest personal sympathy. Thus Rachmaninoff, the composer, is left to be regarded by America as well as Europe as a more or less "exotic plant." Their interest in him must be a passing one at best; one does not adopt an alien's cause as one's own. A real amalgamation, such as that of Tchaikovsky with the German people, is very rare. It is an almost isolated case, and decades were needed to establish even this union, which was founded on congeniality of temperament. Furthermore, the development of such relations would be more difficult nowadays than in Tchaikovsky's time. A wave of the narrowest and most timid nationalism has swept the whole world. Not only are the continents jealously beginning to guard their cultural and material "belongings," but all the small States into which the larger countries have been divided since the World War are following their example. A Lithuanian composer, for instance, would energetically protest if he were confused with a Lettish one when, not so very long ago, both were provincial representatives of one and the same great nation, Russia. I have allowed myself this little digression in order to illustrate the difficult position of a composer who has lost his country, a position made all the more intolerable by the fact that his former countrymen have been forced by the pressure of their present government to take the grotesque step of boycotting all his works and of forbidding them to cross their own frontiers.

Luckily, Rachmaninoff is not a man who could be induced by such actions to swerve from the path dictated to him by his artistic conscience. We are justified in expecting great things from him, great things yet to come.

If, despite the pessimists' ominous croaking, which is lately growing more and more persistent, music is to continue (and none with common sense is likely to doubt it), we need not fear for Rachmaninoff's fate. His name both as pianist and as composer is stamped in the annals of musical history with indelible letters. So long as that history survives, so long will the name of Rachmaninoff be honoured.

PICTURES AND MUSIC

THE pictures in this book are due to the kindness of the Composer's sister-in-law, *Miss Sophie Satin*, New York, and *Frau Lilly Diedrichs, formerly Wogau*, Stockholm, as well as the firm *Dührkoop-Werkstätten*, Hamburg.

The pages of music are: one of the little *Songs Without Words* by the fourteen years old Rachmaninoff, which Tshaikovsky enjoyed so very much at Rachmaninoff's last examination of harmony, and the beginning and the end of the examination problem in 1890 when Rachmaninoff finished the fugue class of the Moscow Conservatoire. At the author's request the Composer has written them down from memory, which a span of forty years has not been able to destroy, in the autumn of 1931. The fifth part of the *Vesper Mass* was taken from the archives of the Russian Music Publishers (Editions Russes) in Paris, as the work is no longer on the market. The author takes great pleasure in sincerely thanking the managers of the Grandes Editions Russes in Paris for their readiness in lending him, not only this rare piece of music, but all other works composed by Rachmaninoff.

THE FAMILY OF RACHMANINOFF

THE details about the family history of the Rachmaninoffs have been taken from a book, which is published in Russia and bears the title *Historic Dates About the Family of Rachmaninoff*, Kiev, 1895.

The material for this book was collected by a member of the family, Fedor Rachmaninoff. After his death his brother, Ivan Rachmaninoff, Rector and Professor of Applied Mathematics at the Kiev University, completed the book. He commissioned the Librarian of the archives of the Foreign Ministry in Moscow, I. F. Tomakov, to complete the material collected by his brother with copies from the documents in the archives of the Foreign Ministry and the Ministry of Justice. These documents, collected by Tomakov, made it possible to write a complete history of the Rachmaninoffs from the time of their settling down in Russia up to the middle of the eighteenth century. The continuation of the history is based on traditions, family papers, and personal recollections.

The book contains approximately one hundred pages and is divided into two chapters: (1) "The History of the Family of Dragosh"; (2) "The History of the Family of Rachmaninoff." It is supplemented by a copy of the family tree of Perfilyi Rachmaninoff, who was Lord High Steward (Stolnik) to the Tsar during the middle of the seventeenth century.

We can find a reference to the family of Rachmaninoff in the sixth part of the genealogical register of the Russian Nobility. (*Families of the Russian Nobility.*)

Vesper - Mass

V.

"Lord, now lettest thou thy servant depart in peace"... (St Luke, 2, 29).

S. Rachmaninoff

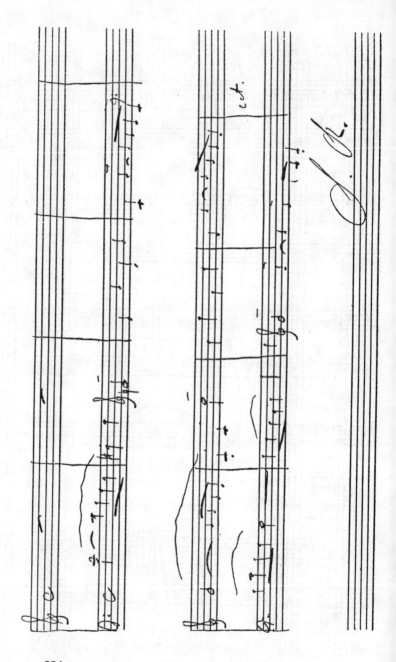

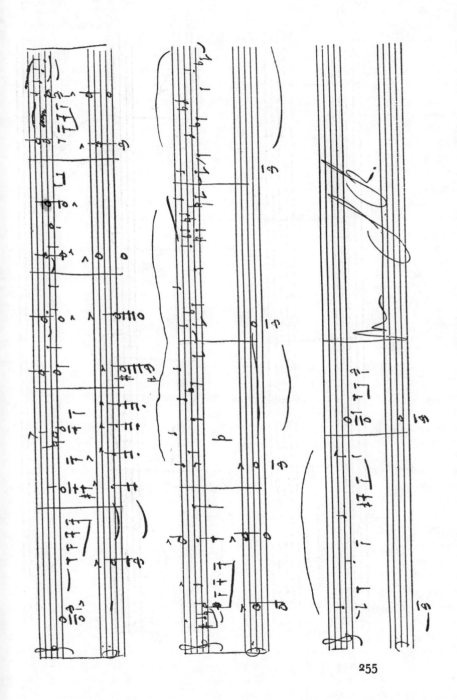

255

LIST OF THE
WORKS OF SERGEI RACHMANINOFF

Op. 1 First Concerto for Piano and Orchestra, F sharp minor, dedicated to Alexander Siloti. 1890–91. (Reduction for two Pianos by the author.) Edition *Gutheil*. New edition, completely recasted, November 10, 1917. (Orchestra Score and Reduction for two Pianos by the author.) *Grandes Editions Musicales Russes.*

    Pp. 103–110, 185, 214, 216, 235

Op. 2 Two Pieces for Violoncello and Piano: 1. Prélude. 2. Dance Orientale. 1892. *Gutheil.*

    Pp. 84, 215

Op. 3 Five Pieces for Piano, dedicated to A. S. Arensky. 1. Elegie. 2. Prélude. 3. Mélodie. 4. Polichinelle. 5. Serenade. 1892. *Gutheil.*

    Pp. 90, 236

    No. 3 (Prélude in C sharp minor).

    Pp. 90, 91, 110, 117, 148, 193, 208, 210, 214, 215, 220, 224, 245

Op. 4 Six Songs. 1. "Oh stay, my love, forsake me not!" (Mereshkovsky, English Version by Edward Agate), dedicated to Mme A. A. Lodyshenskaya. 1890. 2. Morning ("I love thee well!") (M. L. Janov, English Version by Edward Agate), dedicated to Y. S. Sakhnovsky. 1892. 3. In the silent night ("When silent night doth hold me") (Foeth, English Version by Edward Agate), dedicated to Mlle W. D. Scalon. 1889. 4. "Oh never sing to me again" (Poushkin, English Version by Edward Agate), dedicated to Mlle N. A. Satin. 5. The harvest of sorrow (Count Alexis Tolstoy, English Version by Rosa Newmarch), dedicated to Mme E. N. Lyssikova. 1893. 6. "So many hours, so many fancies" (Count A. Golenistchev-Koutousov, English Version by Edward Agate), dedicated to Countess O. A. Golenistchev-Koutousov. 1893. *Gutheil.*

    Pp. 219

Op. 5 Fantasia (First Suite) for two Pianos, dedicated to Peter Tchaikovsky. 1. Barcarole. 2. "Oh night, oh love." 3. Tears. 4. Easter. 1893. *Gutheil.*

    Pp. 89, 91, 93, 100–101, 215

Op. 6 Two Pieces for Violin and Piano. 1. Romance. 2. Danse Hongroise. 1893. *Gutheil.*

P. 215

Op. 7 Fantasia for Orchestra "The Rock" (Lermontov). 1893. (Orchestra Score and Reduction for Piano Duet by the author.) *Jurgenson.*

Pp. 89, 92, 93, 110, 140, 216

Op. 8 Six Songs. 1. The Water Lily ("From reeds on the river") (Plechtcheyev-Heine, English Version by Edward Agate), dedicated to A. D. Jaroshevsky. 2. "Like blossom dew-freshen'd to gladness" (Plechtcheyev-Heine, English Version by Edward Agate), dedicated to M. A. Slonov. 3. Brooding ("The days in turn pass all to soon") (Plechtcheyev-Shevtchenko, English Version by Edward Agate), dedicated to L. G. Jakovlev. 4. The Soldier's Wife ("For a life of pain I have giv'n my love") (Plechtcheyev-Shevtchenko, English Version by Edward Agate), dedicated to Mme M. W. Olferyeva. 5. A Dream ("My native land I once enjoyed") (Plechtcheyev-Shevtchenko, English Version by Edward Agate), dedicated to N. D. Scalon. 6. A Prayer ("O Lord of grace! I stand before Thee self-confessed") (Plechtcheyev-Goethe, English Version by Edward Agate), dedicated to Mme M. A. Deisha-Sionitzkaya. September 1893. *Gutheil.*

P. 219

Op. 9 Trio Elégiaque for Piano, Violin, and Violoncello, D minor, in memory of Peter Tchaikovsky. October 25–December 15, 1893. Second Edition, revised and recast by the author. *Gutheil.*

Pp. 92, 93, 216

Op. 10 Seven Pianoforte Pieces, dedicated to Paul Pabst. 1. Nocturne. 2. Valse. 3. Barcarole. 4. Mélodie. 5. Humoreske. 6. Romance. 7. Mazurka. 1894. *Gutheil.*

P. 215

Op. 11 Six Piano Duets. 1. Barcarole. 2. Scherzo. 3. Russian Song. 4. Valse. 5. Romance. 6. "Slava." 1894. *Gutheil.*

P. 215

Op. 12 Caprice Bohémien for Orchestra, dedicated to P. Lodyshensky. 1894. (Orchestra Score and Reduction for Piano Duet by the author.) *Gutheil.*

P. 208, 217

Op. 13 First Symphony for Orchestra, D minor. 1895. Unpublished.

Op. 14 Twelve Songs. 1. "I wait for thee!" (Davydova, English Version by Edward Agate), dedicated to Mlle L. D. Scalon. 2. The Little Island (Balmont-Shelley, English Version by Edward Agate), dedicated to Mlle Sophie Satin. 3. "How few the joys" (Foeth, English Version by Edward Agate), dedicated to Mme S. A. Pribitkova. 4. "I came to her" (Kolzov, English Version by Edward Agate), dedicated to Y. S. Sakhnovsky. 5. Midsummer Nights (Rathaus, English Version by Edward Agate), dedicated to Mme M. I. Gutheil. 6. "The world would see thee smile" (A. Tolstoy, English Version by Edward Agate), dedicated to A. N. Ivanovsky. 7. "Believe it not" (A. Tolstoy, English Version by Edward Agate), dedicated to Mlle A. G. Klokatcheva. 8. "Oh, do not grieve!" (A. Apouchtine, English Version by Rosa Newmarch), dedicated to Mme N. A. Alexandrova. 9. "As fair as day in blaze of noon" (N. Minsky, English Version by Edward Agate), dedicated to Mme E. A. Lavrovskaya. 10. Love's Flame (N. Minsky, English Version by Edward Agate), dedicated to Mme E. A. Lavrovskaya. 11. Spring Waters (Tyoutchev, English Version by Rosa Newmarch), dedicated to Mlle Anna Ornazkaya. 12. 'Tis Time!" (Nadson, English Version by Edward Agate), 1896. *Gutheil*.

Pp. 109, 219, 224

Op. 15 Six Songs for Female or Boys' Voices, with Piano accompaniment. 1. "Be praised" (Nekrasov). 2. The Night (Ladyshevsky). 3. The Spruce Tree (Lermontov). 4. Dreaming Waves (K. R.). 5. Captivity (Zyganov). 6. The Angel (Lermontov). 1896. *Jurgenson*.

P. 109

Op. 16 Six Moments Musicaux. Dedicated to A. Satayevich. 1. Andantino, B flat minor. 2. Allegretto, E flat minor. 3. Andante cantabile, B minor. 4. Presto, E minor. 5. Adagio sostenuto, D flat major. 6. Maestoso, C major. 1896. *Jurgenson*.

Pp. 109, 221

Op. 17 Second Suite for two Pianos. Dedicated to A. Goldenweiser. 1. Introduction. 2. Valse. 3. Romance. 4. Tarantella. 1901. *Gutheil*.

Pp. 112, 113, 222, 224

Op. 18   Second Concerto for Piano and Orchestra, C minor, dedicated to Dr. N. Dahl. 1901. (Orchestra Score and Reduction for two Pianos by the author.) *Gutheil.*

Pp. 112, 113, 117, 143, 148, 183, 208, 222, 223, 224, 242, 204.

Op. 19   Sonata for Violoncello and Pianoforte, C minor, dedicated to A. Brandoukov. December 12, 1901. *Gutheil.*

Pp. 113, 222, 224

Op. 20   "The Spring," Cantata for Baritone Solo, Female and Male Voices and Orchestra (Nekrassov). Dedicated to N. S. Morosov. January–March 1902. *Gutheil.*

Pp. 113, 143, 222, 225, 242

Op. 21   Twelve Songs. 1. Fate (suggested by Beethoven's Fifth Symphony) (Apouchtin, English Version by Rosa Newmarch), dedicated to Fedor Chaliapin. February 1900. 2. By the Grave ("In gloom of night I stand alone"), Nadson, English Version by Rosa Newmarch. April 1902. 3. Twilight ("Alone and lost in dreams") (M. Guyot, English Version by Edward Agate), dedicated to Mme N. Wrubel. 1902. 4. The Answer ("They wonder'd a while") (Victor Hugo L. Mey, English Version by Edward Agate), dedicated to E. Kreutzer. April 1902. 5. The Lilacs ("At the red of the dawn") (Beketova, English Version by Rosa Newmarch), April 1902. 6. Loneliness ("O, heart of mine") (Apouchtin, English Version by Edward Agate), dedicated to Princess A. Lieven. April 1902. 7. "How fair this spot" (G. Galina, English Version by Rosa Newmarch), April 1902. On the Death of a Linnet (Shoukovsky, English Version by Edward Agate), dedicated to Mlle O. A. Troubnikova. April 1902. 9. Mélodie ("On slumber-laden wings"), dedicated to N. Lanting. April 1902. 10. Before the Image (Count Golenistchev-Koutousov, English Version by Edward Agate), dedicated to Mme M. A. Ivanova. April 1902. 11. "No Prophet I" (Krouglov, English Version by Edward Agate). April 1902. 12. Sorrow in Springtime (G. Galina, English Version by Rosa Newmarch), dedicated to W. A. Satin. April 1902. *Gutheil.*

Pp. 113, 210, 222, 224

Op. 22   Variations for Pianoforte on a theme by Chopin, dedicated to J. Leshetitsky. 1903. *Gutheil.*

Pp. 113, 223, 238

LIST OF WORKS

Op. 23 Ten Préludes for Pianoforte, dedicated to A. Siloti. 1. Largo, F sharp minor. 2. Maestoso, B flat major. 3. Tempo di Minuetto, D minor. 4. Andante cantabile, D major. 5. A la Marcia, G minor. 1901. 6. Andante, E flat major. 7. Allegro, C minor. 8. Allegro vivace, A flat major. 9. Presto, E flat minor. 10. Largo, G flat major. *Gutheil.*

Pp. 113, 114, 223, 236

Op. 24 The Miserly Knight. Opera in three acts. Text by Poushkin. 1904–1905. Pianoforte Score by the author. *Gutheil.*

Pp. 126, 129–131, 214, 226–229

Op. 25 Francesca da Rimini. Opera in two acts with a Prologue and an Epilogue (Libretto by Modest Tchaikovsky). 1904–1905. Pianoforte Score by the author. *Gutheil.*

Pp. 126, 129, 130, 131, 214, 226–229

Op. 26 Fifteen Songs, dedicated to M. S. and Mme A. M. Kersin. 1. The Heart's Secret. (A. Tolstoy, English Version by Edward Agate.) August 14, 1906. 2. "All once I gladly owned" (Tyouchev, English Version by Edward Agate). August 15, 1906. 3. "Come let us rest" (A. Tchekhov, English Version by Edward Agate). August 14, 1906. 4. Two Partings. A Dialogue (Kolzov, English Version by Edward Agate). August 22, 1906. 5. "Beloved let us fly" (Count Golenistchev-Koutousov, English Version by Edward Agate). August 22, 1906. 6. "Christ is risen" (Mereshkovsky, English Version by Rosa Newmarch. August 23, 1906. 7. To the Children (Khomyakov, English Version by Rosa Newmarch). September 9, 1906. 8. "Thy pity I implore!" (Mereshkovsky, English Version by Edward Agate). August 25, 1906. 9. "Let me rest here alone" (Bounin-Shevtchenko, English Version by Edward Agate). September 4, 1906. 10. "Before my window" (G. Galina, English Version by Rosa Newmarch). September 17, 1906. 11. The Fountains (Tyouchev, English Version by Edward Agate). September 6, 1906. 12. "Night is mournful" (Bounin, English Version by Rosa Newmarch). September 3, 1906. 13. "When Yesterday we met" (Polonsky, English Version by Rosa Newmarch). September 3, 1906. 14. The Ring ("Here the tapers I hold") (Kolzov, English Version by Edward Agate). September 10, 1906. 15. "All Things depart" (Rathaus, English Version by Edward Agate). September 5, 1906. *Gutheil.*

Pp. 139, 218, 232

Op. 27 Second Symphony, E minor, dedicated to S. I. Taneyev. (Orchestra Score, Reduction for Piano Duet by W. Wilshau.) 1907. *Gutheil.*

Pp. 139, 141, 142, 161, 210, 229, 231, 242

Op. 28 First Sonata for Pianoforte, D minor. May 14 1907. *Gutheil.*

Op. 29 "The Isle of Death," Symphonic Poem for Orchestra, dedicated to N. Struve. April 17, 1907. (Orchestra Score, Reduction for Pianoforte by Otto Taubmann.) *Gutheil.*

Op. 30 Third Concert for Pianoforte and Orchestra, D minor, dedicated to Joseph Hofmann. 1909. (Orchestra Score and Reduction for two Pianos by the author.) *Gutheil.*

Op. 31 Liturgy of Saint John Chrysostomus for Mixed Chorus. Summer 1910. *Gutheil.*

Op. 32 Thirteen Préludes for Pianoforte. 1. Allegretto vivace, C major. August 30, 1910. 2. Allegretto, B flat minor. September 2, 1910. 3. Allegro vivace, E. major. September 3, 1910. 4. Allegro con fuoco, E minor. August 28, 1910. 5. Moderato, G minor. August 23, 1910. 7. Moderato, F major. August 24, 1910. 8. Vivo, A minor. August 24, 1910. 9. Allegro moderato, A major. August 26, 1910. 10. Lento, B minor. September 6, 1910. 11. Allegretto, B major. August 23, 1910. 12. Allegro, G sharp minor, August 23, 1910. 13. Grave, D flat major. September 10, 1910. *Gutheil.*

Pp. 167, 235, 236

Op. 33 Etudes Tableaux for Pianoforte. 1. Allegro non troppo, F minor. August 11, 1911. 2. Allegro C major. August 16, 1911. 3. Non Allegro, Presto E flat minor. August 23, 1911. 4. Allegro con fuoco, E flat major. August 17, 1911. 5. Moderato, G minor. August 15, 1911. 6. Grave, C sharp minor. August 13, 1911. *Gutheil.*

Pp. 167, 240

Op. 34 Fourteen Songs. 1. The Muse ("From childhood's early days") (Poushkin, English Version by Edward Agate), dedicated to R. E. June 6, 1912. 2. "The Soul's Concealment" (Korfinsky, English Version by Edward Agate), dedicated to Fedor Chaliapin. July 5, 1912. 3. The Storm ("I saw the maid on rocky strand") (Poushkin, English Version by Edward Agate), dedicated to L. V. Sobinov. July 7, 1912. 4. "Day to Night comparing went the Wind her way" (Balmont, English Version by Edward Agate), dedicated to L. V. Sobinov. July

9, 1912. 5. Arion ("Full many souls the vessels held") (Poush-kin, English Version by Edward Agate), dedicated to L. V. Sobinov. June 8, 1912. 6. The Raising of Lazarus ("O Lord of Heaven!") (Khomiakov, English Version by Edward Agate), dedicated to Fedor Chaliapin. June 4, 1912. 7. "So dread a fate I'll never believe" (Maikov, English Version by Edward Agate), dedicated to Mlle W. F. Komisarshevskaya. March 7, 1910, recast June 13, 1912. 8. Music ("How it flows, how it grows!") (Polonsky, English Version by Edward Agate), dedicated to P. Tsh. June 12, 1912. 9. The Poet ("You know him well") (Tyoutchev, English Version by Edward Agate), dedicated to Fedor Chaliapin. June 12, 1912. 10. The Morn of Life ("The Hour I mind me") (Tyoutchev, English Version by Edward Agate), dedicated to L. V. Sobinov. 11. "With holy Banner firmly held . . ." (Foeth, English Version by Edward Agate), dedicated to Fedor Chaliapin. June 11, 1912. 12. "What Wealth of Rapture!" (Foeth, English Version by Edward Agate), dedicated to L. V. Sobinov. June 19, 1912. 13. Discord ("What if fate should decree that apart we remain") (Polonsky, English Version by Edward Agate), dedicated to Mme Felia Litvinne. June 17, 1912. 14. Vocalise. Dedicated to Mme A. W. Neshdanova. Without date. *Gutheil.*

Pp. 167, 240

Op. 35 "The Bells," a Choral Symphony for Solo Soprano, Tenor and Baritone, Female and Male Voices and Orchestra (Text by Edgar Allan Poe, translated by Konstantin Balmont), dedicated to Willem Mengelberg and the Concertgebouw Orchestra. July 27, 1913. (Orchestra Score, Reduction for Pianoforte by A. Goldenweiser.)

Pp. 158, 171, 172, 173, 177, 201, 204, 208, 210, 216, 233, 239, 240, 242, 244, 248

Op. 36 Second Sonata for Pianoforte, B flat minor. Dedicated to M. Pressmann. September 13, 1913. *Gutheil.* Second Edition, entirely recast, Summer 1931, *Edition Tair*, Paris.

Pp. 171, 199, 236

Op. 37 Vesper Mass for Boys' and Men's Voices, in Memory of Stepan Smolensky. 1915. *Grandes Editions Russes.*

Pp. 171, 175, 177, 204, 243, 250

Op. 38 Six Songs. Dedicated to N. Konshin. 1. "In my Garden at Night" (A. Bloch-Isaakian, English Version by Kurt Schindler). September 12, 1916. 2. To her ("Grasses dewpearl'd so tearfully") (A. Byelyi, English Version by Edward Agate). September 12, 1916. 3. Daisies ("Behold, my friend, the daisies sweet and tender") (Igor Severyanin, English Version by Kurt Schindler). 4. The Pied Piper (V. Bryousov, English Version by Kurt Schindler). September 12, 1916. 5. Dreams ("Say, oh wither art bound?") (Sologoub, English Version by Edward Agate). 6. "A-ou" ("Was it a dream?") (Balmont, English Version by Kurt Schindler). September 14, 1916. *Grandes Editions Russes.*

 Pp. 183, 218, 240, 241

Op. 39 Nine Etudes Tableaux for Pianoforte. 1. Allegro agitato, C minor. October 8, 1916. 2. Lento assai, A minor. 3. Allegro molto, F sharp minor. September 14, 1916. 4. Allegro assai, B minor. September 24, 1916. 5. Appassionato, E flat minor. February 17, 1917. 6. Allegro, A minor. September 8, 1911, recasted September 27, 1916. 7. Lento lugubre, C minor. 8. Allegro moderato, D minor. 9. Tempo di Marcia, D major. February 2, 1917. *Grandes Editions Russes.*

 Pp. 183, 236, 237

Op. 40 Fourth Concerto for Pianoforte and Orchestra, G minor. 1927. (Orchestra Score and Reduction for two Pianos by the author.) *Edition Tair*, Paris.

 Pp. 199, 234, 235

Op. 41 Three Russian Folksongs for Choir and Orchestra. Dedicated to Leopold Stokovsky. 1. "See! A wooden bridge is jutting." 2. "Oh, my Johnny!" 3. "Quickly, quickly from my cheeks the powder off!" (Orchestra Score and Reduction for Pianoforte by the author.) *Edition Tair*, Paris.

 Pp. 199, 241

Op. 42 Variations on a theme by Corelli for Pianoforte. Summer 1932. *Edition Tair*, Paris.

 Pp. 199, 238

WORKS WITHOUT INDICATING THE OPUS NUMBER

Concerto for Pianoforte and Orchestra. (A composition of early years.) Unpublished.

Quintet for String Instruments. Unpublished.

LIST OF WORKS

Trio for Pianoforte, Violin, and Violoncello. The manuscript is in possession of P. Lodyshensky. Unpublished.

"Manfred," Symphonic Poem for Orchestra. Unpublished.

"Deos meos," Motet for Mixed Choir. The manuscript is in possession of the Moscow Conservatoire. Unpublished.

Sacred Concerto for Mixed Choir in three parts. The manuscript is in possession of the former Synodical School in Moscow. Unpublished.

Symphonic Poem for Orchestra (on a Poem of Rostislav). Unpublished.

"Aleko," Opera in one Act (Libretto by V. Nemirovich-Danchenko from the Poem "The Gipsies," by Poushkin). 1892. (Piano Score by the author.) *Gutheil*.

"Pentelei" (The Consoler), for Mixed Choir *a capella* (Text by A. Tolstoy). 1901. *Gutheil*.

"Polka Italienne" for Piano Duet, dedicated to S. J. Siloti. *J. Jurgenson*, Petersburg.

"Polka by V. R." for Piano. *Grandes Editions Russes*.

"Letter to K. S. Stanislavsky" (to the Ten Years' Jubilee of the Moscow Art Theatre), for a Voice and Piano. 1909. *Gutheil*.

"From St. John's Gospel" (Chapter xv, 13), for a Voice and Piano. 1915. *Jurgenson*.

TRANSCRIPTIONS FOR PIANOFORTE

"Lilac" (Song by Rachmaninoff, Op. 21, No. 5). *Gutheil*.

"The Brook" (Song by Schubert). *Edition Tair*, Paris.

"Liebesleid," by Fritz Kreisler. Unpublished in Europe.

"Liebesfreud," by Fritz Kreisler. Unpublished in Europe.

"Menuetto" from the "Arlesienne" Suite by Bizet. Unpublished in Europe.

"Prélude, Gavotte, and Gigue" from the Violin Partita in E major, by J. S. Bach. *Edition Tair*, Paris.

"Scherzo" from "Midsummer Night's Dream." Music by Mendelssohn. *Edition Tair*, Paris.

ARRANGEMENTS

Tchaikovsky, P.—"The Sleeping Beauty," Ballet. Reduction for Piano Duet. *Jurgenson.*

Tchaikovsky, P.—Suite from the Ballet, "The Sleeping Beauty," for Piano Duet. *Jurgenson.*

Glazounov, A.—Sixth Symphony, Op. 58. Reduction for Piano Duet. *M. P. Belayev.*

INDEX

Academic Grand Theatre, Moscow, 201

Academy for Singing, Berlin, 148

"Agrarian Unrest," 122

d'Albert Eugen, 49

Altani Hypolit, 80, 81, 86, 118, 119, 120, 131, 132

America, *see* U.S.A.

"America," furnished rooms in Moscow, 80, 102

Amfiteatrov, A. A., 90

Andreyev, Leonid, 152

Apouchtin, 113

Arakcheyev Military College, 20

Arbat, street in Moscow, 90

Archbishop of Moscow, 180

Archimedes, 185

Arensky, Anton, 53, 54–59, 60, 61, 67, 69, 75, 77–79, 80, 212

Armistice Day, 191

Ascold's Grave, Opera by Verstovsky, 107

Astrakhan, 163

Atlantic Ocean, 190

Avranek, conductor, 125

Aylmer, Felix, 9

Bach, J. S., 48, 50, 63, 67, 198, 236, 241

Baklanov, George, singer, 131, 132

Baku, 163

Balakirev, Mili, 51, 64, 96, 97

Balmont, Konstantin, 171, 200, 202, 220, 239, 241

Baltimore, 175

Barnay, Ludwig, 45

Barzevich, violinist, 93

Bechstein, 136

Beethoven, Ludwig van, 49, 50, 63, 68, 113, 194, 224, 238

Behring Serum, 35

Belayev Circle, 96, 100

Belayev, M. P., 96, 97, 99, 114, 138, 242

Belayev, V., 8, 9

Belgium, 145

Belopolskaya, Mme, 52

Belyi, Andrei, 241

Berger, Francesco, 110

Berlin, 58, 172, 197, 199

Berlioz, Hector, 160

Besekirsky, violinist, 82

Bessel, editor, 82

Bizet, Georges, 198

Black Monk, by Tchekhov, 151

Block, Alexander, 153, 241

Blue Bird, by Maeterlinck, 140, 152

Blumenfeld, Felix, 100, 101

Böcklin, Arnold, 139, 237

Bohemian String Quartet, 148

Boito, Arrigo, 130

Boris Godounov, by Moussorgsky, 64, 130

"Borissovo," estate, 37, 38, 101

Borki Memorial Day, 125

Borodin, Alexander, 22, 24, 59, 64, 96, 147, 212

Boston, 189, 190, 194

Boston Symphony Orchestra, 154, 158, 161, 189, 237

Bounin, Ivan, 152

Boutakov, General Peter, 20, 22, 27, 29

Boutakova, Lyoubov, 20, 22, *see also* Rachmaninoff, Lyoubov

Boutakova, Sophie (granny), 20, 22, 30, 33, 37–39, 101

Brahms, J., 212, 228

Brandoukov, Anatol, 93, 112, 115, 137

Breitkopf & Härtel, 9

Brest, 134

British Battle Squadron, 190

Brooklyn, 157

Bruckner, Anton, 230

Bryoussov, Valeri, 241

Budapest, 197

Byron, Lord, 215

Cambridge, U.S.A., 157

Campbell-Mackenzie, Sir Alexander, 110

Carmen, by Bizet, 107, 125

Caruso, Enrico, 117

Casals, Pablo, 112

Cavalry Guards, 20

Chaliapin, Fedor, 104, 107, 108, 112, 114, 118–121, 126, 130–133, 143, 149, 150, 199, 214, 224, 227, 240

Chevillard, conductor, 144

Chopin, Frédéric, 38, 50, 69, 103, 104, 167, 194, 213, 224, 236, 238

Cincinati Symphony Orchestra, 189

Clairefontaine, 205

Clementi, 21

267

INDEX

269

INDEX

271